Macintosh® HyperCard® Script Language Guide
The HyperTalk™ Language

Addison-Wesley Publishing Company, Inc.

Reading, Massachusetts   Menlo Park, California   New York
Don Mills, Ontario   Wokingham, England   Amsterdam   Bonn
Sydney   Singapore   Tokyo   Madrid   San Juan

Varityper is a registered trademark, and VT600 is a trademark, of AM International, Inc.

Simultaneously published in the United States and Canada.

ISBN 0-201-17632-7
ABCDEFGHIJ-DO-898
First printing, July 1988

Contents

Chapter 9   **Properties 173**

Figures and tables

Preface

About This Guide

This book provides detailed information about HyperTalk™, the scripting language of HyperCard®. Even a small knowledge of HyperTalk enables you to customize buttons and other parts of HyperCard stacks for your own purposes, and you can use HyperTalk to make the stacks that you create act the way you want.

To get the most out of this book, you should have read the *HyperCard User's Guide,* and you should have used HyperCard enough to be familiar with its basic features. While you're using HyperCard, you can find information about HyperTalk in the HyperCard Help system. The Help system makes use of some of HyperCard's best features, such as computer-supported cross-referencing and fast text searching.

Some of the concepts in this book, such as message handling and objects, may be new to you. Use this guide as it suits your own style of learning: you might be the kind of person who understands best by thoroughly studying the explanations, or you might be the kind who learns by skimming the material and then playing with HyperTalk—writing scripts or copying the examples and trying them out.

What's in this book?

Here's a brief description of the contents of this guide:

Chapter 1, "HyperTalk Basics," introduces the basic concepts of HyperTalk, showing how it is used in the HyperCard environment. This chapter also explains how to create and modify scripts in HyperCard objects.

Chapter 2, "Handling Messages," describes how HyperTalk works, how it carries out actions, and how it responds to events in the HyperCard environment.

Chapter 3, "Naming Objects," explains how to refer to objects—the parts of HyperCard that contain HyperTalk scripts and that respond to and initiate actions.

Chapter 4, "Values," explains how to create and refer to HyperTalk's values—the information it acts upon. It also describes HyperTalk's operators and explains how HyperTalk evaluates expressions.

Chapter 5, "Keywords," describes the handlers within which you write all HyperTalk scripts, to enable objects to respond to messages and function calls. It also describes the control structures of HyperTalk that let you specify how and when sections of scripts execute, and it describes other keywords: do, global, and send.

Chapter 6, "System Messages," describes the messages that HyperCard generates in response to events (such as mouse clicks) that happen in its environment.

Chapter 7, "Commands," describes each of HyperTalk's built-in commands—the action statements that make HyperCard do things.

Chapter 8, "Functions," describes HyperTalk's built-in functions—named values that reflect conditions in the HyperCard environment.

Chapter 9, "Properties," describes the properties of HyperCard objects—characteristics that determine how objects look and act.

Chapter 10, "Constants," describes HyperTalk's built-in constants—named values that don't change.

Appendix A, "External Commands and Functions," contains general information about XCMDs and XFCNs, extensions to HyperTalk that can be written by expert programmers to increase the power of HyperCard.

Appendix B, "ControlKey Parameters," lists the values generated by various keystrokes in combination with the Control key.

Appendix C, "Extended ASCII Table," lists the decimal values of the standard Macintosh character set used by HyperCard.

Appendix D, "Operator Precedence Table," summarizes the order in which HyperTalk performs operations when it evaluates expressions.

Appendix E, "HyperCard Limits," lists various minimum and maximum sizes and numbers of elements defined in HyperCard.

Appendix F, "HyperTalk Changes in HyperCard Version 1.2," explains the differences in the language appearing with version 1.2.

Appendix G, "HyperTalk Syntax Summary," shows the syntax of HyperTalk's command and function parameters in abbreviated form.

Appendix H, "HyperTalk Vocabulary," lists alphabetically each of the primary terms that HyperTalk understands along with its category, a page reference to where it is explained in this guide, and provides a brief description of its meaning.

Notation conventions

Before you read this guide, you should know about a few typographic conventions. Words or phrases in `typewriter type` are HyperTalk language elements or are those that you type to the computer literally, exactly as shown. New terms are shown in **boldface type** when first used or defined.

In descriptions of HyperTalk syntax for commands and other language elements, words in *italic* type describe general elements, not specific names—you must substitute the actual instances. Square brackets ([ ]) enclose optional elements which may be included if you need them. (Don't type the square brackets.) In some cases, optional elements change what the message does; in other cases they are helper words that have no effect except to make the message more readable. Syntax descriptions for some language elements have particular formats shown at the beginning of their chapters.

It doesn't matter whether you use uppercase or lowercase letters in commands or variable names; message names that are formed from two words are shown in small letters with a capital in the middle (`likeThis`) merely to make them more readable. The keywords `of` and `in` are interchangeable—the syntax descriptions use the one that sounds more natural.

Chapter 1

HyperTalk Basics

This chapter explains HyperTalk's place in the HyperCard system, describes some of HyperTalk's characteristics, and shows how to create and edit the scripts of HyperCard objects.

Most concepts are discussed only briefly in this chapter, with more detailed discussion left for later chapters

What is HyperTalk?

HyperTalk is the scripting language of the HyperCard environment. It allows you to perform actions on HyperCard **objects:** buttons, fields, cards, backgrounds, and stacks.

You use HyperTalk to send **messages** to and from HyperCard objects. You generate a message by (among other means) clicking the mouse, opening a card, or typing a statement into the Message box. How a given object responds to a particular message depends on the object's **script.** All HyperCard scripts are written in HyperTalk.

Objects

There are five kinds of objects in HyperCard: buttons, fields, cards, backgrounds, and stacks. (See Figure 1-1.)

Buttons and fields

Buttons are action objects or "hot spots" on the screen. For example, clicking a button with the Browse tool can take you to the next card in a stack.

Fields contain editable text. The Browse tool hand pointer changes to an I-beam when it's over an unlocked field. (The card or background might also contain **Paint text** characters. Such characters are not editable once they are placed; they become part of the picture on the card or background.)

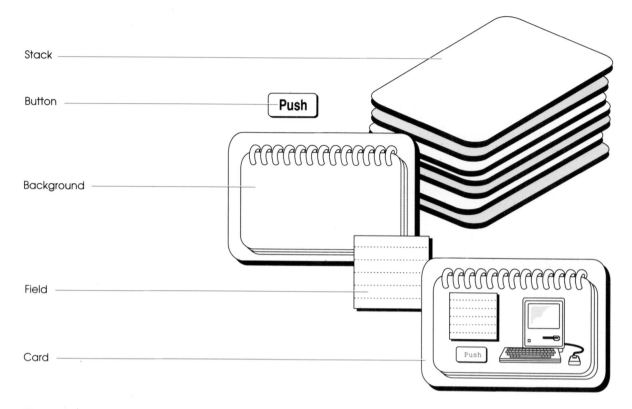

Stack

Button

Background

Field

Card

Figure 1-1
HyperCard objects

Cards, backgrounds, and stacks

The basic unit of information is the **card:** when you look at the screen of a Macintosh®
computer running HyperCard, what you see foremost is a card. Each card is
associated with one **background,** and a background may be (and usually is) shared by
more than one card. The card overlays the background; both are the size of the card
window, which is the size of the original Macintosh screen (512 by 342 pixels). What
you see in the card window belongs to the card, or, if an area of the card is
transparent, to the background The card and background both can contain pictures,
which are bitmaps, and buttons and fields. Cards are grouped in **stacks;** each stack is a
Macintosh file.

The card that is currently displayed, the background associated with it, and the stack
they are in are termed the **current** card, background, and stack. The concept of being
current doesn't apply to buttons or fields.

Chapter 3 contains details about referring to objects.

Messages

HyperCard objects interact with each other, with the user, with HyperCard, and with the Macintosh environment by sending messages. Some messages are descriptions of things that happen in the environment, such as that the mouse has been clicked or a card opened: these are **system messages.** They are like news flashes announced to the community of objects. For example, if you click the mouse button down, HyperCard sends the message `mouseDown`; when you let the mouse button up, HyperCard sends the message `mouseUp`.

Messages are sent to various objects in a particular order. For example, system messages generated by the mouse go first to the topmost button or field (if any) under the pointer on the screen. Next those messages go to the card, then to the background, then the stack, then the Home stack, and finally to HyperCard itself. (You'll find a detailed discussion of this hierarchical sequence in Chapter 2.)

HyperTalk **commands** are also messages—orders to do some particular thing, like add two numbers or go to another card. A command, whether executed in a script or typed into the Message box, is sent as a message.

Scripts

Every HyperCard object has a script (although the script can be completely empty). A script is a collection of any number of **handlers.** The lines inside a handler are HyperTalk statements; each statement ends with a return character. Statements always appear within handlers in a script. Any part of a statement following HyperTalk's double-hyphen comment character (--) is ignored by HyperCard.

Handlers

A handler is a collection of HyperTalk statements; a handler is invoked when a particular message is received by the object whose script contains the handler. A simple handler looks like this:

```
on mouseUp
   go to next card
end mouseUp
```

The first line of a handler always begins with one of two words—either `on` (which begins a message handler) or `function` (which begins a function handler). The last statement of a handler always begins with the keyword `end`. All HyperTalk statements always appear within handlers in a script.

You must place handlers in the scripts of objects that will receive the messages you want the handlers to respond to. The message-passing **hierarchy,** which determines where messages are sent, is described in Chapter 2.

Message handlers

The example shown above is a **message handler.** This particular message handler is in the script of a button; it handles the message mouseUp, and goes to the next card.

The message to which a handler responds begins with the word following the word on. In this case, the message is mouseUp. When you release the mouse button while the Browse tool is inside a button's rectangle on the screen, HyperCard sends the message mouseUp to the button. HyperCard looks in the button's script for a handler matching the mouseUp message. If it finds a match, it executes the HyperTalk statements between on mouseUp and end mouseUp—in this case, go to next card.

Function handlers

In addition to message handlers, scripts can contain user-defined **function handlers.** Function handlers begin with the word function in place of the word on; the name of the function they handle is the second word. A function handler looks like this:

```
function day
   return first item of the long date
end day
```

This function handler responds to a HyperTalk statement containing the function's name followed by parentheses—a **function call.** Here's an example:

```
put day() into message box
```

The function call is day()—the rest of the line and the function call together form a statement. When the function call is made, HyperCard looks for the matching function handler. If it finds one, it executes the lines between function day and end day. The value derived from the expression first item of the long date is returned to the put statement in place of day(). In the example, the value returned by the function (Friday, for example) is put into the Message box.

Function calls use the same object hierarchy as messages; it's described in Chapter 2. Message and function handler structures are described in detail in Chapter 5.

Where's the script?

You get access to an object's script by choosing the object from the Objects menu. The Objects menu has five object Info items, one for each of the five types of objects: the current card, its background, the stack it belongs to, and the buttons and fields belonging to the card and background.

Figure 1-2
The Objects menu

❖ *You must be at level 5:* The user level must be set to 5 (click the Scripting button on the User Preferences card in the Home stack) for you to be able to look at scripts.

To edit the script of the current card, background, or stack, choose the appropriate Info menu item for the object whose script you want. This action brings up information about the object in a dialog box (see Figure 1-3). To open the object's script, click the Script button.

To get to the script of a button or field, first select the button or field (with the Button tool or Field tool), then choose the appropriate Info item from the Objects menu. It is not necessary to be in Edit Background mode to open the script of an existing background button or field. You must be in Edit Background mode, however, to create new background buttons and fields. (It may also help you to select background buttons and fields, because when you're in Edit Background mode, HyperCard doesn't display card buttons and fields.)

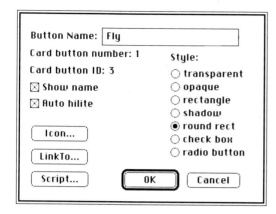

Figure 1-3
Button Info dialog box

❖ *Shortcuts:* To get to the Info dialog box of a button or field quickly, double-click the button or field with the Button or Field tool chosen. To open the script directly, hold down the Shift key while you double-click the object or choose its Info menu item from the Objects menu.

The script editor

The HyperCard script editor lets you create and modify handlers in an object's script (although you can't use it to change the font, size, or style in which the script is displayed). You don't have access to the menu bar while you're editing.

You have to finish editing the script and close the dialog box by clicking its OK or Cancel button before you can do anything else. Closing the script editor box with the OK button or pressing Enter saves the script with its object; closing it with the Cancel button leaves the script the way it was when you opened it.

❖ *Shortcuts:* To save and close a script quickly, press the Enter key. To close the script quickly without saving changes, press Command-period. To choose the Browse tool, press Command-Tab.

You can use the arrow keys to move the text insertion point around in the script.

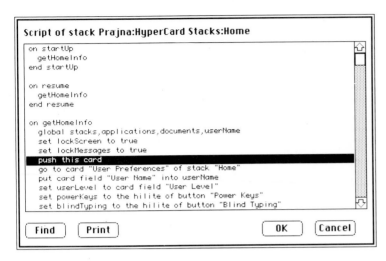

Figure 1-4
Script editor box

Manipulating text

The script editor works in the standard Macintosh text edit manner. The mouse manipulates an I-beam pointer with which you can place an insertion point or select text. You perform cut, copy, and paste operations using Command-X, Command-C, and Command-V, respectively. The selection that you've cut or copied remains in the Clipboard until you cut or copy again, in case you want to paste the material more than once. It remains after you close the script, so you can open another script and paste the material in. You can also paste it into a field as regular text or on a card or background as Paint text.

Searching and printing

Clicking the Find button in the dialog box (or pressing Command-F) brings up a search dialog box. The script editor locates and selects the first occurrence, following the current insertion point, of a string you type into the find window. Searching is not sensitive to uppercase and lowercase distinctions. Here are additional commands you can evoke for searching and printing in the Script editor:

□ To go to the next occurrence of the same string, press Command-G.

□ To copy the current selection from the script into the find window and to locate its next occurrence, press Command-H.

□ To print the current selection of the script (or, if nothing is selected, the entire script), press Command-P or click the Print button.

□ To select the entire script, press Command-A.

Formatting scripts

The HyperCard script editor indents nested control structures for you. It automatically indents all of the lines inside a handler structure when you press the Tab key or close its dialog box. (See Figure 1-5.) When `if` and `repeat` structures are nested inside each other or within handlers, the lines are indented further. (You can't nest handler structures inside each other or any other structure.)

❖ *Error checking:* Automatic formatting provides some degree of error checking while you write a script: if you press the Tab key and the last line isn't flush with the left margin of the script editor dialog box, you probably left something out or made a syntax error in a HyperTalk command.

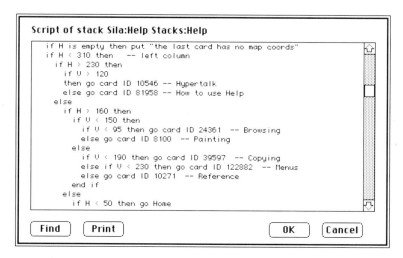

Figure 1-5
Nested control structures

Line length

The script editor doesn't wrap lines too long to fit in its dialog box. There is no specific restriction on the length of lines in scripts (although any single script cannot exceed 32,000 characters, including spaces, returns, and other invisible characters). Lines too long to fit in the dialog box simply extend out of sight.

You can break a single statement into multiple lines by pressing Option-Return where you want a line to break. This "soft" return appears in HyperCard scripts as a logical NOT symbol (¬). HyperCard treats lines broken in this way as single HyperTalk statements continuing to the next actual return character.

❖ *You can't break a literal:* You can't put a "soft" return inside a quoted literal expression. (Literals are described in Chapter 4.)

Table 1-1 is a summary of the script editor commands you can evoke from the keyboard.

Table 1-1
Script editor command summary

Key press	Action
Command-X	Cut selection to Clipboard
Command-C	Copy selection to Clipboard
Command-V	Paste Clipboard contents at insertion point
Command-F	Find text string
Command-G	Find next occurrence of same text string
Command-H	Find current selection
Command-P	Print selection or (if no selection) entire script
Command-A	Select entire script
Tab	Format script
Option-Return	Carry command onto new line ("soft" return)
Enter	Save changes and close script
Command-period	Close script without saving changes

Chapter summary

Here is a summary of the material covered in this chapter:

☐ HyperTalk controls the properties of HyperCard objects: buttons, fields, cards, backgrounds, and stacks.

☐ HyperCard objects interact by sending and receiving messages.

☐ How an object responds to a message is specified by its script, which is written in HyperTalk.

☐ Scripts are collections of message handlers and function handlers.

☐ You can create and edit scripts with the HyperCard script editor.

Chapter 2

Handling Messages

This chapter explains how HyperCard objects send and receive messages and how HyperCard executes scripts.

The HyperCard environment

HyperCard provides the environment in which HyperTalk scripts execute. The HyperCard environment consists of objects connected by a message-passing hierarchy and the HyperTalk language through which they communicate.

Although you could write a stand-alone program in a single HyperTalk script, you would not be making use of the power and flexibility of the HyperCard environment. Instead, you use HyperTalk to define the ways in which objects interact with each other and with the user.

HyperCard is user oriented. When using HyperCard, the user opens and closes cards, reads and changes text in fields, draws pictures on cards, and so on. HyperCard constantly sends messages to objects in response to these actions (and the user's inactivity when doing nothing), and the objects in turn respond with other messages and other actions. The basic purpose of HyperTalk scripts is to enable objects to handle those messages and to specify succeeding actions by sending further messages.

Most of the time, scripts carry out specific actions for the user: setting properties of objects, going to other cards, and so on. HyperTalk can do automatically almost everything the user can do manually with the mouse and keyboard.

Sending messages

All HyperCard actions are initiated by messages sent to objects. Messages are sent to objects in four ways:

- □ An event (such as a mouse click) can cause HyperCard to send a system message.
- □ Handler statements (other than keywords) are sent as messages when a handler executes.
- □ HyperCard sends the contents of the Message box as a message when the user presses Return or Enter.
- □ HyperCard sometimes sends a message when it executes a command.

System messages

HyperCard sends system messages constantly in response to events in the Macintosh environment. For example, if you move the pointer so that it's over a button on the screen, as soon as the pointer enters the button's rectangle, HyperCard sends the message `mouseEnter` to the button. As long as the pointer remains inside the button rectangle, HyperCard continuously sends the message `mouseWithin` to the button. As soon as you move the pointer outside the button area, HyperCard sends the message `mouseLeave` to the button.

HyperCard sends other system messages when you press certain keys on the keyboard, close a field, select a menu item, or when you quit HyperCard. When you open a card, HyperCard sends the message `openCard` to the card itself; when you leave the card it sends `closeCard`. Similar messages are sent to cards when their backgrounds and stacks are opened and closed. If nothing at all is happening, HyperCard continuously sends the message `idle` to the current card.

One of the most commonly used messages is `mouseUp`. Buttons often contain handlers that respond to the `mouseUp` message; the `mouseUp` message is sent to a particular button when you click it. (HyperCard actually sends two messages to a button when it is clicked: `mouseDown` and `mouseUp`. The `mouseUp` message is sent only if you release the mouse button with the pointer over the same screen button it was over when you pressed it down.)

HyperCard also sends mouse messages to a locked field when you click it. If the field isn't locked, `mouseDown` and `mouseUp` aren't sent—the click opens the field for text editing and HyperCard sends the message `openField` to the field. (You can send mouse messages to an unlocked field, however, by holding down the Command key while you click the field.)

Clicking outside all buttons and fields sends `mouseDown` and `mouseUp` directly to the current card.

Chapter 6 describes all of HyperCard's system messages.

Statements as messages

When a handler executes, its statements are sent as messages, first to the object that contains the currently executing handler, then to succeeding objects in the object hierarchy (described later in this chapter). When an object gets a message it can handle—that is, for which it has a handler in its script—the statements contained in the handler are in turn sent as messages. When all statements in the handler (and in any other handlers invoked along the way) have executed, the action stops.

Message box messages

When you type something into the Message box and press Return or Enter, HyperCard does one of two things: either it sends what you typed as a message to the current card, or, if what you typed is a valid expression, HyperCard evaluates it and puts the result into the Message box. (See Chapter 4 for an explanation of values.)

If you try to use a keyword other than send in the Message box, HyperCard displays an error dialog box. A **keyword** is a word whose meaning is predefined in HyperTalk; keywords are never sent as messages from scripts but are interpreted directly. The following list contains all of HyperTalk's keywords:

```
do          next
else        on
end         pass
exit        repeat
function    return
global      send
if          then
```

Send works in the Message box; you use it to direct a message to a specific object rather than sending it to the current card. Chapter 5 explains HyperTalk's keywords.

Messages resulting from commands

HyperCard sometimes sends a system message to the current card while executing a command. For example, when you create a card with the New Card menu command, HyperCard sends the message newCard to the card as soon as it's created; when you delete a card it sends deleteCard. Similar messages are sent when other objects are created and deleted. These messages are among the results of commands executing, rather than commands themselves—they are like announcements of what is happening.

❖ *External commands can send messages:* Expert programmers can write definitions for new commands in development languages such as Pascal, C, and 68000 assembly language. Such external commands act much like built-in HyperTalk commands. External commands can send messages to the current card when they execute. See Appendix A for general information about external commands.

Receiving messages

As senders and receivers of messages, objects all work exactly the same way. Every object has a script, and the type of object makes no difference to the execution of its handlers.

❖ *How objects differ:* As elements of the HyperCard user interface, objects differ according to their function: buttons share a set of properties or characteristics that determine how they look and act; fields also share a set of properties, but it is different from the set of button properties.

When a message is sent to an object, HyperCard checks the object's script for a handler whose name—the second word on the first line of the handler—matches the message name—the first word of the message. If it finds a match, it executes each statement in the handler. (See Figure 2-1.) After the handler has run, the message is sent no further, unless it is explicitly passed with the `pass` keyword (discussed in Chapter 5).

If message name matches any handler name...

...then execute the lines in that handler.

```
on openStack
    global helpExit
    push recent card
    pop card into it
    if "help" is not in it then put it into helpExit
end openStack
```

Figure 2-1
Matching messages with handlers

If the object has no handler for the message, the message passes to the next object in the hierarchy, and the process repeats.

If no object in the hierarchy has a handler matching a message name, HyperCard looks for a command by that name. Commands are like built-in handlers that cause some action to take place; `mouseUp` and most other system messages have no built-in handlers and cause no action. If a message gets all the way through the hierarchy and is not a system message or a command, HyperCard displays an error dialog box with the words `Can't understand` followed by the name of the message.

❖ *External commands can be in stacks:* External commands can exist in stack files, as well as in the HyperCard application itself. See Appendix A for general information about external commands.

Object hierarchy

The objects in HyperCard have an **object hierarchy.** The object hierarchy determines the path by which messages are passed from one object to another: buttons and fields are at the same level, followed (in order) by card, background, stack, and the Home stack (the one stack that HyperCard requires). Any message that traverses the entire hierarchy goes to HyperCard itself.

Where messages go

The position of an object in the hierarchy determines whether or not the object will receive a given message, and where subsequent messages that the object sends will go. Most system messages are initially sent by HyperCard to the current card, as shown in Figure 2-2.

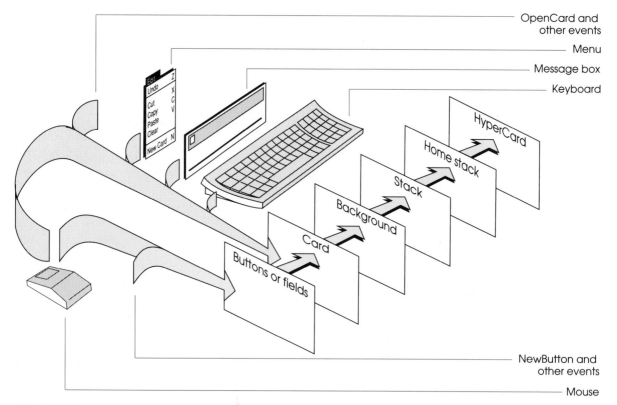

Figure 2-2
Object hierarchy

Messages to buttons and fields

Any mouse message (for example, `mouseEnter`) is sent initially to the topmost button or field, if there are any, under the pointer. Any buttons or fields that are layered farther under the one initially receiving the message are ignored. Figure 2-3 shows layered buttons and fields. If the topmost button or field doesn't have a handler for the mouse message, the message is passed to the current card.

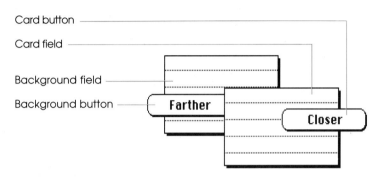

Figure 2-3
Layered buttons and fields

❖ *Background buttons and fields come before cards:* HyperCard first sends mouse messages to the topmost button or field under the pointer, whether the button or field belongs to the card or the background, before passing the message on to the card. Background buttons and fields, however, are always farther away than card buttons and fields.

Other than mouse messages, the only system messages that are sent first to buttons are `newButton` and `deleteButton`; for fields they are `newField`, `deleteField`, `openField`, and `closeField`. The entry point in the hierarchy for all other system messages is the current card.

For a complete list of all system messages, see Chapter 6.

The current hierarchy

The current hierarchy consists of the buttons and fields belonging to the current card and its background, the card and background themselves, and their stack. System messages and those typed directly into the Message box always traverse the current hierarchy. Messages sent from executing handlers traverse the hierarchy to which their containing object belongs—in most cases, the current one. Figure 2-4 shows how a message traverses the current hierarchy.

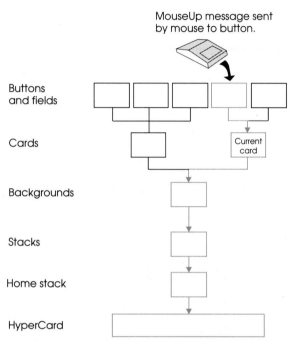

Figure 2-4
Message traversing current hierarchy

When a handler executes, HyperCard sends each statement as a message, unless it begins with a keyword. It sends the message first to the object containing the executing handler, as shown in Figure 2-5. If that object doesn't have a handler for the message, the message is passed down the object hierarchy; if none of the succeeding objects has a handler for it, the message ends up at HyperCard itself.

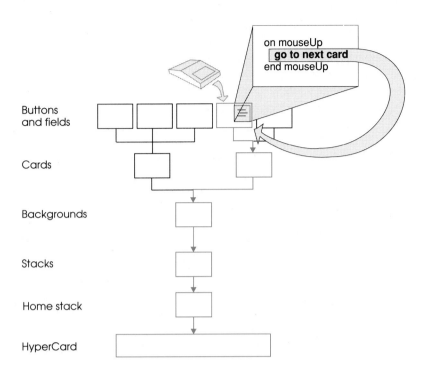

Figure 2-5
Command sent as a message

❖ *Function calls use the message-passing hierarchy:* Function calls work like messages in the way they traverse the object hierarchy. When you make a function call with the syntax that uses parentheses, HyperCard looks in the script of each object in the hierarchy for a matching function handler. If none is found, the function call is passed to HyperCard itself.

The target

The object to which the message is first sent is the **target.** If HyperCard finds a handler in the target that matches the message name, the handler's statements start executing. If, however, the target has no matching handler, the message is passed down the hierarchy. HyperCard may find a matching handler in another object, which then begins executing as shown in Figure 2-6.

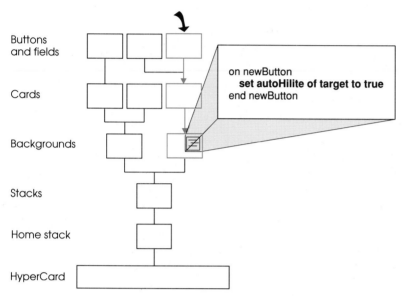

Figure 2-6
The target

The function `the target` returns the value of the original target, so that handlers in succeeding objects can determine where a message was originally sent. In Figure 2-6, although the executing handler is in the background script, `the target`, used in the background handler, identifies the button that originally received the message.

The dynamic path

When a message is traversing the hierarchy of a card different from the current one, HyperCard inserts a **dynamic path** into the static path the message normally follows. The **static path** is the route defined by an object's own hierarchy. For example, a card passes messages to its own background, the background passes them to its own stack, and so on. When that hierarchy is not the one stemming from the current card (the one currently visible), HyperCard passes messages through the current card's hierarchy as well—that's the dynamic path.

Examples of situations in which a message traverses a hierarchy different from the current one, invoking the dynamic path, are

☐ when an executing handler contains a command that takes you to another card (such as go or a command to create or delete the current card)

☐ when you use the send keyword to send a message to an object not in the current hierarchy

When any message that has not been received by a handler reaches the stack, HyperCard checks to see if the current card is in a different hierarchy. If so, HyperCard passes the message to the current card, and it traverses the current card, background, and stack, before it passes to the Home stack.

If any handler receives the message and passes it explicitly with the pass keyword, HyperCard does not invoke the dynamic path unless the current hierarchy is in a different stack from the static path. If either of the hierarchies is in the Home stack, the message is not passed again to the Home stack.

The go command and the dynamic path

Figures 2-7 and 2-8 show how a handler containing a go command invokes the dynamic path.

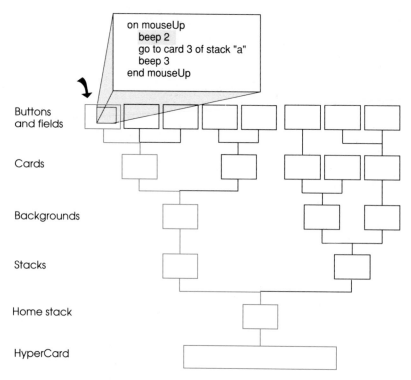

```
on mouseUp
  beep 2
  go to card 3 of stack "a"
  beep 3
end mouseUp
```

Buttons and fields

Cards

Backgrounds

Stacks

Home stack

HyperCard

Figure 2-7
Static path before the go command executes

In Figure 2-7, the mouseUp handler executes the statement beep 2, which is sent as a message along the current hierarchy beginning with the button containing the handler. After the go executes, the current card has changed. Nonetheless, the button handler continues to execute, sending subsequent statements as messages through its own hierarchy. In addition, however, HyperCard now sends messages to the card, background, and stack of the new current hierarchy, as shown in Figure 2-8.

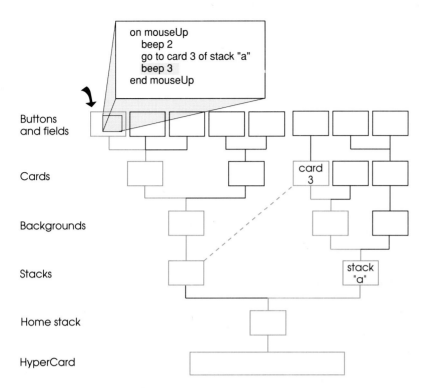

```
on mouseUp
    beep 2
    go to card 3 of stack "a"
    beep 3
end mouseUp
```

Buttons
and fields

Cards

card
3

Backgrounds

Stacks

stack
"a"

Home stack

HyperCard

Figure 2-8
Dynamic path after the go command executes

The send keyword and the dynamic path

It's possible to send a message directly to an object, whether or not it's in the current hierarchy, by using the send keyword. For example, you can type the following statement into the Message box:

```
send "greetings" to stack "a"
```

HyperCard looks in the script of the object to which the message is sent (in this case, stack "a") for a matching handler, just as if it were in the current hierarchy. If the matching handler isn't found (in this case, a handler named greetings), the message goes down the hierarchy stemming from the object to which it was sent (that is, from stack "a"). If the target of the send is a stack other than the current one, HyperCard invokes the dynamic path.

Figure 2-9 shows the path of a message directed with the send keyword.

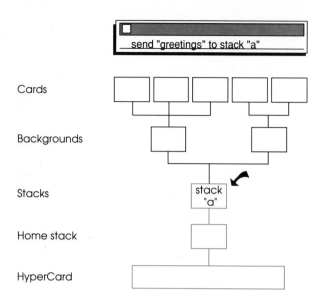

Figure 2-9
Using the send keyword

So the executing handler, the one currently in control, need not belong to any particular object. It doesn't need to be in the hierarchy belonging to the current card. Which handler has control is determined solely by which object receives a message.

You can use the send keyword to direct a message to

□ any object in the current stack

□ any other stack on any disk or file server accessible to your Macintosh (but not any individual object in those stacks)

□ HyperCard itself

For details about the send keyword, see Chapter 5.

Handlers calling handlers

When a handler executes, HyperCard sends each statement as a message first to the object containing the executing handler. So other handlers in the same script, as well as those in any other script lower in the hierarchy, can be used as subroutines. A handler can also call itself, which is known as **recursion.**

Subroutine calls

You can use handlers in HyperCard the way you use procedures or subroutines in other languages. You invoke a subroutine call in HyperTalk by executing a statement that begins with the name of a handler. That name is sent as a message, first to the object that contains the executing handler, then along the current object hierarchy.

You can include a subroutine in a script by writing a handler in the same script (or any other script lower in the object hierarchy) with whatever name you'd like to call it by. In the following example, the handler greetings is defined in the same script as the one from which the message greetings is sent:

```
on mouseUp
  greetings
end mouseUp

on greetings
  Put "You've just been drafted!" into the Message box
end greetings
```

When HyperCard executes the statement consisting of the subroutine handler name, and a match is found between the name and its handler, control passes to the subroutine handler. After it has finished executing, control passes back to the calling handler. But it's entirely possible for the subroutine handler to issue a similar message, beginning execution of a third handler. The third handler must finish executing before control passes back to the second handler, which must finish executing before control passes back to the first. The execution of a handler that has invoked another handler is suspended until the handler it has called finishes executing.

❖ *Stopping execution:* A handler can avoid giving control back to pending handlers by executing the exit to HyperCard keyword statement. You can interrupt an executing handler at any time (and bypass pending handlers) by pressing Command-period.

Any handler can act as a subroutine for any other handler. The called handler either has to be in the same script or in a script lower in the object hierarchy. However, you can also use the send keyword to send the message (the subroutine handler name) directly to the object that contains the handler. (See Chapter 5 for details on using send.) Generally, handlers that act as subroutines are placed in the same script as the handlers that call them.

❖ *Handlers can't be nested:* Handlers can't be defined with one inside another—a handler definition must not appear between the on statement and the end statement of another handler.

Recursion

The term for a handler calling itself is *recursion.* In the following example, the handler decrement subtracts 1 from a number in the Message box until the number is reduced to 1 (a number must be in the Message box before you call the handler). To do the subtraction, the handler summons itself:

```
on decrement
  subtract 1 from the message box
  if the value of the message box > 1 then decrement
end decrement
```

Generally, subroutine calls and recursion don't cause any problems. In fact, they are natural consequences of the good programming technique of separating scripts into functional units. However, HyperCard has a limit on the number of pending handlers. The actual number depends on the complexity of the handlers and other factors. It doesn't matter whether a handler is invoking itself or another handler—either type of invocation causes another level of pending execution.

In particular, watch out for endless recursion as in the following handler (if it were in a stack script or the script of every card):

```
on openCard
  go to next card
end openCard
```

The go next card command results in an openCard message, so the handler recurses again and again, and you get an error dialog box. Keep control in a single handler instead, as with the following script (if it were in the first card's script):

```
on openCard
  repeat for the number of cards -1
    go to next card
  end repeat
end openCard
```

Using the hierarchy

Where you place a handler in the hierarchy determines when it will be called. All objects that are higher in the hierarchy can call handlers in objects lower in the hierarchy. Lower objects can't call handlers in higher objects unless they use the send keyword. Messages that are sent when a statement in a handler executes always go first to the object containing the executing handler. Then they traverse the hierarchy stemming from that object until they find a matching handler or reach HyperCard itself. Therefore, the farther down the hierarchy a handler is placed, the greater the number of objects that can pass messages to it.

Sharing handlers

In effect, every object has access to the handlers of all the objects lower than it in the hierarchy. If you want every card in a stack to have a certain capability (that is, to respond to a certain message), you put the appropriate handler in the stack script. Every card can use the handler by passing the message down to the stack.

Figures 2-10 and 2-11 show the effect of placing a handler at different positions in the hierarchy. The example handler responds to the message moveOn (the message name is for example only). The handler takes you to the next card:

```
on moveOn
  go to next card
end moveOn
```

You can place the handler in the script of the current card, as in Figure 2-10. Then, if you send moveOn from the Message box, you invoke the handler and go to the next card. From any other card, however, the moveOn message has no effect.

In Figure 2-11, the handler is invoked by sending moveOn to any card in the stack (because the handler is in the script of the stack).

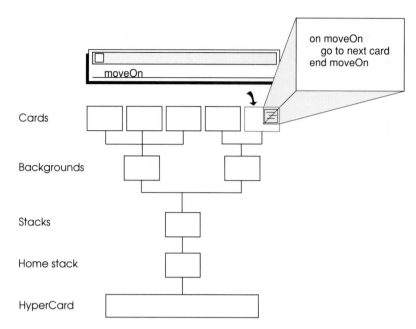

Figure 2-10
Handler in card script

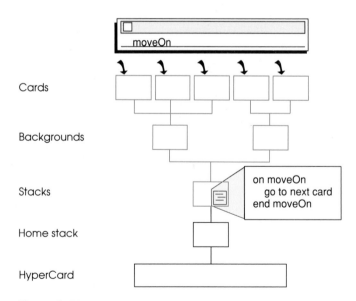

Figure 2-11
Handler in stack script

Intercepting messages

You can also make any card you want an exception in the way it responds to a given message, without affecting the other cards in the stack, by putting a special handler for the message in that card's script: you write two different handlers with the same message name—one in the stack script and one in the card script. Then, for that same message, if the message comes through that particular card, the card's handler runs; from any other card, the stack's handler runs.

For instance, in the previous example, putting the handler in the stack script caused the message moveOn to take you to the next card from any card in the stack:

```
on moveOn
  go to next card
end moveOn
```

But if you want the last card in the stack to be an exception, from which the message moveOn takes you back to the Home card, put the following handler in the last card's script:

```
on moveOn
  go to stack "home"
end moveOn
```

Figure 2-12 illustrates this example of one object intercepting a message.

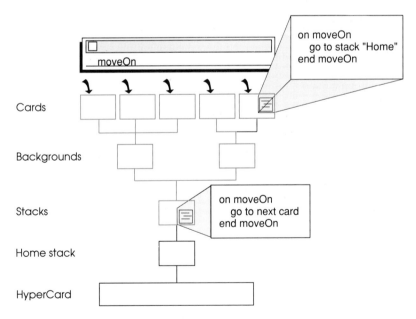

Figure 2-12
Intercepting a message

❖ *A handler can intercept a HyperTalk command:* In the same way that you can give one card a unique way of handling a message that would ordinarily be handled in the background or stack script, you can write a handler with the same name as a HyperTalk command and place it anywhere in the hierarchy. But remember that your handler is the one that will ordinarily run in response to the command message, not HyperCard's built-in one. HyperTalk functions can be redefined in a similar manner, and the same warning applies.

Parameter passing

When a HyperTalk message is sent, the first word is the message name. For example, in the message

```
searchScript "WildCard","Help"
```

the message name is `searchScript`. Any other words (or characters) are the **parameters.** In the example, the parameters are `"WildCard"` and `"Help"`. Each receiving object in the hierarchy looks for a message handler with a matching name. If the object finds a matching handler, the parameters are passed into the handler.

Parameters are passed into handlers as a list of comma-separated expressions. (Chapter 4 describes expressions.) These expressions are evaluated before the message is sent and, when the message is received, placed into a list of comma-separated **parameter variables** appearing on the first line of the matching handler definition. (See Figure 2-13.) That is, parameters are passed by value into handlers.

Parameter variables are local variables of the handler in which they appear. Parameter variables are also called **formal parameters,** to contrast them to the **actual parameters** which are the parameter values passed to them.

❖ *Function handler parameters:* HyperCard passes parameters into function handlers and message handlers in the same way, except that the syntax of the function call requires the parameters to be placed between parentheses. Placement of the parameter variables on the first line of function handlers is identical to that of message handlers.

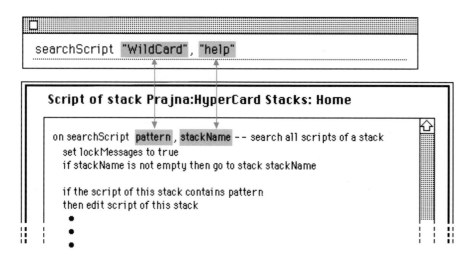

```
searchScript "WildCard" , "help"
```

Script of stack Prajna:HyperCard Stacks: Home

```
on searchScript pattern , stackName -- search all scripts of a stack
    set lockMessages to true
    if stackName is not empty then go to stack stackName

    if the script of this stack contains pattern
    then edit script of this stack
        •
        •
        •
```

Figure 2-13
Parameter passing

The value of the first expression in the message is placed into the first parameter variable in the handler, the value of the second expression into the second parameter variable, and so on. If there are more expressions in the message's parameter list than there are parameter variables in the first line of the handler, the extra parameters are ignored. If there are more parameter variables than parameters, the extra parameter variables are given an empty value (equal to a string of zero length).

❖ *Passing parameters to redefined commands:* HyperTalk command parameters are often more complex than a comma-separated list of expressions. Some built-in commands take parameters to which user-written handlers have no access. So, if you redefine a command, you may not be able to pass all of the parameters to your handler.

Chapter summary

Here is a summary of the material covered in this chapter:

☐ The HyperCard environment consists of objects related to each other in a hierarchy using HyperTalk as the means of communicating.

☐ Messages sent to objects initiate all HyperCard actions.

☐ Messages are generated by system events, executing handlers, statements typed into the Message box, and the execution of some commands.

☐ When an object receives a message, HyperCard tries to match the message name with a handler in the object's script; if it finds a match, it executes the handler; otherwise it passes the message to the next object.

☐ The object hierarchy determines how messages are passed from one object to another.

☐ You can send a message directly to any object in the current stack, to another stack, or to HyperCard using the send keyword.

☐ A handler can initiate execution of another handler as a subroutine call.

☐ Every object can use the handlers of objects lower than it in the hierarchy by passing messages; conversely, an object can intercept a message to perform a different action.

☐ The values of a series of expressions following the first word of a message statement are passed to variables in the first line of the receiving handler.

Chapter 3

Naming Objects

This chapter explains how to refer to HyperCard's objects.

A HyperCard object has three characteristics:

☐ It can send and receive messages.

☐ It has **properties,** which are its defining characterstics, and one of those properties is its script.

☐ It has a visible representation on the Macintosh screen (although the object need not always be visible).

You refer to an object when you use the `go` keyword (to go to a particular card, background, or stack) or the `send` command (to send a message to a particular object), and when you want to manipulate an object's properties. Fields are unique because they are HyperCard objects and are also sources of values (described in Chapter 4).

You can think of HyperCard itself as an object, because it can send and receive messages and it has global properties, including a "script" of built-in handlers or commands. When this guide talks about objects, however, it usually refers to buttons, fields, cards, backgrounds, and stacks.

Object descriptors

You refer to objects using **object descriptors.** An object descriptor is formed by combining a generic name with its specific designation. Generic names are `stack`, `card`, `background` (abbreviated `bkgnd`), `button` (abbreviated `btn`), or `field`.

To refer to background buttons, you must include that designation with the generic name (`background button "buttonName"`), and you must do the same for card fields (`card field "fieldName"`). You can also include the default designation, but it's not required (`card button "buttonName"` refers to the same button as `button "buttonName"` and `background field "fieldName"` refers to the same field as `field "fieldName"`).

The only specific designation of a stack is its name. (See "Stack Descriptors," later in this chapter.) The specific designation of all other objects (buttons, fields, backgrounds, and cards) can be the objects's name, number, or ID number. The unambiguous form of a designation begins with an object's generic name, immediately followed by its particular name, number, or ID number. (See Figure 3-1.)

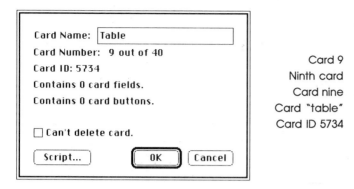

Card 9
Ninth card
Card nine
Card "table"
Card ID 5734

Figure 3-1
Card Info dialog box and descriptors for the same card

Object names

Names are optional for cards, backgrounds, buttons, and fields. You assign a name for any of these objects by typing into the Name box in the object Info dialog box, which appears when you choose the object's Info item from the Objects menu. Object names can include any characters, even spaces. It's safest to put quotation marks around an object name when you use it in a statement (background button "belly") to ensure that HyperCard recognizes it literally and doesn't look for a variable or stack by that name.

❖ *Be careful with names:* It's difficult to manipulate a name that extends out of the naming window although you can scroll it left and right (and up and down if it has more than one line) by dragging. It's also difficult to refer by name to an object if you put a double quotation mark in its name. Also, if you use numbers for an object's name, HyperCard gets confused: it takes card "1812" to mean a card whose *number,* rather than name, is 1812.

Object ID numbers

HyperCard generates an object ID number for each object within a stack. This number is unique for that type of object within its enclosing object. For example, each button (the type of object) on a card (the enclosing object) has a different ID number. Object ID numbers never change and, if an object is deleted, are not reassigned to newly created objects (until the HyperCard object limit, listed in Appendix E, has been reached). An object's ID number is its generic name, followed by the word ID (in uppercase or lowercase), followed by an integer (for example, card id 5734).

❖ *The ID number of a copied object is different:* If you copy an object and paste it into a different enclosing object, the copy is then a different object from the original, and it has a different ID number. For example, if you copy a card and paste it into a different stack, the ID number of the pasted card is different from the ID number of the card you copied. Therefore, you can't assume that you have "moved" the card when you copy it, paste it, and delete the original—a button that took you to the original will probably not take you to the copy.

Because ID numbers are unique and unchanging for all objects within a stack, HyperCard uses them internally to identify objects (for example, to identify the target of a `go` command generated with the LinkTo feature in the Button Info dialog box). HyperCard can generally find objects faster if they are identified by ID number. Also, if you ask for the name of an object that has no name (`put the name of last card`), HyperCard returns its ID number. (See Chapter 9 for information about the `name` object property.)

Object numbers

Buttons, fields, cards, and backgrounds always have numbers by which you can refer to them. An object's number represents its position within its containing object: buttons and fields are ordered within a card or background; cards and backgrounds are ordered within their stack. There are three ways to express an object's number: use an integer following its generic name (`card 2`), use one of the numeric constants `one` through `ten` following its generic name (`card two`), or use one of the ordinal constants `first` through `tenth` preceding its generic name (`second card`).

❖ *Descriptor phrasing:* Be careful to phrase descriptors so that they mean what you intend. For example, using a field descriptor such as `card field id 7`, you could mean that the name of the card is in the background field with ID number 7, or you could be referring to the card field with ID number 7. HyperCard assumes that you're referring to the card field. If you want HyperCard to get the card name from the background field, enclose its descriptor in parentheses:

`card (field id 7).`

Object numbers are contiguous from 1 through the number of currently existing objects within the enclosing object: card buttons and card fields within their card; background buttons and background fields within their background; cards within their stack (not their background); and backgrounds within their stack. If you delete an object, its number is reassigned to the object following it in order, and so on for the succeeding objects as well.

Special ordinals

In addition to the ordinal constants `first` through `tenth`, HyperTalk has three special ordinals: `middle`, `last`, and `any`. The values of the special ordinals are resolved according to the number of objects in the set. `Middle` resolves to half the number of objects plus 1. `Last` resolves to the number of objects. `Any` resolves to a random number between 1 and the number of objects. (The special ordinals also work with chunk expressions, which are described in Chapter 4.)

Object numbers and tab order

The sequence of object numbers determines tab order for fields: you can move from field to field within a background and card using the Tab key—it moves from the lowest number field to the highest through the background fields first, then the card fields. The sequence also determines which button or field gets a message when several are layered on top of each other (the highest numbered one is closest and gets the message), and it determines which card or background is `next` or `previous` within a stack.

❖ *Reassigning object numbers:* You can reassign object numbers of buttons and fields with the Bring Closer and Send Farther menu commands. See the *HyperCard User's Guide* for details.

Special object descriptors

You can use the special descriptor `this` to refer to the current card, background, or stack. For example:

```
put the id of this card into whereFound
```

You can't use `this` with buttons or fields.

You can refer to the card or background preceding the current one, within the stack, as `previous`, which can be abbreviated `prev`. Similarly, you can refer to the card or background following the current one as `next`. For example:

```
go to next background
```

You can refer to the card that was current immediately prior to the current one as `recent`.

You use `me` within a script to specify the object containing the currently executing handler. For example:

```
put the textHeight of me into height -- in a field's script
```

❖ *Using special descriptors with fields as containers:* In all versions of HyperCard, you can use a special object descriptor (other than `this`) to identify a field as an object: to get or set its properties, or as the target of `send`. For example, the following statements always work:

```
put the name of me into myName
send mouseUp to me
```

A field, however, is both an object and a container. In versions of HyperCard prior to version 1.2, you can't use a special object descriptor to refer to a field as a container into which to put a value. For example, the following statement in a field script would work only in HyperCard versions 1.2 and later:

```
put "*" before line 1 of me
```

See Chapter 4, "Values," for information about containers.

Stack descriptors

A stack is a HyperCard document. In some cases when you're writing a script or using the Message box, you can refer to a stack by its name alone. To do that, the stack must be in the current folder, in the folder containing the Help stacks, or in the current disk or server (and not in a folder). When the stack is located anywhere else, you must let HyperCard know the full pathname by which it can find the stack.

A full pathname is a concatenation of the volume name, directory name(s), and filename, separated by colons. The volume name is the name of the disk or server containing the stack. The directory names are the names of all the folders, if any, that HyperCard has to open to get to the stack. (HyperCard sometimes might have to open several folders because folders may contain other folders to any depth.) The filename is the stack name.

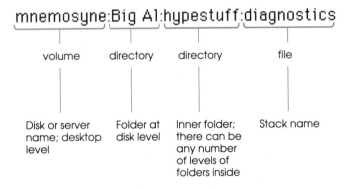

Figure 3-2
A pathname

The only unambiguous way to refer to a stack in a script or in the Message box is the word `stack` followed by its name in quotation marks. When you refer to a stack you can use the full pathname to specify the stack's exact location: `go to stack "myDisk:myFolder:mystack"`. You can also type the full pathname on the stack search path card in the Home stack. If HyperCard can't find a stack you request, it displays a dialog box that allows you to click your way through the directories until you reach the stack. HyperCard notes your path and, once you've found the stack, automatically records its full pathname on the stack search path card in the Home stack.

❖ *Ambiguous stack descriptors:* HyperCard will try to derive a proper stack name from an ambiguous expression in a place where it expects a stack descriptor, but it cannot always succeed. In that case, HyperCard displays the directory dialog box to allow the user to find the stack file.

Naming a stack

You must name a stack when you create it. (For all other objects, names are optional.) You create a stack with the New Stack command in the File menu. A dialog box appears in which you type the name for the new stack. (See Figure 3-3.)

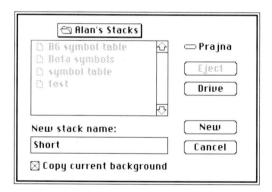

Figure 3-3
New Stack dialog box

Combining object descriptors

To refer to objects within a stack, you combine object descriptors using either of the prepositions `of` or `in` between an object descriptor and that of its enclosing object. Combined object descriptors proceed left-to-right from the smaller to the larger:

```
first field of last card of this background
```

This syntax lets you refer directly to any object within the current stack—you don't have to go to the card containing a particular field to get its contents or put something into it. For example, if the current card were the first in the stack, you could still execute the following command:

```
put the selection into field "undoHolder" of last card
```

You cannot refer to an object within another stack. You have to go to the stack before you can address its objects directly.

You can further combine field descriptors with chunk expressions, which are described in Chapter 4, "Values."

Chapter summary

Here is a summary of the material covered in this chapter:

- □ You refer to a HyperCard object using an object descriptor—its generic name and its specific designation.

- □ Cards, backgrounds, buttons, and fields always have unique ID numbers that never change, they always have object numbers that may change, and they may optionally be given names.

- □ You can use special ordinals—`middle`, `last`, and `any`—to refer to objects by their position within their enclosing object.

- □ You can refer to the current card, background, or stack with `this`. You can refer to the card or background preceding the current one with `previous`, and to the one following the current one with `next`. You can refer to the card that was current prior to the current one with `recent`.

- □ The term `me`, in a script, refers to the object containing the script.

- □ The only unambiguous object descriptor for a stack is the word `stack` followed by the stack's filename within quotation marks.

- □ You can combine object descriptors to refer directly to any object in the current stack.

Chapter 4

Values

This chapter describes the expressions you use to refer to **values:** the information on which HyperCard operates. It also describes HyperTalk's **operators,** the elements of the language that you use in expressions to manipulate and calculate values.

HyperCard does not have data types: values are stored simply as strings of characters. (Numbers are sometimes represented internally in a more efficient format, as described later in this chapter.)

An **expression** is a description of how to get a value. It may be as simple as a single source of a value, or it can be a complex expression built with operators.

Sources of values

The **sources of values** in HyperTalk are

☐ constants

☐ literals

☐ functions

☐ properties

☐ numbers

☐ containers

These sources of values are the most basic expressions.

Constants

A **constant** is a named value that never changes. It's different from a variable in that you can't change it, and it's different from a literal in that its value is not always the string of characters making up the name. For example, the constant empty is the same as the null string (the literal " "), and the constant space is the same as the literal " ". All HyperTalk constants are described in Chapter 10.

Literals

A **literal** is a text string whose value *is* the string, exactly as it appears. Literals are denoted by double quotation marks at both ends of the string. (You must use the straight double quotation mark, not the printer's double quotation marks typed with the Option–left bracket and Option–Shift–left bracket keys.) Any character except double quotation mark, return, or "soft" return (generated by pressing Option-Return) can be part of a literal string. A literal can be of any length. For example, "This is a literal string" is a literal.

❖ *Unquoted literals are not recommended:* In some places you can use an unquoted single word as an unquoted literal (as long as the word doesn't begin with a digit). The value of an unquoted literal is the literal of itself—as though you had entered put "fred" into fred. But unquoted literals are not allowed in complex expressions (those built with operators). It's always safer to put double quotation marks around a word you want HyperCard to take as a literal.

Functions

A **function** is a named value that HyperCard calculates when the statement in which the function is used executes. The value of a function varies according to conditions of the system or according to the value of parameters you pass to the function when you use it.

For example, the built-in function named the time returns the current time in place of itself in a HyperTalk statement:

```
put the time into msg
```

If the current time were 5:12 P.M., the above example would put 5:12 PM into the Message box.

You can also define your own functions in scripts using the function handler structure described in Chapter 5.

All built-in HyperTalk functions are described in Chapter 8.

Properties

A **property** is a named value representing one of the defining characteristics of a HyperCard object or the HyperCard environment. Different types of objects have different properties, according to their purpose. For example, fields share a set of properties, many of which are different from the set shared by buttons.

You get the value of most properties by using the property name as a function in a script or in the Message box. For example, the following statement retrieves the location property (two integers separated by a comma) of button 1, and it puts the value into the Message box:

```
put the location of button 1 into msg
```

You can also change most properties with the set command. All HyperCard properties are described in Chapter 9.

Numbers

A **number** in HyperCard is a character string consisting of any combination of the numerals 0 through 9, representing a decimal value. A number can include one period (.) representing the decimal point, but it can have no other punctuation nor a space character. A number can be preceded by a hyphen or minus sign to represent a negative value (HyperCard doesn't recognize a plus sign as part of a number). Numbers that consist only of numerals are integers. Numbers that include a period are real, and, when used with mathematical operators, are manipulated with floating-point operations.

Standard Apple Numerics Environment

HyperCard performs mathematical operations with Standard Apple Numerics Environment (SANE®) routines, but you don't have to worry about how to represent the values. You always enter numbers into HyperCard containers as numeric strings.

When performing a mathematical operation, HyperCard automatically converts the strings representing the numbers to SANE numeric values. If you put the result of the operation into a variable, it's stored as a SANE numeric value; if you put it into a field or the Message box, HyperCard automatically converts it back to a string with a precision of up to 19 decimal places. The same conversion takes place if you put the variable into a field or the Message box at a later time, or if you use it in a way that implies a string (`character 2 of varName`). So although SANE values are used internally for handling numbers with speed and precision, you can always think of HyperTalk numbers as strings.

Precision

The precision of the decimal string, resulting from putting a SANE numeric value into a field or the Message box, is controlled by the `numberFormat` global property (see Chapter 9 for a detailed description). For example, the command

```
set numberFormat to 0.00
```

would result in a string with at least one digit to the left of the decimal point and exactly two digits to the right of the decimal point.

The `numberFormat` property does not affect the precision with which mathematical operations are executed, only the precision with which the results are displayed. When you put a number into a field or the Message box to display it, however, HyperCard converts it to a decimal string. So any extra precision it may have had (beyond the `numberFormat` specification in effect at the time) is lost.

Number handling

The following example shows how number handling works. These three HyperTalk statements put the constant `pi` into a variable, set the `numberFormat` property, and put the value of the variable into the Message box, respectively:

```
put pi into joe
set numberFormat to 0.00
put joe into msg
```

The result shown in the Message box is 3.14159265358979323846. In this case, `pi` is entered into the variable `joe` as a string, and it remains a string, so `numberFormat` has no effect. If, however, you perform a mathematical operation on the variable, HyperCard converts it to a SANE numeric value:

```
put pi into joe
add 0 to joe
set numberFormat to 0.00
put joe into msg
```

The result shown in the Message box is 3.14. In this case, `numberFormat` takes effect when `joe` is converted from a SANE numeric value to a string as it's put into the Message box.

Containers

A **container** in HyperCard is a place where you can store a value. Containers include fields, variables, the current selection, and the Message box. Containers other than fields can store values of any length, including zero length. Containers other than the Message box can have more than one line in them; each line ends with a return character (which can be the only character in the line).

Fields

A **field** is a HyperCard object for holding and displaying editable text. Fields are unique objects because they are also containers—a field's value is the text string it contains.

You can refer to fields directly by name, number, or ID number. (See Chapter 3, "Naming Objects," for more description of how to refer to fields.)

Fields belong to cards or to backgrounds; the text held by a field, however, always remains with the card, even if the field belongs to the background. A field can contain up to 30,000 characters, including spaces, return characters, and other invisible characters. If you put more than that many characters into a field, the extras are ignored.

Text in fields always remains editable—you can search through it with the `find` command, and you can change it with the I-beam pointer of the Browse tool (assuming the field isn't locked).

❖ *About Paint text:* You can also put text onto cards and backgrounds as **Paint text**—pictures that look like characters. Paint text can't be edited once it has been fixed onto the card or background (although you can paint over it or erase it as you can any part of a picture). See the *HyperCard User's Guide* for more information on Paint text.

Variables

A **variable** is a named container that has no visible representation other than its name. Its value is a character string of any length. The variable name is a HyperTalk **identifier.** An identifier can be of any length, it always begins with an alphabetic character, and it can contain any alphanumeric character plus the underscore character (_).

You assign a value to a variable with the `put` command. It is illegal to read from a nonexistent variable—you must create it by putting something into it before you use it. The constant `empty`, the null string, counts as something to put into a variable.

HyperCard assumes that an unquoted word used in an expression is a variable when it can't interpret the word as some other source of value (the string is not a function, constant, property, or other container name). If you haven't put a value into a variable by that name, HyperCard treats it as an unquoted literal.

Scope of variables: HyperCard has both local and global variables. A **local variable** is valid only during the current invocation of the currently executing handler. You don't need to declare a local variable before you use it—just put something into it. A **global variable** is valid for all handlers. You must declare a variable as global by using the `global` keyword in each handler before you use the variable:

```
global useMeEverywhere,useMeToo
```

HyperTalk assumes a variable to be local unless you specifically use the `global` keyword.

For more details on the `global` keyword, see Chapter 5.

Parameter variables: You create parameter variables when you put their names after the message name in a handler:

```
on messageName firstParam,secondParam
```

When the handler is called, these variables are assigned the values, if any, of the items in a comma-separated list of expressions following the message name in the calling statement. Parameter variables are local to their handler. Chapter 2, "Handling Messages," gives more explanation of parameter passing.

The variable It: The local variable named `It` is the destination of the commands `get`, `ask`, `answer`, and `read`. For example, `get the name of field 1` puts the value of that background field's name into `It`. `Convert` puts its results into `It` if another destination isn't specified.

For information on commands, see Chapter 7.

The selection

The **selection** is a container that holds the currently selected area of text. You can put values into, before, or after the selection or put the selection (or any chunk of the selection) into another container.

Starting with this selection...

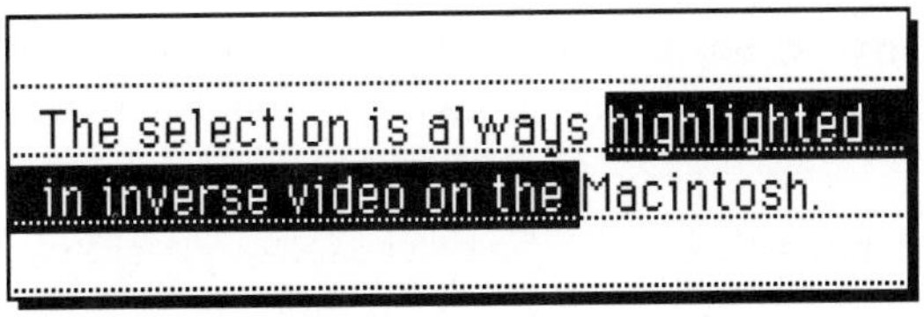

The selection is always highlighted in inverse video on the Macintosh.

...this HyperTalk command...

put "easy to change using a" into the selection

...produces this result.

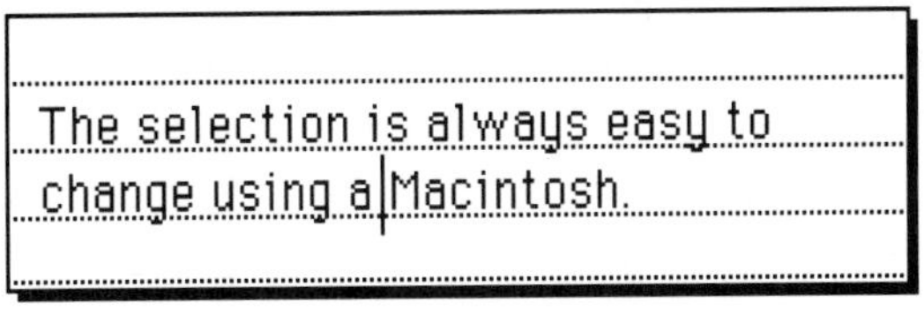

The selection is always easy to change using a Macintosh.

Figure 4-1
Manipulating the selection

For example, if the phrase `I'm the selected text` is selected, and you issue the command

put the selection into the Message box

then `I'm the selected text` appears in the Message box. (Both instances of the word `the` in the example are optional.)

❖ *Found text isn't selected:* Text found by the `find` command is indicated by a box around it—it is not placed into `selection`. HyperTalk versions prior to 1.2 don't have a construct to indicate directly where the text was found, but you can use `contains` and other operators to locate the text. HyperCard versions 1.2 and later have functions that return information about found text; they are described in Appendix F, "HyperTalk Changes in HyperCard Version 1.2." The `find` command is described in Chapter 7; operators are described later in this chapter.

You must select some text with the mouse or the `click` or `drag` command before you can manipulate the selection container.

The Message box

The **Message box** is a special container. Typically, you use the Message box to send a HyperTalk message directly to an object or to HyperCard. The Message box is a single-line container. If you put more than one line from a multiple-line container into the Message box (put card field 2 into msg), only the first line is copied into the Message box.

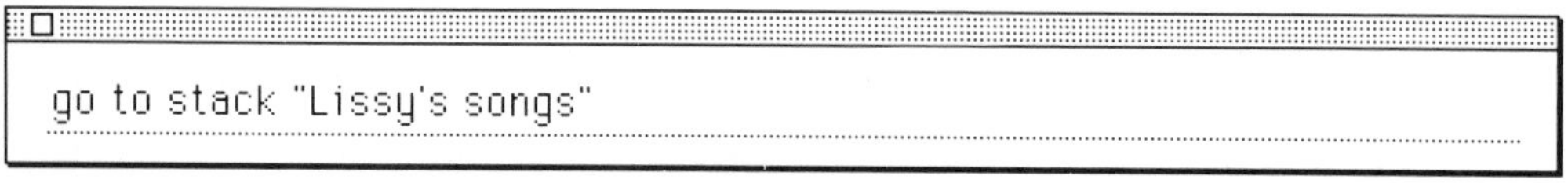

```
go to stack "Lissy's songs"
```

Figure 4-2
The Message box

The Message box is the default destination for the `put` command.

If you put something into the Message box when it's hidden, HyperCard shows it automatically. You can toggle the Message box between being hidden or shown by pressing Command-M.

The Message box can be specified by just the word `message` or its abbreviation `msg`. Optionally, you can follow either of those with either `box` or `window`, and you can precede either with the word `the`.

Complex expressions

You can build complex expressions using values and operators. As a complex expression is evaluated, the values of its basic components are manipulated to derive a final value in place of the entire expression. (The original values are not changed in the process.) Complex expressions are evaluated according to rules of precedence, and restrictions apply to the values that can be used, depending on their operators.

❖ *Chunk expressions are different:* Chunk expressions are a different type of expression: they designate pieces of the strings representing values. Chunk expressions are described in the last section of this chapter.

Factors

A **factor** is a single element of value in an expression. The following constructs are factors:

☐ a simple source of value

☐ an expression enclosed in parentheses

☐ a factor (which must evaluate to a number) with a hyphen or a minus sign in front of it

☐ a factor (which must evaluate to `true` or `false`) with the word `not` in front of it

An expression can be just a factor, or it can be any two expressions with an operator between them.

The difference between a factor and an expression is important to the syntax of HyperTalk commands and functions. Where a built-in HyperTalk command parameter permits an expression, you can specify as complex an expression as you wish. HyperCard derives the final value before passing the parameter to the command. For example, the `add` command accepts a complex expression as its first parameter:

```
add 46+12*monthlyRate to total
```

In contrast, where a built-in HyperTalk function requires a factor, HyperCard will take the value of the first factor as the parameter to pass to the function. For example, the `sqrt` function takes the first factor following its name as its parameter. This is illustrated by the following expression, which you can type into the Message box or use in a command:

```
the sqrt of 4 + 12
```

In the example, the `sqrt` function takes the factor `4` as its parameter, rather than the value of the expression `4 + 12`. So the entire expression evaluates to 14, rather than 4, which would be the value if `sqrt` accepted an entire expression. (To specify the entire expression `4 + 12` as the parameter, you can enclose it in parentheses, which turns it into a factor.)

❖ *Two hyphens always indicate a comment:* You can put a hyphen in front of a factor to create another factor, and you can put another hyphen in front of that and still have a factor. However, two hyphens in sequence indicate a comment, so you must separate the hyphens with a space or enclose the inner factor in parentheses for HyperCard to recognize the construct as a factor.

HyperTalk's built-in commands and functions are described in Chapters 7 and 8, respectively.

HyperTalk operators

Operators are used in complex expressions to derive values from other values. Operators fall into several categories:

□ Arithmetic operators work on numbers and result in numbers.

□ Comparison operators work on numbers, text, and Boolean values (`true` or `false`) and result in Boolean values.

□ Logical operators work on Boolean values and result in Boolean values.

□ Text operators manipulate text strings and result in text strings.

Parentheses alter the order of expression evaluation.

Operator precedence

Different operators have different orders of precedence that determine how things get evaluated. The order in which HyperCard performs operations is shown in Table 4-1.

Table 4-1
Operator precedence

Order	Operators	Type of operator
1	( )	Grouping
2	−	Minus sign for numbers
	not	Logical negation for Boolean values
3	^	Exponentiation for numbers
4	* / div mod	Multiplication and division for numbers
5	+ −	Addition and subtraction for numbers
6	& &&	Concatenation of text
7	> < <= >= ≤ ≥	Comparison for numbers or text
	is in contains	Comparison for text
	is not in	Comparison for text
8	= is is not <> ≠	Comparison for numbers or text
9	and	Logical for Boolean values
10	or	Logical for Boolean values

Operators of equal precedence are evaluated left to right, except for exponentiation, which goes right to left. For example, $2^3{}^4$ means "3 raised to the fourth power, then 2 raised to that power," whereas $1-2-3$ means "2 subtracted from 1, then 3 subtracted from that." If you use parentheses, HyperCard evaluates the parenthetical expression first.

Operators and expression type

The operator you use must match the values you're using it with: `"tom" + "cat"` would cause an error, because numeric values are required for addition. On the other hand, `tom + cat` would be acceptable if `tom` and `cat` were names of containers with numbers in them, and `"tom" & "cat"` would be acceptable because the `&` operator works on text strings (the result of this operation would be the text string `tomcat`). Text operators work on any value, because any value in HyperTalk can be treated as a text string; they always yield text strings.

Because numeric values are automatically converted to strings when necessary (see "Numbers" earlier in this chapter), they can be manipulated by both text operators and arithmetic operators. For example, `5 & 78` yields `578`, and `5 + 78` yields `83`.

Comparison operators try to treat both of their operands as numbers; if they can't be regarded as numbers, HyperCard treats them as text and does a lexical comparison. For example, `9 < 10` results in `true`, because `9` is less than `10` arithmetically. But, `"9x" < "10x"` results in `false`, because the operands can't be regarded as numbers and `9` is greater than `10` lexically.

Table 4-2 is a list of all the operators in HyperTalk.

Table 4-2
HyperTalk operators

Operator	Description
( )	Grouping: Expressions within the innermost pair of parentheses are evaluated first. Parentheses don't force a new level of evaluation; they change the sequence in which the current level of evaluation proceeds.
–	Minus: Arithmetic operator that makes negative the number to its right, or, if it is between two numbers, subtracts the one on the right from the one on the left.
+	Plus: Arithmetic operator that adds two numbers it appears between.
*	Multiply: Arithmetic operator that multiplies two numbers it appears between.
/	Divide: Arithmetic operator that divides the number to its left by the number to its right.
div	Divide and truncate: Arithmetic operator that divides a number to its left by a number to its right, ignoring any remainder, resulting in just the whole part.

Table 4-2 *(continued)*
HyperTalk operators

Operator	Description
mod	Modulo: Arithmetic operator that divides the number to its left by the number to its right, ignoring the whole part, resulting in just the remainder.
^	Exponent: Arithmetic operator that raises the number to its left to the power of the number to its right.
not	NOT: Logical operator that results in true if the expression on its right is false, and false if the expression on its right is true.
and	AND: Logical operator that results in true if both the expression to its left and the expression to its right are true.
or	OR: Logical operator that results in true if either the expression to its left or the expression to its right is true.
=	Equal: Comparison operator that results in true if the expression to its left and the expression to its right have the same value. The expressions can be arithmetic, text string, or logical.
is	Is: Same as =.
<>	Not equal: Comparison operator that results in true if the expression to its left and the expression to its right have different values. The expressions can be arithmetic, text, or logical.
≠	Not equal: Same as <>. The ≠ character is obtained on the Macintosh keyboard by pressing Option-equal (=).
is not	Is not: Same as <>.
<	Less than: Comparison operator that results in true if the expression to its left has less value than the one to its right. The expressions can be both arithmetic or both text.
>	Greater than: Comparison operator that results in true if the expression to its left has greater value than the one to its right. The expressions can be both arithmetic or both text.
<=	Less than or equal to: Comparison operator that results in true if the expression to its left has less value than the one to its right or the same value. The expressions can be both arithmetic or both text.
≤	Less than or equal to: Same as <=. The ≤ character is obtained on the Macintosh keyboard by pressing Option-comma (,).

Table 4-2 *(continued)*
HyperTalk operators

Operator	Description
>=	Greater than or equal to: Comparison operator that results in `true` if the expression to its left has greater value than the one to its right or the same value. The expressions can be both arithmetic or both text.
≥	Greater than or equal to: Same as >=. The ≥ character is obtained on the Macintosh keyboard by pressing Option-period (.).
contains	Contains: Comparison operator that results in `true` if the text string yielded by the expression on its right is found in the text string yielded by the expression on its left.
is in	Is in: Converse of `contains`; comparison operator that results in `true` if the text string yielded by the expression on its left is found in the text string yielded by the expression on its right.
is not in	Is not in: Opposite of `is in`; comparison operator that results in `true` if the text string yielded by the expression on its left is not found in the text string yielded by the expression on its right.
&	Concatenate: Text string operator that joins the text string yielded by the expression on its left to the text string yielded by the expression on its right.
&&	Concatenate with space: Text string operator that joins the text string yielded by the expression on its left to the text string yielded by the expression on its right, with a space between them.

Chunk expressions

You use a chunk expression to specify a particular piece—a **chunk**—of the value of any source of value: constant, literal, function, property, number, or container. Chunk expressions can specify any character, word, item, or line in the source.

Syntax

The form of a chunk expression designates the smallest part of the chunk first, then specifies each larger, enclosing part. You separate each part of the expression with the preposition `of` or its synonym `in`. For example,

```
first character of second word of third line of field 1
```

specifies a single character in the field.

You modify the specification of the kind of chunk—character, word, item, or line—with the number of the particular one you want. The number can be an ordinal constant preceding the kind (`tenth word`) or an integer following the kind (`line 2`). You can also use a numeric constant in place of the integer (`line two`), or any numeric expression that resolves to an integer.

You can use the special ordinals `middle`, `last`, and `any` to specify a chunk within its enclosing part. HyperCard resolves a special ordinal to a number using the total number of chunks of the specified type within its enclosing part: `middle` resolves to one more than half the total, `last` resolves to the total, and `any` resolves to a random number between 1 and the total. For example,

```
put "Joe" into any word of line 2 of field 1
```

replaces a random word in the line with `Joe`.

It isn't necessary to specify the enclosing parts of the source in strict, hierarchical order. You can designate any smaller part within any larger part:

```
character 35 of field 1
```

And, although you must go left-to-right from smaller to larger, you don't have to specify any smaller part than you want:

```
third item of It
```

Characters

Characters are designated by the chunk name `character` (or `char`). Spaces count as characters in any part of a source except words. (Words are delimited by spaces.) Commas count as characters except in items. (Items are delimited by commas.) Return characters count as characters in whole sources and items. (A return character delimits the last word on the line as well as the line itself.)

For example, if field 6 contains the phrase

```
It was the turtle, not I, who spilled the beans.
```

the chunk expression

```
character 25 of field 6
```

yields a comma (the one after `not I`).

Words

Words are composed of any characters, including punctuation, delimited by spaces, and are designated by the chunk name `word`:

`word 2 of "Where's my cubicle?"`

yields `my`.

Items

Items are composed of any characters, including punctuation, delimited by commas, and are designated by the chunk name `item`:

`item three of "cat's, rat's, bat's, gnat's"`

yields " `bat's`" (including the space character in front).

Lines

Lines are composed of any characters, including punctuation, delimited by return characters, and are designated by the chunk name `line`.

The chunk name `line` strictly denotes text between the beginning of a container and the first return character, between two return characters, or between the last return character and the end of the container.

It doesn't matter how many display lines it takes to display one container line. For example, a single line in a field might occupy several lines on the display if the text wraps around (which it does if the field isn't wide enough to accommodate the whole line).

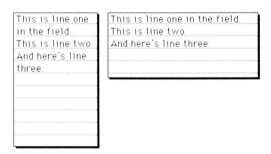

Figure 4-3
Lines in a field

Ranges

The preposition `to` in a chunk expression specifies a range of a chunk within the larger chunk:

```
word 1 to 5 of line 2 of field "fred"
```

The numbers given in a range are inclusive. For example:

```
char 2 to 5 of "HyperTalk"
```

yields `yper`.

You specify the range with integers (or with constants or numeric expressions that resolve to integers) following the chunk name, rather than with ordinal numbers preceding the chunk name. That is, you must say `char 1 to 3 of "george"`; you can't say `first to third char of "george"`.

When the first number in a range is greater than the second, you get the first chunk only. For example, `char 5 to 3 of "HyperTalk"` yields the character `r`.

Figure 4-4 shows some chunk expressions, labeled in various valid forms of chunk expression syntax, in a hypothetical `card field 1`.

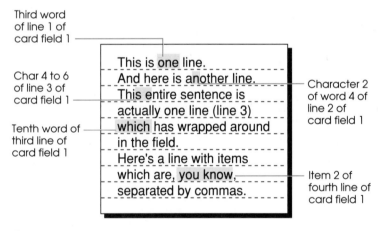

Figure 4-4
Chunk expressions

Chunks and containers

Combining a chunk expression with the object descriptor of a field lets you refer directly to any piece of text down to a single character within the current stack:

```
put char 2 of line 2 of field 1 of last card
```

❖ *You can't specify chunks in another stack:* You can't combine a stack name with a chunk expression; you must go to the stack first.

Chunks as destinations as well as sources

Chunk expressions can be used to specify a part of the value in a container wherever a container name is used. So, the chunk can specify the destination of a value—where you're putting it—as well as the source of a value—where you're getting it. For example,

```
put "George" into word 3 of field 1
```

replaces only the third word in the field with the value George, leaving the rest of the field's former contents intact.

Nonexistent chunks

If you specify chunks that don't exist as sources of values, you get nothing. That is,

```
put char 5 of "hey" into msg
```

puts empty into the Message box.

If you specify a nonexistent chunk as the destination of a put command, the outcome depends on the kind of chunk. If you put a value into a character or a word that doesn't exist in a container, you put just the value. That is, if field 1 is empty, the statement:

```
put "hey" into word 5 of field 1
```

puts hey (with no characters before it) into background field 1.

If you put a value into a nonexistent line, however, HyperCard puts in a return character, and if you put a value into a nonexistent item, HyperCard puts in a comma. (In both cases, you put a null chunk delimited by its particular delimiting character.) For example, if field 1 is empty, the statement:

```
put "hey" into line 5 of field 1
```

puts four return characters (four null lines) followed by hey into background field 1. Similarly,

```
put "hey" into item 5 of field 1
```

puts four commas (four null items) followed by hey into the first line of background field 1.

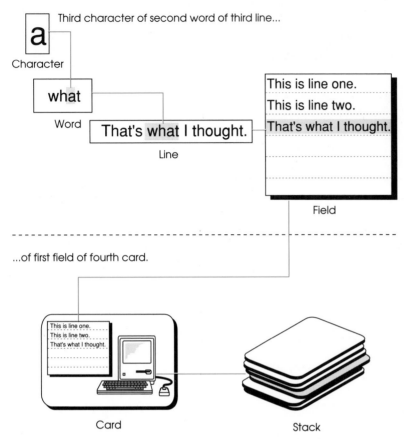

Figure 4-5
Combining chunks and objects

Chapter summary

Here is a summary of the material covered in this chapter:

☐ HyperTalk's values can always be treated as strings of characters.

☐ The most basic expressions in HyperTalk are constants, literals, functions, properties, numbers, and containers.

☐ Containers—fields, variables, the selection, and the Message box—are places to store values.

☐ Complex expressions are built with values and operators.

☐ Operators are used to manipulate and calculate values.

☐ Chunk expressions can specify any chunk—character, word, item, or line—either in a source of value or as the destination of a `put` command.

Chapter 5

Keywords

This chapter describes all of HyperTalk's keywords.

A **keyword** is a word whose meaning is predefined in HyperTalk. You cannot redefine keywords as variable names. Keywords are not sent as messages when they execute in scripts, nor can they be used in the Message box (except for `send`). Some keywords provide the structure for handlers; others control the flow of execution within handlers.

HyperTalk has two kinds of handlers: message and function handlers, denoted by the initial keywords `on` and `function`, respectively. Message and function handlers are defined in the same way (except for the initial keyword), but they differ in how they are invoked and in how they return values.

In this chapter, the heading for each keyword is followed by a syntax statement. Words in italic are general elements. Square brackets ([ ]) denote optional elements (don't type the square brackets).

Keywords in message handlers

The `on` keyword identifies a HyperCard message handler. Message handlers are written to define your own messages, or to modify or redefine what happens in response to any message (including a HyperTalk command). The general syntax of a message handler looks like this:

```
on messageName [parameterList]
   [statementList]
end messageName
```

MessageName is an identifier: a string starting with a letter and containing no spaces or punctuation marks except underscore; *parameterList* is a series of zero or more parameter variables (separated by commas if more than one); and *statementList* is zero or more HyperTalk statements.

The handler dictates the method by which its object responds to *messageName*. When somebody sends a message called *messageName* to an object, HyperCard checks all of that object's message handlers to see if it has one named *messageName*. If so, the object responds according to that handler, and the message is sent no further (assuming the script has no `pass` statement, described later in this chapter). If the object has no handler to match *messageName*, HyperCard passes the message to the next object in the hierarchy.

❖ *You can override HyperTalk:* If you name a message handler the same as a built-in command, your name overrides the built-in one if yours is anywhere along the object hierarchy between the object sending the message and HyperCard.

Program flow runs through the handler until it encounters an `end`, `exit`, `pass`, or `return` statement (discussed later in this section). A message handler can return a value through the built-in function `the result` (discussed in Chapter 8).

On

on *messageName* [*parameterList*]

The on keyword marks the beginning of a message handler and connects the handler with a particular message. *MessageName* is the first word of the message to which the handler responds, and it is the name of the handler.

The optional *parameterList* allows the message handler to receive some values sent along with the message. This list is a series of local variable names, called parameter variables or formal parameters, separated by commas. When the message is sent, each source following the message name is evaluated; when the handler receives the message, each value is plugged into the parameter variable that appears in the corresponding position following on *messageName,* the first value in the list going into the first parameter variable, and so on.

Chapter 2, "Handling Messages," explains more about parameter passing. See also the param, params, and paramCount functions in Chapter 8, "Functions."

End

end *messageName*

The end keyword begins the last line of a handler— it is reached when all of the handler's statements have been executed (except for any bypassed conditional blocks). When the end statement is reached, the message that initiated execution of the handler is sent no further. If the message that initiated this handler's execution was part of some other handler, control passes back to the other handler.

Exit

exit *messageName*
exit to HyperCard

The exit *messageName* statement ends execution of the handler.

The exit to HyperCard form makes program flow return directly to HyperCard, bypassing any pending handlers that have not finished executing.

Pass

```
pass messageName
```

The `pass` statement ends execution of the handler and sends the entire message that initiated execution of the handler to the next object in the hierarchy. (Ordinarily, a message is sent no further than the object containing the executing handler.)

Return

```
return expression
```

The `return` statement ends execution of the handler and, when it appears within a message handler structure, places the value of *expression* into the HyperTalk function `the result`.

The value of `the result` set by the `return` statement is valid only immediately after it executes; each new statement resets `the result`. (See "Result" in Chapter 8, "Functions," for examples.)

Message handler example

The following example shows a handler that originates a message which in turn initiates execution of a second handler. (The second handler could be in the same script as the first or anywhere farther along the object hierarchy.)

```
on mouseUp
  heyNow 5,10 -- heyNow is the message name that's sent
end mouseUp

on heyNow timeVar,timeVar2 --Handler name is heyNow, matching message name
  play "boing" tempo 200 "c4e c dq c f eh" -- Happy Birthday
  wait timeVar seconds
  play stop
  play "harpsichord" "ch d e f g a b c5w"
  wait timeVar2 seconds
  play stop
end heyNow
```

Execution of the first handler is initiated when its object receives a `mouseUp` message. The `mouseUp` could be generated by the user clicking the mouse or typing `mouseUp` in the Message box and pressing Return. It could also originate from another handler executing the statement `mouseUp` or could be sent explicitly to the handler's object with a `send` command.

When the `mouseUp` handler executes, it sends its one command statement (`heyNow 5,10`) as a message, first to its own object. The message name (the first word of the message) matches the handler name (the word following `on` in the first line of the handler), so the statements in the second handler begin executing. (If the current object had no `heyNow` message handler, that object would pass the entire message on to the next object in the hierarchy.)

The values of the parameters following `heyNow` in the first handler are passed into the parameter variables following `heyNow` in the second handler. So when the second handler is executing, `timeVar` has the value 5, and `timeVar2` has the value 10.

Keywords in function handlers

The `function` keyword identifies a HyperCard function handler. You can use this structure to define your own functions, which then can be called from any place in a statement where their values are needed. (User-defined functions are called like built-in HyperCard functions except that you must always use parentheses—see "Return," later in this section.)

Like message handlers, function handlers cannot be nested inside each other (or inside message handlers). The general syntax of a function handler looks like this:

```
function functionName [parameterList]
   statementList
end functionName
```

FunctionName is an identifier: a string starting with a letter and containing no spaces or punctuation marks except underscore; *parameterList* is a series of zero or more parameter variables separated by commas; and *statementList* is zero or more HyperTalk statements.

User-defined function handlers use the object hierarchy in the same way as do message handlers. That is, when the function name appears in a statement or in the Message box, HyperCard searches through all of the scripts along the current object hierarchy for a matching function handler. If a match is found, the function handler executes. If none is found, the function call is passed to HyperCard; if there is no built-in function of that name, HyperCard displays an error dialog box.

❖ *You can override HyperTalk:* If you name a function handler the same as a built-in function, yours overrides the built-in one if it's called with the function call syntax that uses parentheses. Of course, your function handler must also be in the script of an object lower in the hierarchy than the originator of the function call. You can make calls to built-in functions using the function call syntax with `the` preceding the function name, which bypasses any function handlers and always invokes the built-in function.

Program flow runs through the function handler until it encounters an `end`, `exit`, `pass`, or `return` statement (discussed later in this section). A function handler returns a value directly into the statement in which its name was used.

Function

`function` *functionName* [*parameterList*]

The `function` keyword marks the beginning of a function handler and connects the handler with a particular function call. *FunctionName* is the function call to which the handler responds, and it is the name of the handler.

The optional *parameterList* allows the function handler to receive some values sent along with the function call. This list is a series of local variable names, called parameter variables, separated by commas. When the function call is made, each source appearing between parentheses following the function name is evaluated; when the handler begins to execute, each value is plugged into the parameter variable that appears in the corresponding position following `function` *functionName,* the first value in the list going into the first parameter variable, and so on.

For more details on passing parameters to function handlers, see "Return" later in this section.

End

`end` *functionName*

The `end` statement is the last line of the handler, reached when all of the handler's statements have been executed (except for any bypassed conditional blocks).

When the `end` statement is reached, control passes back to the handler containing the function call that originated the function handler's execution.

Exit

`exit` *functionName*
`exit to HyperCard`

The `exit` *functionName* statement ends execution of the handler.

The `exit to HyperCard` form makes program flow return directly to HyperCard, bypassing any pending handlers that have not finished executing, including the handler containing the function call.

Pass

```
pass functionName
```

The `pass` statement ends execution of the handler and sends the entire function call that initiated execution of the handler to the next object in the hierarchy. (Ordinarily, a function call is sent no further than the object containing the executing handler.)

Return

```
return expression
```

The `return` statement ends execution of the handler and, when it appears within a function handler structure, dictates the returned value of the function.

The value of *expression* replaces the function in the calling statement.

The function appears in the calling statement in the form
functionName (*expressionList*) :

```
put square(17) into card field 1
```

ExpressionList is a series of zero or more expressions separated by commas whose values are assigned to the parameter variables in the *parameterList* of the function handler. In the above example, the *expressionList* comprises only the number 17.

A user-defined function handler that would respond to the function call example `square(17)`, shown above, is

```
function square x
  return x * x
end square
```

In the example, the function handler has one parameter variable to receive one value passed to it by the calling statement. The value 17 is passed to the function handler where it is assigned to the parameter variable `x`; the value of `x * x` is returned by the `return` statement, replacing `square(17)` in the calling statement. So, the effect of the calling statement is to put the value 289 into card field 1.

❖ *Parentheses required:* User-defined functions are always followed by parentheses (which are empty if there are no parameters to pass). Unlike built-in functions (explained in detail in Chapter 8), user-defined functions can't be called with `the` or `of`.

Function handler example

The following function handler determines whether a number passed to it as a parameter is even or odd, returning the constant `true` if it's even or `false` if it's odd:

```
function evenNumber numberPassed
  return numberPassed mod 2 is 0
end evenNumber
```

A calling statement that would invoke the `evenNumber` function handler could be one like the following:

```
if evenNumber(numberVariable) then add 1 to evenNumberCount
```

In the calling statement, `numberVariable` can be the name of any variable or other source of value (including an actual number). HyperCard evaluates `numberVariable` before it passes the function call along the hierarchy, and its value is given to the parameter variable `numberPassed` when the `evenNumber` function handler is found. The part of the calling statement following `then` is arbitrary—the point of the example is to show how the function handler receives a value, examines it, and returns another value into the calling statement, based on the result of its execution.

Repeat

The `repeat` structure causes all of the HyperTalk statements between its first and last lines to execute in a loop until some condition is met or until an `exit` statement is encountered. The general syntax of a `repeat` structure looks like this:

```
repeat  controlForm
    statementList
end repeat
```

ControlForm is one of the forms of the `repeat` statement described below, and *statementList* is any number of HyperTalk statements. `Repeat` structures can be used only within message handlers or function handlers.

❖ *Note:* If you want to try the examples in this chapter, be sure to put them within handlers.

Repeat

The `repeat` statement is the first line of a `repeat` structure. It has five forms differentiated by the second word of the statement. Additionally, the `repeat with` form has two variations.

Repeat forever

```
repeat [forever]
```

The loop repeats forever, or until an `exit` statement is encountered (whichever comes first):

```
put 1 into Message box
repeat
  add 1 to Message box
  if Message box contains 6 then exit repeat
end repeat
```

The example ends with 6 in the Message box.

For information on `exit repeat`, see "Exit Repeat" later in this chapter.

For information on `if`, see "If Structure" later in this chapter.

Repeat for

```
repeat [for] number [times]
```

Number is a source that yields a number specifying how many times the loop is executed:

```
put 1 into Message box
repeat for 5 times
  add 1 to Message box
end repeat
```

The example ends with 6 in the Message box.

Repeat until

```
repeat until condition
```

Condition is an expression that evaluates to `true` or `false`. The loop is repeated as long as the condition is false. The condition is checked prior to the first and any subsequent executions of the loop:

```
put 1 into Message box
repeat until Message Box contains 6
  add 1 to Message box
end repeat
```

The example ends with 6 in the Message box.

Repeat while

```
repeat while condition
```

Condition is an expression that evaluates to `true` or `false`. The loop is repeated as long as the condition is true. The condition is checked prior to the first and any subsequent executions of the loop:

```
put 1 into Message box
repeat while Message Box < 6
  add 1 to Message box
end repeat
```

The example ends with 6 in the Message box.

Repeat with

There are two variations of the `repeat with` form: one that increments a variable and one that decrements.

```
repeat with variable = start to finish
```

Variable is a local or global variable name, and *start* and *finish* are sources of integers. The value of *start* is assigned to *variable* at the beginning of the loop, and is incremented by 1 with each pass through the loop. Execution ends when the value of *variable* equals the value of *finish*.

```
repeat with increment = 1 to 6
  put increment into the Message box
end repeat
```

The example ends with 6 in the Message box. (This structure works much like a FOR...NEXT loop in BASIC.)

```
repeat with variable = start down to finish
```

The `down to` form is the same as the `to` form above, except that the value of *variable* is decremented by 1 with each pass through the loop. Execution ends when the value of *variable* equals the value of *finish*.

```
repeat with decrement = 6 down to 1
  put decrement into the Message box
end repeat
```

The example ends with 1 in the Message box.

Exit

```
exit repeat
```

The `exit` statement sends control to the end of the `repeat` structure, ending execution of the loop regardless of the state of the controlling conditions specified in the `repeat` statement.

```
put 1 into the Message box
repeat with increment = 1 to 100
  add increment to the Message box
  if Message box > 20 then
    beep 5
    exit repeat
  end if
end repeat
```

The example ends with 22 in the Message box.

An `exit` statement can appear anywhere within the structure.

For information on `if`, see "If Structure" later in this chapter.

Next

```
next repeat
```

When a `next` statement is encountered, control returns immediately to the top of structure. (Usually, flow doesn't return to the top of the structure until an `end` statement is encountered.)

```
repeat 20
  put random(9) into tempVar
  if tempVar mod 2 = 0 then next repeat
  put tempVar after field "oddNumbers"
end repeat
```

The example appends only the odd random numbers to the field, skipping any even ones.

A `next` statement can appear anywhere within the structure.

For information on `if`, see "If Structure" later in this chapter.

End

```
end repeat
```

The `end` statement marks the end of the loop; it's the last line of a `repeat` control structure. When the controlling conditions specified in the `repeat` statement have been satisfied or an `exit` statement encountered, control goes beyond the `end` statement:

```
repeat for 5 times
  beep
end repeat
```

If

The `if` structure tests for the specified condition and executes the following statement or series of statements if the condition is true. `If` structures can be used only within message handlers or function handlers. The `if` structure has several forms, described below.

❖ *Note:* If you want to try the examples in this chapter, be sure to put them within handlers.

Single-statement If structure

A single-statement `if` structure can occupy only one line as shown below:

```
if condition then statement [else statement]
```

A single-statement `if` structure can also occupy more than one line, but only one statement can follow `then` or `else`:

```
if condition
then statement
[else statement]
```

Condition is an expression that evaluates to `true` or `false`, and *statement* is a single HyperTalk command statement.

In the single-statement `if` structure, only one command statement can follow either `then` or `else` (if present), and the command statement must be on the same line with `then` or `else`.

If the condition between `if` and `then` is true, HyperCard executes the statement between `then` and `else` if `else` is present, or between `then` and the end of the line if `else` is not present following the statement, either on the same line or on the next line.

If the condition between `if` and `then` is false, HyperCard executes the statement between `else` and the end of the line if `else` is present, or it ignores the rest of the line if `else` is not present:

```
if Message box > 10 then beep 5 else beep 15
```

In this example, if the Message box holds a value greater than 10, the Macintosh beeps 5 times; if the value in the Message box is 10 or less, the Macintosh beeps 15 times.

Multiple-statement If structure

A multiple-statement `if` structure accommodates more than one executable statement following `then` and, optionally, more than one statement following `else`:

```
if condition then
   statementList
[else
   statementList]
end if
```

You can also end a multiple-statement `then` clause with a single-line `else`, in which case no `end if` statement is needed:

```
if condition then
   statementList
else statement
```

Condition is an expression that evaluates to true or false, and *statementList* is any number of HyperTalk statements.

In the multiple-statement `if` structure, more than one command statement can follow either `then` or `else` (if present), and the first command statement must be on the line following `then` or `else`. That is, if you want to have more than one statement in a block following `then` or `else`, put a return character after the respective `then` or `else`. Such a multiple-statement block must be ended explicitly: a `then` block can be ended with either `end if` or `else`; an `else` block must be ended with `end if`.

If the condition between `if` and `then` is true, HyperCard executes the statement(s) between `then` and `else` if `else` is present, or between `then` and `end if` if `else` is not present.

If the condition between `if` and `then` is false, HyperCard executes the statement(s) between `else` and `end if` if `else` is present, or it ignores what's between `then` and `end if` if `else` is not present:

```
if number of this card is 10 then
  put "We're done!" into msg
  go Home
else
  put "And the next question is:" into msg
  go next card
end if
```

Nested If structures

`If` structures can be nested; that is, statements following a `then` or an `else` can include more `if` structures. Each nested multiple-line `if` structure must have its own `end if`, and an `else` always goes with the closest preceding `if` clause.

```
repeat
  ask "Guess a random number between 1 and 10:" with empty
  if it is empty then
    exit repeat
  else
    if it is random(10) then
      put "You guessed it!"
    else
      put "Sorry, try again."
    end if
  end if
end repeat
```

Do

do *expression*

The `do` keyword causes HyperCard to get the value of *expression,* then send it as a message. If more than one line is in the source, only the first one is sent.

```
on getFromlist -- create 3 card fields putting data into the first 2
  put "card field 1" & return & "card field 2" into list
  do "put" && line 1 of list && "into card field 3"
  -- try this with: put line 1 of list into card field 3
  -- commenting out the do "put"... line before running it
end getFromlist
```

Global

```
global variableList
```

VariableList is one or more HyperCard variable names separated by commas.

The `global` keyword makes a variable name known and its contents available to any script of any object in HyperCard. The following two lines are individual examples of `global` statements:

```
global myVar
global pages,sections,chapters
```

The following example handlers show a global variable being used for two handlers to access the same value:

```
on mouseUp
  global myVariable -- load the global here
  put 3 into myVariable
  writeResult
end mouseup

on writeResult
  global myVariable -- can use the global as long as we define it here
  put myVariable -- the value remains 3
end writeResult
```

Changing the value of a global variable in any script changes its value everywhere. The `global` keyword must be used in each handler in which the global variable is used.

Global variables are not saved in between sessions of HyperCard or when HyperCard is suspended by launching another application with the `open` command.

Send

```
send "messageName [parameterList]" [to object]
```

MessageName is a string beginning with a letter and containing no spaces or punctuation marks other than underscore; *parameterList* is one or more expressions (separated by commas if more than one); and *object* is a HyperCard object descriptor or HyperCard itself. If no object is specified, HyperCard is the object.

The `send` keyword sends a message directly to a particular object, bypassing any handlers in the intervening object hierarchy that might otherwise intercept the message.

```
send "hideIt" to field 3
send "addSums travel,food,hotel" to stack "expenseAccount"
send mouseUp to button "pushMe"
send "doMenu print card" to HyperCard
```

You can send a message directly to any object in the current stack or to another stack, but not to a specific object in another stack.

If the object has no message handler for *messageName,* the message is passed along the object hierarchy stemming from the object to which the message was sent. If the object does have a matching handler, the handler executes, but the card to which it belongs does not necessarily open. Messages sent by executing the statements of the object's handler are sent along the receiving object's hierarchy.

Chapter 2, "Handling Messages," has more information about how the `send` command interacts with the object hierarchy.

Quotation marks around the message are not required if the message is a single word. Parameter expressions are evaluated before they are sent, even though the entire message has quotation marks around it.

❖ *You can use it in the Message box:* The `send` keyword, unlike all other keywords, works in the Message box.

Chapter 6

System Messages

This chapter describes the messages HyperCard sends in response to events, such as mouse clicks, that you initiate in its environment.

Most system messages are sent by HyperCard to the current card, but those having to do with a specific button or field are sent to that object. The receiving object has the first chance to respond to the message before it goes on to the next encompassing object, as described in Chapter 2, "Handling Messages." The receiving object can respond to the system message with a handler that begins

on *messageName*

where *messageName* is one of the system messages in the following lists.

The tables in this chapter correspond to the type of object to which the listed system messages are sent initially. If that object has no handler with a name matching the system message, it passes the message on to succeeding objects in the hierarchy. So, for example, a card can have a handler for a message sent initially to a button.

Messages and commands

Most system messages are informational—they cause no action if passed all the way to HyperCard, although they may be a result of a HyperTalk command executing. For example, HyperCard sends `deleteButton` to a button while it is executing either a Cut Button or Clear Button menu command. The `deleteButton` message is a result of a command, not the command itself. (Consequently, you can't prevent the deletion of buttons by intercepting the `deleteButton` message with a handler named `deleteButton`).

Other system messages, however, are commands if passed to HyperCard. For example, all menu commands are passed to HyperCard as parameters of the `doMenu` message. (So you can prevent deletion of buttons by intercepting `doMenu`. But see the section "Redefining Commands" at the beginning of Chapter 7 before trying it.) All system messages that are HyperTalk commands are noted as such in this chapter and are also listed in Chapter 7. If a message that reaches HyperCard is neither a system message nor a command, HyperCard displays a "Can't understand" error dialog box.

Although system messages are usually sent by HyperCard, they can be sent by other objects as well. For example, a handler could invoke a `mouseUp` handler in another object by executing a statement such as

```
send "mouseUp" to button 1 of card 1
```

Messages sent to a button

The only messages that are sent initially to buttons are those having to do with a specific button. They are of two types: those announcing the button's creation or deletion, and mouse messages.

When buttons and fields are layered on top of each other, mouse messages are sent only to the closest one. (But background buttons and fields can never overlay those belonging to the card.) Whether a button or field belongs to the card or the background, however, makes no difference regarding where a message is sent initially: all buttons and fields precede the card.

Table 6-1 shows the system messages HyperCard sends initially to buttons.

Table 6-1
Messages sent to a button

Message	Meaning

newButton	Sent to a button as soon as it has been created. Although the new button can have no script with which to respond to this message (unless it was created by pasting), the message will pass to objects lower in the hierarchy which can respond with handlers such as
	
	`on newButton`
	`  set autoHilite of the target to true`
	`end newButton`

deleteButton	Sent to a button that is being deleted, just before it disappears.
mouseDown	Sent to a button when the mouse button is pressed down while the pointer is inside its rectangle. (This message may also be sent to a field or card; see Tables 6-2 and 6-3.)
mouseStillDown	Sent to a button repeatedly while the mouse button is held down and the pointer is inside its rectangle. (This message may also be sent to a field or card; see Tables 6-2 and 6-3.)
mouseUp	Sent to a button when the mouse button is released while the pointer is inside its rectangle. The pointer must be in the same button rectangle it was in when the mouse button was pressed down for the message to be sent. (This message may also be sent to a field or card; see Tables 6-2 and 6-3.)

Table 6-1 *(continued)*
Messages sent to a button

Message	Meaning
mouseEnter	Sent to a button as soon as the pointer is moved within its rectangle. (This message may also be sent to a field; see Table 6-2.)
mouseWithin	Sent to a button repeatedly while the pointer is inside its rectangle. (This message may also be sent to a field; see Table 6-2.)
mouseLeave	Sent to a button as soon as the pointer is moved outside its rectangle. (This message may also be sent to a field; see Table 6-2.)

Messages sent to a field

The only messages that are sent initially to fields are those having to do with a specific field. They are of three types: those announcing the field's creation or deletion, those announcing its opening for text entry or closing afterwards, and mouse messages.

When buttons and fields are layered on top of each other, mouse messages are sent only to the closest one. (But background buttons and fields can never overlay those belonging to the card.) Whether a button or field belongs to the card or the background, however, makes no difference regarding where a message is sent initially: all buttons and fields precede the card.

Table 6-2 shows the system messages HyperCard sends initially to fields.

Table 6-2
Messages sent to a field

Message	Meaning
newField	Sent to a field as soon as it has been created.
deleteField	Sent to a field that is being deleted, just before it disappears.
openField	Sent to an unlocked field when it is opened for text editing, by clicking in the field or moving the text insertion point from the previous field with the Tab key.
closeField	Sent to an unlocked field when it is closed after text editing by clicking outside the field, moving the text insertion point to the next field with the Tab key, pressing the Enter key, going to another card, or quitting HyperCard. The message is not sent unless some text was actually changed.
mouseDown	Sent to a locked field when the mouse button is pressed down while the pointer is inside it. MouseDown is not sent to a scrolling field when the mouse is clicked in the scroll bar. You can send mouseDown to an unlocked field by holding down the Command key while clicking the mouse in the field. (This message may also be sent to a button or card; see Tables 6-1 and 6-3.)
mouseStillDown	Sent to a locked field repeatedly while the mouse button is held down and the mouse pointer is inside it. (This message may also be sent to a button or card; see Tables 6-1 and 6-3.)
mouseUp	Sent to a locked field when the mouse button is released while the pointer is inside it. The pointer must be in the same field it was in when the mouse button was pressed down for the message to be sent. (This message may also be sent to a button or card; see Tables 6-1 and 6-3.)
mouseEnter	Sent to a field as soon as the pointer is moved into it. (This message may also be sent to a button; see Table 6-1.)
mouseWithin	Sent to a field repeatedly while the pointer is inside it. (This message may also be sent to a button; see Table 6-1.)
mouseLeave	Sent to a field as soon as the pointer is moved outside it. (This message may also be sent to a button; see Table 6-1.)
tabKey	Sent to a field when the Tab key is pressed while the text insertion point is in the field. (This message may also be sent to the current card; see Table 6-3.)

Messages sent to the current card

System messages not sent to buttons or fields are sent initially to the current card, even when they concern the background or the stack.

Mouse messages are sent to the card only when there is no button or field, belonging to either the card or the background, under the pointer.

Table 6-3 shows the system messages HyperCard sends initially to the current card.

Table 6-3
Messages sent to the current card

Message	Meaning
newCard	Sent to a card as soon as it has been created.
deleteCard	Sent to a card that is being deleted, just before it disappears.
openCard	Sent to a card when you go to it.
closeCard	Sent to a card when you leave it.
mouseDown	Sent to the current card when the mouse button is pressed down and the pointer is not in the current button rectangle or field. (This message may also be sent to a button or field; see Tables 6-1 and 6-2.)
mouseStillDown	Sent to the current card repeatedly while the mouse button is held down. (This message may also be sent to a button or field; see Tables 6-1 and 6-2.)
mouseUp	Sent to the current card when the mouse button is released. (This message may also be sent to a button or field; see Tables 6-1 and 6-2.)
startUp	Sent to the first card displayed when HyperCard is first started.

Table 6-3 *(continued)*
Messages sent to the current card

Message	Meaning
idle	Sent to the current card repeatedly when nothing else is happening and the Browse tool is current.
	An idle handler can interfere with typing. For example, if you have an idle handler that puts text into a field, it can remove the insertion point from another field while the user is typing. An example of such a handler is
| | ```
on idle
  put the time into card field "Time"
  pass idle
end idle
``` |
	If this handler were to execute during typing into another field (idle is sent during a typing pause), and if the time had changed, HyperCard would remove the insertion point from the user's field. The user would have to click in the field or press Tab to replace the insertion point after every pause, which would be annoying and tedious.
returnKey	Sent to the current card when the Return key is pressed, unless the text insertion point is in a field. (This message is also a HyperTalk command. See Chapter 7.)
enterKey	Sent to the current card when the Enter key is pressed, unless the text insertion point is in a field. (This message is also a HyperTalk command. See Chapter 7.)
tabKey	Sent to the current card when the Tab key is pressed, unless the text insertion point is in a field. (In that case, tabKey is sent initially to the field; see Table 6-2.)
	This message is also a HyperTalk command. See Chapter 7.
```

Table 6-3 *(continued)*
Messages sent to the current card

Message	Meaning
arrowKey *var*	Sent to the current card when an arrow key is pressed (and the textArrows property is false; see Chapter 9). The value passed into the parameter variable *var* can be left, right, up, or down, depending on which arrow key is pressed. The beginning of a handler for this message could read: ```on arrowKey whichKey if whichKey = "left" then go previous card . . .``` (This message is also a HyperTalk command. See Chapter 7.)
functionKey *var*	Sent to the current card when a function key on the Apple Extended Keyboard is pressed. The parameter variable *var* can range from 1 to 15. Function keys 1 through 4 are preprogrammed for the Undo, Cut, Copy, and Paste commands, respectively. The beginning of a handler for this message could read: ```on functionKey whichKey if whichKey < 5 then pass functionKey else if whichKey is 5 then doMenu "New Card" else if whichKey is 6 then choose browse tool else if whichKey is 7 then choose button tool . . .``` You can override the preprogrammed functions of keys 1 through 4 in a functionKey message handler. (This message is also a HyperTalk command. See Chapter 7.)
controlKey *var*	Sent to the current card when a combination of the Control key and another key is pressed. The parameter variable *var* can range from 0 to 255. The parameter variable values generated by different keystrokes on the Apple Extended Keyboard are shown in Appendix B. The beginning of a handler for this message could read: ```on controlKey whichKey if whichKey = 16 then doMenu "Print Card" . . .```

Table 6-3 *(continued)*
Messages sent to the current card

Message	Meaning
doMenu *var*	Sent to the current card when a menu item is selected. The parameter variable *var* has the exact name of the menu item selected, including the three periods following menu items that invoke dialog boxes. Uppercase and lowercase don't matter, but you must type the three periods—don't use the Option-semicolon ellipsis character. (This message is also a HyperTalk command, which is listed in Chapter 7. An example handler to intercept the doMenu message is shown in the section "Redefining Commands" at the beginning of Chapter 7.)
newBackground	Sent to the current card as soon as a background has been created.
deleteBackground	Sent to the current card when a background is deleted, just before it disappears.
openBackground	Sent to the current card when a background is first opened by going to a card whose background is different than that of the previous card.
closeBackground	Sent to the current card when a background is closed by going to another card that has a different background.
newStack	Sent to the current card when a stack is created.
deleteStack	Sent to the current card when a stack is deleted, just before it disappears.
openStack	Sent to the current card when a stack is opened by going to a card in a different stack than that of the previous card. In this case the following three messages are sent, in order: openCard, openBackground, and openStack.
closeStack	Sent to the current card when a stack is closed by opening another stack.
help	Sent to the current card when Help is chosen from the Go menu (or Command-? is pressed). You can intercept this message if you want to provide your own Help system for your stack. (This message is also a HyperTalk command. See Chapter 7.)
suspend	Sent to the current card when HyperCard is suspended, when you launch another application with the open command, just before the other application is launched.

Table 6-3 *(continued)*
Messages sent to the current card

Message	Meaning
resume	Sent to the current card when HyperCard resumes running after having been suspended.
quit	Sent to the current card when you choose Quit HyperCard from the File menu (or press Command-Q), just before HyperCard quits.
hide *var*	Sent to the current card when the menu bar is visible and you press Command–Space bar. The parameter variable *var* has only one value for the `hide` system message: `menubar`. (This message is also a HyperTalk command; the command accepts other parameter variable values in addition to `menubar`. See Chapter 7.)
show *var*	Sent to the current card when the menu bar is hidden and you press Command–Space bar. The parameter variable *var* has only one value for the `show` system messsage: `menuBar`. (This message is also a HyperTalk command; the command accepts other parameter variable values in addition to `menuBar`. See Chapter 7.)

Chapter 7

Commands

This chapter describes all the commands in HyperTalk, showing their syntax and meaning.

HyperTalk commands are built-in message handlers that reside in HyperCard itself. When you issue a HyperTalk command, it's passed along the object hierarchy as a message to HyperCard. In most cases there's no handler in any script along the way to intercept the message, so HyperCard receives the message and acts on it.

Some commands (such as `arrowKey`) are system messages as well as commands. This means two things: a system event generates the message (pressing an arrow key generates the `arrowKey` message), and HyperCard has a built-in response to the message (`arrowKey` takes you to another card).

Redefining commands

You can write a message handler that redefines a built-in command (for example, `on doMenu menuItem`). This is especially useful for trapping menu commands you want to modify or that you want to prevent a user from issuing.

Be wary, however: once a command—or any message—has been intercepted by a handler, it's sent no further along the hierarchy; so your newly defined command replaces HyperCard's built-in one. If, for example, you write a handler for the `doMenu` command, be sure to pass the message if you don't want to prevent *every* instance of it from reaching HyperCard:

```
on doMenu menuItem
  if menuItem is "Delete Card" then
    answer "Are you sure?" with "Delete" or "Cancel"
    if It is not "Delete" then exit doMenu
  end if
  pass doMenu
end doMenu
```

If you inadvertently fail to pass `doMenu`, you may find yourself apparently unable to use any menu command, even to fix the `doMenu` handler. (In that case, execute the command `edit script`, for the object containing the handler, from the Message box. If the Message box is hidden and blind typing is false, go to the last card of the Home stack and turn blind typing on.)

Syntax description notation

The syntax descriptions use the following typographic conventions. Words or phrases in `typewriter type` are Hypertalk language elements or are those that you type to the computer literally, exactly as shown. Words in *italic* type describe general elements, not specific names—you must substitute the actual instances. Square brackets ([ ]) enclose optional elements which may be included if you need them. (Don't type the square brackets.) In some cases, optional elements change what the message does; in other cases they are helper words that have no effect except to make the message more readable.

It doesn't matter whether you use uppercase or lowercase letters; names that are formed from two words are shown in small letters with a capital in the middle (`likeThis`) merely to make them more readable. The HyperTalk prepositions `of` and `in` are interchangeable—the syntax descriptions use the one that sounds more natural.

The terms *factor* and *expression* are defined in Chapter 4. Briefly, a factor can be a constant, literal, function, property, number, or container, and an expression can be a factor or a complex expression built with factors and operators. Also, a factor can be an expression within parentheses. The term *yields* indicates a specific kind of value, such as a number or a text string, that must result from evaluation of a factor or expression when a restriction applies (for example, the expression and the destination in an `add` command must yield numbers). However, any HyperTalk value can be treated as a text string.

Add

Syntax

```
add expression to destination
```

Expression yields an arithmetic value and *destination* is a container.

Examples

```
add 3 to It
add field Amount to field Total
```

Description

The `add` command adds the value of *expression* to the value of *destination,* and leaves the result in *destination.*

Script

The following example handler sums numbers in a field, if each line of the field contains one number, and puts the result into the Message box. The name of the field is passed to the handler as a parameter.

```
on sumField whichField
  put 0 into total
  repeat with count = 1 to the number of lines in whichField
    add line count of whichField to total
  end repeat
  put total into msg
end sumField
```

Notes

The value previously in the destination must be a number; it is replaced with the new value.

Answer

Syntax

answer *question* [with *reply* [or *reply2* [or *reply3*]]]

Question and *reply* are expressions that yield text strings.

Examples

answer "Which is the way the world ends?" with "Bang" or "Whimper"
answer myQuestion with myAnswer or field 7

Description

The answer command displays a dialog box with a question and up to three buttons, each representing a different reply.

The dialog box stays on the screen until one of the buttons is clicked; pressing Return or Enter has the same effect as clicking the button farthest to the right, which correlates to the last reply specified with the answer command.

Script

The following example handler produces the dialog boxes in Figure 7-1 (the second one depends on which button you click in the first one):

```
on chooseColor
  answer "Which color do you prefer?" with "Red" or "Blue" or "Yellow"
  if It is "Red" then answer "You picked Red."
  else if It is "Blue" then answer "You picked Blue."
  else if It is "Yellow" then answer "You picked Yellow."
end chooseColor
```

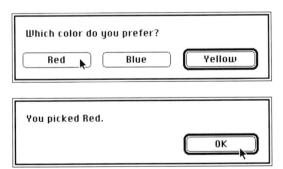

Figure 7-1
Answer command dialog boxes

There is no way for a script to reply to a dialog box by itself, so it's important that a script meant to run unattended not use answer.

The text of the button clicked goes into the local variable It. If no *reply* is specified, HyperCard displays one button containing OK.

Neither the question nor any of the replies can have more than one line. If you use a container that has more than one line of text in it for the question, only the first line appears. If you use a container with more than one line for a reply, the last line is displayed in the button. (Only the center portion shows if the line is too long to fit in the button.) However, all lines go into the local variable It when the button is clicked.

Unless you're using container names, put the question and the replies inside quotation marks if they contain any spaces.

Each reply can be up to 13 characters long (depending on the width of the characters).

See also the ask command.

ArrowKey

Syntax

arrowKey *keyName*

KeyName describes one of the arrow keys: left, right, up, or down.

Examples

arrowKey left
arrowKey down

Description

The arrowKey command takes you to another card. The effects of the arrowKey command are shown in Table 7-1.

Table 7-1
Effects of the arrowKey command

Parameter value	Effect
left	Go to previous card in current stack
right	Go to next card in current stack
up	Go forward through recent cards
down	Go back through recent cards

The arrowKey message, which invokes the arrowKey command if it reaches HyperCard, is normally generated by pressing any of the arrow keys on the keyboard. (Which arrow key you press determines the message's parameter value.) You can also send arrowKey from the Message box or execute it as a line in a script.

Script

The following example handler makes function keys 9, 10, 11, and 12 send the arrowKey message with parameters of left, right, up, and down, respectively:

```
on functionKey whichKey -- map function keys to arrow keys
  if whichKey is 9 then arrowKey left
  else if whichKey is 10 then arrowKey right
  else if whichKey is 11 then arrowKey up
  else if whichKey is 12 then arrowKey down
end functionKey
```

Notes

The textArrows property, available only in HyperCard versions 1.1 and later, alters the effect of pressing the arrow keys (see "TextArrows" in Chapter 9), but it does not affect the arrowKey command.

See also the arrowKey message in Chapter 6.

Ask

Syntax

```
ask question [with defaultAnswer]
ask password question [with defaultAnswer]
```

Question and *defaultAnswer* are expressions that yield text strings.

Examples

```
ask "Who needs this kind of grief?" with "Not me."
ask field 1 with line 1 of field 2
ask password "Please enter your password:"
```

Description

The `ask` command displays a dialog box containing a question with a text window into which the user can type an answer. The optional *defaultAnswer* string specifies an answer which appears inititally in the window, highlighted so it can be easily replaced. The dialog box appears with OK and Cancel buttons.

Script

The following example handler produces the dialog box in Figure 7-2:

```
on phone
  ask "Dial what number:" with "555-1212"
  if It is not empty then dial It
end phone
```

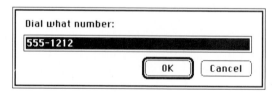

Figure 7-2
Ask command dialog box

The answer goes into the local variable It, either when the OK button is clicked or when Return or Enter is pressed. If the Cancel button is clicked, the dialog box goes away, but the answer is not placed into It.

The ask password form causes the answer to be encrypted as a number (which is placed into the local variable It). The encrypted answer can be stored in a field to be compared to a later answer to ask password if, for example, you want the user to be able to protect data he or she enters into the stack. Password protection built into a stack in this manner is separate from that set up by the Protect Stack menu command.

Neither the question nor the default answer can have more than one line; if you use a container that has more than one line in it, only the first line appears.

Unless you're using container names, put the question and the default answer inside quotation marks if they contain any spaces (or if, as in the example, they are telephone numbers containing a hyphen—to prevent HyperCard from doing subtraction).

See also the answer command, earlier in this chapter.

Beep

Syntax

```
beep count
```

Count is an expression that yields an integer.

Examples

```
beep 5
beep line 3 of field 1
```

Description

The beep command causes the Macintosh speaker to make a beep sound count times. If no count is given, the speaker beeps once.

Script

The following example handler uses the beep command to alert the user that an answer dialog box, to which the user must reply, is being displayed:

```
on openStack
  beep 2
  answer "Do you need instructions?" with "Yes" or "No"
  if It is "Yes" then go to stack "Instructions"
end openStack
```

Choose

Syntax

```
choose toolName tool
```

ToolName is the name of any one of the tools from the HyperCard Tools palette (shown in Figure 7-2).

Examples

```
choose browse tool
choose eraser tool
```

Description

The `choose` command changes the current tool to *toolName* as though you had selected it from the Tools palette. Valid tool names are

browse	oval
brush	pencil
bucket	poly[gon]
button	rect[angle]
curve	reg[ular] poly[gon]
eraser	round rect[angle]
field	select
lasso	spray [can]
line	text

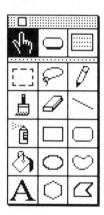

Figure 7-3
Tools palette

Script   The following example shows a typical use of the choose command in a handler:

```
on drawBox
  reset paint
  choose rectangle tool
  set lineSize to 2
  drag from 50,50 to 200,200
  choose browse tool
end drawBox
```

Notes   You must have HyperCard's user level set to Painting, Authoring, or Scripting to use
the choose command, but the Tools palette need not be visible. Setting user levels
is described in the *HyperCard User's Guide* and in the userLevel global property
description in Chapter 9.

Click

Syntax   click at *location* [with *key*[, *key2*[, *key3*]]]

Location is an expression yielding a point: two integers separated by a comma,
representing horizontal and vertical pixel offsets (respectively) from the top-left
corner of the card window. *Key, key2,* and *key3* are one or more of the following key
names, separated by commas: shiftKey, optionKey, or commandKey (or
cmdKey).

Examples   click at 100,100
click at the loc of button "Press me" with optionKey

Description   The `click` command causes the same actions as though you had clicked with the pointer at the specified location on the screen: the system messages `mouseDown` and `mouseUp` are sent to the objects under the pointer (but the visible pointer is not moved from its current location).

Using the `with` *key* form produces the same result as clicking the mouse button while holding down the specified key (or keys).

If *location* is within an unlocked field, the insertion point is set: if there is text at or past *location,* the insertion point is set at *location;* if there is text on the same line as *location* but *location* is beyond the end of text, the insertion point is set at the end of text on that line; if there is no text at *location,* the insertion point is set at the start of the line.

You can select a word by double-clicking it (that is, by executing the `click` command twice in succession at the location of the word). You can select any string of text by clicking at the beginning then clicking `with shiftKey` at the end of the string.

Script   The following example handler selects and displays a word from a locked field when you click on the word (`mouseUp` is not sent to unlocked fields when you click them):

```
on mouseUp
  set lockText of me to false
  click at the clickLoc
  click at the clickLoc
  get the selection
  put It into the Message box
  set lockText of me to true
end mouseUp
```

Notes   The pixel offset values of *location* are not restricted to the size of the screen, but are misinterpreted if greater than `32767`.

See also the `drag` command, later in this chapter.

Close file

Syntax

```
close file fileName
```

FileName is the expression of a text string that is a valid filename.

Examples

```
close file myData
close file "myDisk:myFolder:myFile"
```

Description

The `close` command closes a disk file previously opened with the `open file` command to import or export ASCII text. The expression *fileName* must yield a valid Macintosh filename, including pathname if required.

Script

The following example handler reads any size text file into a global variable named `temp`:

```
on importText
  global temp
  put "MyFilename" into filename
  open file filename
  repeat
    read from file filename for 16384
    if It is empty then exit repeat
    put It after temp
  end repeat
  close file filename
end importText
```

Notes

If the specified file is not open, you get an error message. Use the `close file` command to close files explicitly after you use them. HyperCard automatically closes all open files when an `exit to HyperCard` statement is executed, when you press Command-period, or when you quit HyperCard.

You must provide the full pathname of the file if it's not at the same directory level as HyperCard. (See "Stack Descriptors" in Chapter 3 for an explanation of pathnames.)

See also the `open file`, `read`, and `write` commands, later in this chapter.

Close printing

Syntax

```
close printing
```

Description

The `close printing` command ends a print job previously begun with the `open printing` command.

Script

The following example handler executes a printing job, printing a specified number of cards, beginning on a specified card:

```
on printRange low,high
  push card
  open printing
  go to card low
  print (high-low) + 1 cards
  close printing
  pop card
end printRange
```

Notes

Also see the `open printing` command, later in this chapter.

Convert

Syntax

```
convert container to format [and format]
```

Container is a container name and *format* is a format specification.

Examples

```
convert timeVariable to seconds
convert line 1 of second card field to long date and short time
```

Description   The `convert` command converts a date or time in the specified container to the format specified. The optional second format specification is used when a date and time are both included. Valid format specifications and their meanings are

seconds	Seconds since midnight, January 1, 1904.
dateItems	A comma-separated list of numbers representing (in order): year, month, day, hour, minute, second, and day of week.
long date	The date in text form: `Tuesday, June 30, 1987.`
short date	The date in slash-separated numeric form: `6/30/87.`
abbreviated date	The date in text form with abbreviated day of week: `Tue, June 30, 1987.`
long time	The time in colon-separated form including seconds: `11:15:15 AM.`
short time	The time in colon-separated form without seconds: `11:15 AM.`
abbreviated time	same form as short: `11:15 AM.`

Script   The following example handler counts the seconds elapsed while a command in the Message box executes:

```
on mouseUp
  put the long time into startTime
  convert startTime to seconds
  if msg is not empty then do msg
  put the long time into endTime
  convert endTime to seconds
  answer "That took" && endTime - startTime && "seconds."
end mouseUp
```

Notes   The modifier `abbreviated` can be shortened to `abbrev` or `abbr`.

Delete

Syntax

```
delete chunk [of container]
```

Chunk is a chunk expression referring to some text in a specified field and *container* specifies a container.

Examples

```
delete line 1 of field 1
delete char 1 to 5 of line 4 of field "Charlie" of second card
```

Description

The `delete` command removes specified text from the designated container in the current stack.

Script

The following example handler finds and deletes a name from a list with one name per line:

```
on zapaName
  put "Spragens" & return & "Kamins" & return & "Bond" into list
  ask "Delete which name from the list?" with empty -- enter a name
  repeat with count = the number of lines in list down to 1
    if It is in line count of list then delete line count of list
  end repeat
end zapaName
```

Notes

Using the `delete` command is not the same as using `put empty into` with the same chunk of text specified. For example, if you delete a line in a field with a statement like

```
delete line 4 of field 7
```

you delete the return character as well as the text; what was previously the fifth line becomes the fourth. The following statement leaves the return character in line 4:

```
put empty into line 4 of field 7
```

Even if you delete all of the text in a field, the field remains defined on the card or background, unlike selecting the field and choosing Cut Field or Clear Field from the Edit menu.

When you delete text in a field on a card other than the current one, the current card does not change.

Chapter 3 describes how to designate a card. Chunk expressions are described in Chapter 4. See also the `put` command, later in this chapter.

Dial

Syntax

```
dial expression [with modem [modemCommands]]
```

Expression yields an arithmetic value and *modemCommands* are commands for your modem.

Examples

```
dial charlie -- if charlie is a variable containing a number
dial "415-555-1212"
dial "407-996-1010" with modem "ATS0=0S7=1DT"
dial "407-973-6000" with modem
```

Description

The `dial` command, without the `with modem` option, generates the touch-tone sounds for the digits in *expression* through the Macintosh speaker. Holding the telephone handset up to the speaker works on some phones; for others you need a device that feeds the Macintosh audio output to the telephone.

If you use the `with modem` option, the `dial` command sets up telephone calls using the Apple Modem 300/1200, the Apple Personal Modem, or any Hayes-compatible modem attached to the Macintosh serial port. The *modemCommands* parameters are those described in the manual for your modem. Their default value is `"ATS0=0DT"`.

If *expression* yields a number including a hyphen (as in 555-1212), enclose it within quotation marks to prevent HyperCard from doing subtraction with the hyphen before passing the number to the `dial` command (which ignores characters other than numbers). Similarly, it's a good idea to enclose the *modemCommands* within quotation marks.

Divide

Syntax

```
divide destination by expression
```

Destination is a container and *expression* yields an arithmetic value.

Examples

```
divide field "total" by 3
divide farenheit by celsius -- if farenheit and celsius are variables
```

Description

The `divide` command divides the value of *destination* by the value of *expression* and puts the result into *destination*.

Script

The following example handler figures the percentage represented by a fraction of two numbers specified as parameters:

```
on percent var1,var2
  divide var1 by var2
  put trunc(var1 * 100) & "%"
end percent
```

Notes

The value previously in the destination must be a number; it is replaced with the new value.

Division by 0 puts the result `INF` into *destination*. Division is carried out to a precision of up to 19 decimal places.

See also the `numberFormat` global property in Chapter 9, and the discussion of numbers in Chapter 4.

DoMenu

Syntax

```
doMenu menuItem
```

MenuItem is an expression that yields a menu command.

Examples

```
doMenu "open stack..."
doMenu thisCommand -- thisCommand is a variable containing a command
doMenu calculator -- desk accessory from the Apple menu
```

Description

The `doMenu` command performs the menu command specified by *expression* as though you had chosen the item directly from the appropriate HyperCard menu.

Script

If you choose the Finder menu item while running HyperCard under MultiFinder, you could leave a stack that's on a file server open and inaccessible to other users. The following example handler closes the current stack and goes to the Home stack:

```
on doMenu menuChoice
  if menuChoice is "Finder" then go to "Home"
  pass doMenu
end doMenu
```

Notes

Both the specified command and the menu in which it resides must be available at the current user level (as described in the *HyperCard User's Guide*). If there are periods following the menu command, you must include them in *menuItem* (you can't use the ellipsis character in their place).

You don't have to specify which menu the command comes from. But be aware that some menu commands change with conditions (for example, Paste Card can change to Paste Button, depending on the contents of the Clipboard).

❖ *Don't lock yourself out:* If you write a handler to intercept `doMenu`, be sure to pass the message after examining the new menu item. Otherwise, you may find yourself apparently unable to use any menu command, even to fix the `doMenu` handler or to quit HyperCard. (In that case, execute the command `edit script`, for the object containing the handler, from the Message box. If the Message box is hidden and blind typing is false, go to the last card of the Home stack and turn blind typing on.)

Drag

Syntax

```
drag from start to finish [with key[, key2[, key3]]]
```

Start and *finish* are expressions, each of which yields a point: two integers separated by a comma, representing horizontal and vertical pixel offsets (respectively) from the top left of the Macintosh screen. *Key, key2,* and *key3* are one or more of the following key names, separated by commas: `shiftKey`, `optionKey`, or `commandKey` (or `cmdKey`).

Examples

```
drag from 100,100 to 200,200
drag from the loc of button 1 to the mouseLoc with commandKey,shiftKey
```

Description

The `drag` command performs the same action as though you had dragged manually, except that in order to select text in a field using the `drag` command, you must use `with shiftKey`.

Script

The following example handler draws random-sized ovals filled with random patterns on a new card:

```
on mouseUp
  doMenu "New Card" -- so we don't draw on the current card
  choose oval tool
  set filled to true
  repeat until the mouseclick
    set pattern to random(40)
    drag from random(512),random(342) to random(512),random(342)
  end repeat
  choose browse tool
  doMenu "Delete Card" -- get rid of the card we just made
  go previous card -- take us back to the card we started from
end mouseUp
```

Notes

Using the `with` *key* form produces the same result as dragging while holding down the specified key.

You can use `drag` with any tool selected, but it has no effect with some Paint tools.

The location of the actual pointer doesn't change from where it was before the command was issued.

See also the `click` command earlier in this chapter, and the `dragSpeed` property (used with the `set` command) in Chapter 9.

Edit script

Syntax

```
edit script of object
```

Object is a factor that yields a designator of an object: a stack, card, background, field, or button.

Examples

```
edit script of button 1
edit script of this stack
```

Description

The `edit script` command opens the script of the specified object with the HyperCard script editor as though you had clicked the Script button in the object's Info dialog box.

Script

The following example handler enables you to edit the script of any button or field merely by positioning the pointer over it and pressing the Option key:

```
on mouseWithin
  if the optionKey is down then edit script of the target
end mouseWithin
```

Notes

If the `edit script` command is issued from a script, execution of the current handler is suspended until the script editor dialog box is closed.

Refer to Chapter 1, "HyperTalk Basics," for an explanation of how the script editor works.

EnterKey

Syntax

```
enterKey
```

Description

The `enterKey` command sends a statement typed into the Message box to the current card or, if a field is open for text editing, `enterKey` closes the field.

Notes

The `enterKey` message, which invokes the `enterKey` command if it reaches HyperCard, is normally sent by pressing the Enter key on the keyboard. But you can also execute it as a line in a script.

Closing a field with `enterKey` doesn't send the `closeField` system message.

See also the `enterKey` message in Chapter 6.

Find

Syntax

```
find expression [in field fieldDesignator]
find chars expression [in field fieldDesignator]
find word expression [in field fieldDesignator]
```

Expression yields a series of one or more text strings separated by spaces, and *fieldDesignator* is a background field name, number, or ID number.

Examples

```
find "money" in field SofPlenty
find chars "Wild" in field 1
find word msg in second field
```

Description

The `find` command searches through all the card and background fields (visible or not) in the stack for the text strings yielded by *expression*. The search begins on the current card and continues through the last card, the first card, and on to the card previous to the current card. Choosing Find from the Edit menu (or pressing Command-F) puts the `find` command in the Message box with the text insertion point after it between double quotation marks.

❖ *Use at least three characters:* The `find` command executes faster if you use as many three-character combinations as possible in the search string. That is, three characters are fast, six are faster than three, nine are faster than six, and so on.

Script

The following example handler queries the user for search criteria, then executes the `find` command:

```
on doMenu var
  global findString
  if var is "Find..." then
    ask "Find what string:" with findString
    if It is not empty then
      put It into findString
      answer "Match" && findString && "how:" with "Chars" or "Word" or "All"
      if It is "Chars" then find chars findString
      else if It is "Word" then find word findString
      else find findString
    end if
  else pass doMenu
end doMenu
```

If you include `in field` *fieldDesignator,* you restrict the search to the specified background field. You can't restrict the search to a card field.

The `find` form finds the match only at the beginnings of words. The `find chars` form finds the match anywhere within words. The `find word` form matches only complete words.

If the match is on a different card, it becomes the current card; otherwise the current card doesn't change and HyperCard sounds a beep. If it finds a match, HyperCard puts a box around the word containing the found string, if the field containing the string is visible. If a match is found in a hidden field, the field's card becomes the current card, but the field remains hidden.

As the `find` command evaluates the expression passed to it, it places the resulting values internally between quotation marks as a single parameter string. The following examples show text expressions on the left and the resulting parameter string on the right:

```
find "my" && "word"   find "my word"
find "my" & "word"    find "myword"
find a & b & c        find "xyz" -- if a = "x", b = "y", c = "z"
find a && b && c      find "x y z"
```

If more than one search string (separated from each other by spaces) is included in the parameter string, all of them must be on a single card or its background for a successful search. However, they can be in any order on the card and only the first is shown with a box around it.

Press Command-F to display the parameter string from the most recently executed `find` command in the Message box.

An unsuccessful search sets HyperTalk's `the result` function to `not found`. After a successful search `the result` is empty. (See "Result" in Chapter 8.)

FunctionKey

Syntax

```
functionKey keyNumber
```

KeyNumber is an expression that yields an integer between 1 and 15.

Examples

```
functionKey 1
functionKey 15
```

Description

The `functionKey` command has built-in Undo, Cut, Copy, and Paste functions for *keyNumber* values 1 through 4, respectively. Any other value of *keyNumber* has no built-in effect.

Script

The following example handler uses the `functionKey` command to implement the message `undo` as a command:

```
on undo
  functionKey 1 -- preprogrammed as undo in HyperCard
end undo
```

Notes

The `functionKey` message, which invokes the `functionKey` command if it reaches HyperCard, is normally generated by pressing one of the function keys on the Apple Extended Keyboard. But you can also send it from the Message box or execute it as a line in a script.

You can program function keys 5 through 15, or reprogram keys 1 through 4, by writing an `on functionKey` handler in the script of any object in the hierarchy between the current card and HyperCard.

See also the `functionKey` system message in Chapter 6.

Get

Syntax

get *expression*

Expression yields any value.

Examples

```
get the long name of field 1
get the location of button "newButton"
get 2+3 -- puts 5 into It
get the date
```

Description

The get command puts the value of any expression into the local variable It. That is, get *expression* is the same as put *expression* into It.

Script

The following example handler saves the current user level, sets the user level to 5, then restores the saved level:

```
on doMything
  get userLevel -- get the current userLevel
  put It into savedLevel -- save userLevel before changing it
  set userLevel to 5 -- set userLevel for my button or script
  -- (put my script here)
  set userLevel to savedLevel -- restore userLevel when leaving
end doMything
```

Go

```
go [to] [stack] stackName
go [to] bkgndDescriptor [of [stack] stackName]
go [to] cardDescriptor [of bkgndDescriptor] [of [stack] stackName]
```

CardDescriptor is the word `card` followed by the name, number, ID number, or ordinal of a card (as described in Chapter 3), or it's the name of a container holding one of those things. *StackName* is the name of a stack or a container holding a stack name. *BkgndDescriptor* is the word `background` (or `bkgnd`) followed by its descriptor, or it's a container holding a background descriptor.

Examples

```
go card 23
go to art ideas
go field 1  -- if bkgnd field 1 contains a stack name
go home
go mid card of clip art -- middle card of stack "clip art"
go next
go to first card of second background of "home"
go "hd:bigFolder:innerFolder:myStack" -- full pathname
```

Description

The `go` command takes you to the specified card or stack. If you name a stack without specifying a card, you go to the first card in the stack. If you don't name a stack, you go to the specified card in the current stack. You can specify a visual effect to be used on opening the card by issuing the `visual effect` command before you use the `go` command.

Script

The following example handler queries the user for a destination, then executes a `go` command with a visual effect:

```
on mouseUp
  ask "Where to?" with "This card"
  if It is empty then put "this card" into It
  put It into goWhere
  visual effect dissolve to black
  go to goWhere
end mouseUp
```

Help

Syntax

```
help
```

Description

The `help` command takes you to the first card of the stack named Help.

Notes

See also the `help` system message in Chapter 6.

Hide

Syntax

```
hide menuBar
hide window
hide part
```

Window can be one of the following:

```
card window
tool window
pattern window
[the] message [window]
[the] message [box]
```

Part is the descriptor of a button or field. The part descriptor can be:

```
[card] button descriptor
background button descriptor
[background] field descriptor
card field descriptor
```

Descriptor is the name, number, or ID of the button or field, or a factor yielding one of those.

Examples

```
hide message
hide bkgnd button "goHome"
hide field id 1
```

Description The `hide` command removes the specified window or object from view. Its effect is the same as setting the `visible` property of the specified window or object to `false`, or clicking a window's close box.

Script The following example handler hides a field or button when the user puts the pointer over the button or field:

```
on mouseWithin
  hide the target
end mouseWithin
```

Notes `Message` can be abbreviated `msg`. `Background` can be abbreviated `bkgnd`. `Button` can be abbreviated `btn`.

The `hide` command does not affect the `location` property of an object or window.

Hidden fields aren't in the tab order. (They are skipped when you move the text insertion cursor from one visible field to the next by pressing the Tab key.) The `find` command does search through them, however, and you can put values into them and put their values elsewhere.

The `card window` parameter works with the `hide` command only in HyperCard versions 1.1 and later.

See also the `show` command, later in this chapter.

Multiply

Syntax

```
multiply destination by expression
```

Destination is a container and *expression* yields a number.

Examples

```
multiply Subtotal by Tax
multiply field 1 by field 3
multiply It by 2 -- puts result into It, replacing old value
```

Description

The `multiply` command multiplies the value in *destination* by the value of *expression* and puts the result in *destination*.

Script

The following example handler adds 6 percent to the value of items in a list:

```
on taxMe
  put "12.45,15.00,150.00,76.95,10.00,14.95" into taxables
  repeat with count = 1 to the number of items in taxables
    multiply item count of taxables by 1.06
  end repeat -- the new values are stored in taxables
end taxMe
```

Notes

The value previously in the destination must be a number; it is replaced with the new value.

The result is calculated to a precision of up to 19 decimal places and, if put into a field or the Message box, is displayed according to the `numberFormat` global property.

See also the `numberFormat` global property in Chapter 9.

Open

Syntax

```
open [document with] application
```

Application is the name of any application and *document* is the name of any document on your Macintosh. Either one can be an expression that yields such a name.

Examples

```
open "MacWrite"
open "Letter" with "MacWrite"
open Field 3
open FavoriteApp
```

Description

The open command launches the named application. A specific document may be opened with its own creator or a compatible application by using with *application*.

Script

The following example handler queries the user for a document and application before executing the open command:

```
on mouseUp
  ask "Open what document?" with empty
  if It is not empty then
    put It into doc
    ask "Use what application?" with empty
    if It is not empty then open doc with It
  end if
end mouseUp
```

Notes

If the document or application you specify isn't at the top level of the file hierarchy (the "disk" level), then the path to it must be specified on the appropriate search path card of the Home stack (use the card titled "Look for documents in" for documents and the card titled "Look for applications in" for applications). Alternatively, you can specify the full pathname with the open command:

```
open "My Hard Disk:Applications:Words:MacWrite"
```

If HyperCard can't find the requested document or application, it displays the directory dialog box to the user.

When you quit the application, you go to the card you were on in HyperCard when you executed the open command. However, any global variables you had previously declared are now gone, and any portions of handlers that remained unfinished when you executed the open command do not finish.

Open file

Syntax

```
open file fileName
```

FileName is the name of any file on your Macintosh, or an expression that yields such a name.

Examples

```
open file "textOnly"
open file field 1
```

Description

The `open file` command opens the data fork of the named file. Usually, the file is an ASCII text file opened in preparation for importing or exporting text. If the specified file doesn't exist, HyperCard creates it.

Script

The following example handler determines if a given file exists by trying to read from it:

```
on checkFile
  put "MyFilename" into filename
  open file filename
  read from file filename for 16384
  if It is empty then answer "File does not exist" with "OK"
  close file filename
end checkFile
```

Notes

If the specified file is already open, you get an error message. Use the `close file` command to close files explicitly after you use them. HyperCard automatically closes all open files when an `exit to HyperCard` statement is executed, when you press Command-period, or when you quit HyperCard.

You must provide the full pathname of the file if it's not at the same directory level as HyperCard. (See "Stack Descriptors" in Chapter 3 for an explanation of pathnames.)

See also `read`, `write`, and `close file`, in this chapter.

Open printing

Syntax

```
open printing [with dialog]
```

Description

The `open printing` command starts a print job to be ended later by a `close printing` command.

The settings specified in the Print Stack dialog box are used unless `with dialog` is specified, in which case the dialog box is displayed and new settings can be chosen.

Script

The following example handler prints a selection of cards:

```
on printSelection
  put "1,3,8,15,21" into myCards
  open printing with dialog
  repeat with count = 1 to the number of items in myCards
    go card item count of myCards
    print this card
  end repeat
  close printing
end printSelection
```

Notes

Printing cards with `open printing` is similar to printing with the Print Stack command in the File menu, except that Print Stack prints all cards in the stack, while `open printing` prints only the ones you specify with the `print card` command, described later in this chapter.

You must use the `close printing` command to end a print job begun with `open printing`. Don't use the `print [document with] application` command while a print job is active.

See also `close printing` and `print card`, in this chapter.

Play

Syntax

```
play "voice" [tempo] ["notes"]
play stop
```

Voice is the name of a digitized sound (`boing` and `harpsichord` are included with HyperCard), *tempo* is the speed at which the sound plays, and *notes* is a list of one or more notes representing the pitch at which the sound plays and the duration of the notes. The quotation marks around *voice* and *notes* are required.

Examples

```
play "boing" tempo 200 "c4e c dq c f eh" -- Happy Birthday
play "harpsichord" "ch d e f g a b c5w"
```

Description

The `play` command makes the Macintosh play notes through its speaker (or through the audio jack if it's plugged in). You can write a song by specifying a series of notes after the `play` command. The `play stop` form stops the current sound immediately; otherwise it plays until it's done and stops by itself. HyperCard continues to execute handlers and perform other actions while a sound plays.

Script

The following example handler goes to each card in a stack and synchronizes playing the specified notes with each card change:

```
on tour
  repeat the number of cards
    play "harpsichord" tempo 200 "ce4 fe ae c5q ae4 cq5"
    go next card
    wait until the sound is "done"
  end repeat
end tour
```

Notes

The *tempo* is a number specifying the speed at which the group of notes is played (100 is a medium tempo; higher numbers are faster). Voice and tempo are specified once for each `play` command.

The notes are specified in the following form:

noteName accidental octave duration

NoteName is the name of the note played (A through G); *accidental* is # or b specifying sharp or flat, respectively; *octave* is a number specifying the pitch of the scale (4 is the "middle C" scale); and *duration* specifies the relative time value of the note played:

w   whole note
h   half note
q   quarter note
e   eighth note
s   16th note
t   32nd note
x   64th note

You can use a period (.) or numeral 3 following *duration* to specify a dotted or triplet note, respectively.

Octave and *duration* may be changed for each note played; if they are not changed, subsequent notes are in the same octave and have the same duration as the previous note.

HyperCard can also play digitized music or voice samples which are stored on disk as format 2 'snd' resources—the resource name is the voice—in the current stack file, the Home stack, the HyperCard application, or the System file. *Inside Macintosh,* Volume V, describes format 2 'snd' resources.

See also the sound function in Chapter 8.

Pop card

Syntax

pop card [*preposition destination*]

Preposition is into, before, or after, and *destination* is a container or any chunk of a container.

Example

pop card into field 3 of card WhereIbeen

Description

The pop card command retrieves the identification (full ID and stack pathname) of a card previously saved with the push card command. If you don't provide a destination for the identification, you go directly to the card whose address is popped.

Script

The following example handler pushes whatever card you're on, goes to another stack, gets the value of a field property, then returns to the original card:

```
on getTheFont
  global myStack,theFont
  push card
  go myStack
  put textFont of field 1 into theFont
  pop card -- goes to the card formerly pushed
end getTheFont
```

Notes

If you don't specify a destination, after the card has been popped, its identification is removed from the memory stack—it can't be popped again. If a destination is given, however, the card's identification is put into the destination container, but you don't go anywhere.

See also the `push card` command, in this chapter.

Print card

Syntax

```
print card
print expression cards
print cardDescriptor
```

Expression yields an integer or the word `all`, and *cardDescriptor* is a card descriptor of a card in the current stack.

Examples

```
print card
print last card
print card id 3011
print all cards
print howMany cards -- howMany contains a number or "all"
```

Description

The `print card` command makes HyperCard print the current card, the same as the Print Card command in the File menu (Command-P). The `print expression cards` form prints the number of cards specified by *expression,* or all the cards in the stack, beginning with the current card. The `print cardDescriptor` form makes HyperCard go to the specified card, print it, and return to the current card.

Script

The following example handler queries the user for a number of cards to print whenever Print Card is chosen from the File menu:

```
on doMenu var
  if var is "print card" then
    ask "Print how many cards?" with one
    open printing
    print It cards
    close printing
  else pass doMenu -- make sure other menu choices continue to work
end doMenu
```

Notes

You don't need to use the `open printing` command before using the `print card` command. If nothing is printing, the `print card` command prints the specified card or cards immediately; if an `open printing` command is in effect, no cards are printed until a page is full (depending on how many cards per page are specified in the printing dialog box) or the `close printing` command is given.

Chapter 3, "Naming Objects," defines card descriptors.

Print

Syntax

`print` *document* `with` *application*

Document is an expression that yields the name of any document on your Macintosh, and *application* is an expression that yields the name of the application to which it belongs (or with which it is compatible).

Examples

```
print "memo" with "MacWrite"
print field 1 with field "Program"
print "hd:Mac docs:letter" with "hd:utilities:MacWrite"
```

Description

The `print` command suspends HyperCard, launches the named application, opens the named document, prints the document, then resumes running HyperCard. The specified application must support printing.

Script

The following example handler queries the user for the name of a document to print and an application with which to print it:

```
on mouseUp
  ask "Print what document?" with empty
  if It is not empty then
    put It into doc
    ask "Use what application?" with empty
    if It is not empty then print doc with It
  end if
end mouseUp
```

Notes

If the document or application you specify isn't at the top level of the file hierarchy (the "disk" level), then the path to it must be specified on the appropriate search path card of the Home stack (use the card titled "Look for documents in" for documents and the card titled "Look for applications in" for applications). Alternatively, you can specify the full pathname with the print command.

Don't use the print command while the open printing command is active.

Push

Syntax

push *cardDescriptor*

CardDescriptor is a factor that yields the descriptor of any card in the current stack.

Examples

```
push recent card
push first card
push card
```

Description

The push command saves the identification of the specified card in a LIFO (last-in, first-out) memory stack (an area of memory, not a HyperCard stack).

Script

The following example handler saves the current card, goes to a random card, then returns to the original card:

```
on nonSense
  push card -- save current card
  go any card
  pop card -- restore current card
end nonSense
```

The card identification can be retrieved later with the `pop card` command (usually so that you can go directly back to the pushed card). The card identification that's saved is the full card ID and stack path name.

Card descriptors are described in Chapter 3.

See also the `pop card` command, earlier in this chapter.

Put

Syntax

put *expression* [*preposition destination*]

Expression yields a text string or number, *preposition* is `into`, `before`, or `after`, and *destination* is a container.

Examples

```
put "Hello" into field 1
put "go " before field "WhereTo"
put empty into It
put It -- puts contents of It into Msg
put "Tom" into first word of field "Name"
put "." after first character of last word of field 3
put field 2 + field 3 into field 4 -- adds numbers in fields
put the date into varName
```

Description

The `put` command causes HyperCard to evaluate *expression* and copy the result into *destination*.

Script

The following example handler initializes three global variables when the stack it's in is opened:

```
on openStack
  global var1,var2,var3
  put 0 into var1
  put empty into var2
  put empty into var3
end openStack
```

If you don't specify the destination, the value is copied into the Message box. (HyperCard shows the Message box if it's hidden.) If you specify a destination that HyperCard doesn't recognize, it creates a new local variable of that name and puts the value into the variable.

Using into with put replaces the contents of the destination, before places the source value at the beginning of the previous contents, and after appends the source value to the end of the previous contents.

If *expression* is a container holding an arithmetic expression, the expression is not evaluated but is copied literally into the destination. Use the value function with the container name to have HyperCard evaluate its contents.

You can delete the contents of a container by putting the constant empty or "" into it (but this doesn't delete the container). You can specify a chunk expression before the destination to insert, replace, or delete a portion of the contents.

See also the delete command, earlier in this chapter.

Read

Syntax

read from file *fileName* until *character*
read from file *fileName* for *numberOfCharacters*

FileName is an expression yielding the name of any file on your Macintosh, *character* is an expression yielding a character, and *numberOfCharacters* is an expression yielding an integer.

Examples

```
read from file "import" until tab
read from file "File Names" until return -- reads one line
read from file "someText" for 16384 -- maximum block size
```

Description

The read command reads from the data fork of the specified file, previously opened with the open file command, into the local variable It. Reading starts at the beginning of a newly opened file and continues from the last point read with each read command.

The until *character* form causes reading to stop when the specified character has been read; the for *numberOfCharacters* form causes reading to stop when the specified number of characters (or bytes) have been read. Return characters at the end of lines count, as do space and tab characters.

Script

The following example handler opens a file, reads to the end of the file while placing its contents into a global variable, and closes the file:

```
on mouseUp
  global fileName, textHolder
  open file fileName
  repeat
    read from file fileName for 16834
    if It is empty then exit repeat
    put It after textHolder
  end repeat
  close file fileName
end mouseUp
```

Notes

You can read only up to 16,384 characters at a time. If you try to read more characters than that, all but the last 16,384 that you read are ignored. The read command puts the characters into the local variable It, replacing its previous contents. So, you must put each block of text that you read into another container (use after with the put command to append each new block of text to the end of the previous contents). Containers other than fields have no practical size limit (they're limited by available memory). If you try to put more than 30,000 characters into a field, the extra characters are ignored.

❖ *HyperCard removes tab characters from fields:* HyperCard reads tab characters from a file into It, and the tab characters remain when you put the text into another variable or a field (where they are displayed as spaces). If you alter any text in the field, however, HyperCard removes the tab characters.

If you specify more than one character with the until *character* form, HyperCard stops reading when it matches the first character specified.

Use the close file command to close files explicitly after you use them. HyperCard automatically closes all open files when an exit to HyperCard statement is executed, when you press Command-period, or when you quit HyperCard.

You must provide the full pathname of the file if it's not at the same directory level as HyperCard. (See "Stack Descriptors" in Chapter 3 for an explanation of pathnames.)

See also the close file, open file, and write commands in this chapter.

Reset paint

Syntax   `reset paint`

Description   The `reset paint` command reinstates the default values of all the painting
                  properties. The painting properties and their default values are

grid	false
lineSize	1
filled	false
centered	false
multiple	false
multiSpace	1
pattern	12
brush	8
polySides	4
textAlign	left
textFont	geneva
textSize	12
textStyle	plain
textHeight	16

Notes   The painting properties are described in Chapter 9, "Properties."

ReturnKey

Syntax   `returnKey`

Description   The `returnKey` command sends a statement typed into the Message box to the
                  current card. (If a field is open for text editing, pressing the Return key enters a return
                  character.)

Notes   The `returnKey` message, which invokes the `returnKey` command if it reaches
                  HyperCard, is normally generated by pressing the Return key on the keyboard. But
                  you can also send it from the Message box or execute it as a line in a script.

                  See also the `returnKey` system message in Chapter 6.

Set

Syntax

```
set [the] property [of object] to value
```

Property is a characteristic of a HyperCard object, *object* is an object descriptor or window name, and *value* is a valid setting for the particular property.

Examples

```
set name of field 1 to "Soccer"
set location of button "newButton" to the mouseLoc
set the visible of field 1 to "false" -- hide the field
set userLevel to 5 -- scripting
```

Description

The set command changes the state of a specified global, painting, window, or object property. If the object to which the property belongs is not specified, the property must be a global or painting property.

Script

The following example handler automatically draws a circle on the current card:

```
on mouseUp
  choose oval tool
  set linesize to 2
  set centered to true
  set dragspeed to 75 -- this changes the speed of expansion
  drag from 255,170 to 385,300
  choose browse tool
end mouseUp
```

Notes

The properties of objects depend on the type of object. Generally, they are the characteristics shown in the Info dialog boxes under the Objects menu.

All of the HyperCard global, painting, window, and object properties are described in detail in Chapter 9, "Properties." See also the show command, later in this chapter.

Show cards

Syntax

show *number* cards

Number is an expression yielding an integer or the word all.

Examples

```
show all cards
show ten cards
show 26 cards
show howMany cards -- howMany is a variable containing a number
```

Description

The show cards command displays the specified number of cards in the current stack in turn, beginning with the next card.

Script

The following example handler "pre-warms" the stack when you open it, so that going to cards in the stack subsequently will be faster, by caching the cards in RAM:

```
on openStack
  set lockScreen to true
  show all cards
  set lockScreen to false
end openStack
```

Notes

The show all cards form shows all cards in the stack. HyperCard doesn't send the openCard system message when a card is displayed by show cards, nor do visual effects occur. After the cards are shown, the last one shown (where you began in the case of show all cards) is the current card.

Show

Syntax

```
show menuBar
show window [at h, v]
show part [at h, v]
```

Window can be one of the following:

```
card window
tool window
pattern window
[the] message [window]
[the] message [box]
```

Part is the descriptor of a button or field. The part descriptor can be

```
[card] button descriptor
background button descriptor
[background] field descriptor
card field descriptor
```

Descriptor is an expression yielding the name, number, or ID of the button or field; *h* and *v* are expressions yielding integers representing horizontal and vertical pixel offsets, respectively, on the screen.

Examples

```
show msg at 100,200
show tool window
show field "Names" at 1,1
```

Description

The show command displays a specified window or object at a specified location on the screen. If positioning offsets aren't given, the window or object is displayed at its previous location.

Script

The following example handler displays the palettes and the Message box at their default locations when HyperCard first starts running:

```
on startUp
  show tool window
  show pattern window
  show msg
end startUp
```

Notes

If they have not been previously torn off the menu bar, the Tools palette appears at 200,70 and the Patterns palette at 300,70. The Message box appears at 22,300. The menu bar always appears at the top of the screen. In effect, the `show` command sets the `visible` and, optionally, `location` properties of the window or object. (See Chapter 9 for a description of the `visible` and `location` properties.)

On the original Macintosh screen, visible horizontal offsets range from 0 to 511, and visible vertical offsets range from 0 to 341.

`Message` can be abbreviated `msg`. `Background` can be abbreviated `bkgnd`. `Button` can be abbreviated `btn`.

`Card window` refers to the position of the entire HyperCard display on the screen; the *h* and *v* offsets specify the distance from the top-left corner of the screen to the top-left corner of the card window, disregarding the title bar at the top of the window. For the other windows, *h* and *v* specify the distance from the top-left corner of the card window to the top-left corner of the other window, disregarding the drag bar at the top of the window.

For buttons and fields, *h* and *v* specify the distance from the top-left corner of the card window to the center of the button or field. The menu bar always shows at the top of the screen. The `tool` window is the Tools palette, `pattern` is the Patterns palette, and `message` or `msg` is the Message box.

See also the `hide` and `set` commands, earlier in this chapter.

Sort

Syntax

```
sort [direction] [style] by expression
```

Direction is `ascending` or `descending`, *style* is `text`, `numeric`, `dateTime`, or `international`, and *expression* is any expression.

Examples

```
sort numeric by second word of field 1
sort descending text by last word of field "Names"
sort by field 2
```

Description

The `sort` command orders all the cards in a stack according to the value of *expression*, which is evaluated individually for each card in the stack.

The default *direction* is `ascending`, and the default *style* is `text`.

Script

The following example handler shuffles the cards in a stack randomly when the user goes to it from another stack:

```
on openStack
  sort numeric by random(the number of cards)
end openStack
```

Notes

The `dateTime` style sorts the stack using one of the forms of date or time (shown with the `convert` command, in this chapter), with earliest placed first in the ascending direction. The `international` style assures correct sorting of non-English text containing diacritical marks and special characters, depending on the international resources in your System file, your version of HyperCard, the Home stack, and the current stack. The `dateTime` style also works correctly with non-English forms of date and time modified by international resources in the System file.

Subtract

Syntax

```
subtract expression from destination
```

Expression yields a number, and *destination* is a container.

Examples

```
subtract 2 from It
subtract field 1 from field 2
```

Description

The `subtract` command subtracts the value of *expression* from the value of *destination,* leaving the result in the destination.

Notes

The value previously in the destination must be a number; it is replaced with the new value.

TabKey

Syntax

```
tabKey
```

Description

The `tabKey` command opens the first unlocked field on the current background or card (placing the text insertion point in the field) and selecting its entire contents. If a field is already open, `tabKey` closes it and opens the next field, selecting its contents.

Script

The following example handler sets the insertion point in the first field, so that the user can type something, when the card is opened:

```
on openCard
  tabKey
end openCard
```

Notes

The `tabKey` message, which invokes the `tabKey` command if it reaches HyperCard, is normally generated by pressing the Tab key on the keyboard. But you can also send it from the Message box or execute it as a line in a script.

The `tabKey` command opens fields in the following order: from the lowest number to the highest, through the background fields first, then through the card fields.

See also the `tabKey` message in Chapter 6.

Type

Syntax

```
type expression [with key[, key2[, key3]]]
```

Expression yields a text string, and *key, key2,* and *key3* are one or more of the following key names, separated by commas: `shiftKey`, `optionKey`, or `commandKey` (or `cmdKey`).

Examples

```
type "Now is the time for all good persons."
type "p" with commandKey -- print card
```

Description

The `type` command enters the value of *expression* at the text insertion point, as though you had typed it manually.

Script

The following example handler chooses the Browse tool, clicks at the center of the specified field, and types a literal string:

```
on autoType
  choose browse tool
  click at the loc of field "whereToType"
  type "Automatic writing apppears before your eyes..."
end autoType
```

Notes

The text insertion point is placed by clicking in an unlocked field with the Browse tool or by sending the `tabKey` message. Manipulating the text insertion point is described in the *HyperCard User's Guide*. Paint text can be typed at the text insertion point on a card or background with the Paint Text tool selected.

Visual

visual [effect] *effectName* [*speed*] [to *image*]

EffectName is one of the following:

barn door close	scroll up
barn door open	venetian blinds
checkerboard	wipe down
dissolve	wipe left
iris close	wipe right
iris open	wipe up
plain	zoom close
scroll down	zoom in
scroll left	zoom open
scroll right	zoom out

Speed is one of the following:

fast	very fast
slow[ly]	very slow[ly]

Image is one of the following:

black	inverse
card	white
gray	

Examples

```
visual effect barn door open
visual dissolve slowly to white
visual checkerboard
```

Description   The `visual` command specifies a visual transition for HyperCard to use the next time it opens a card, as the current card is closed. The default `plain` visual effect causes all of the current image to be replaced immediately by the image of the next card. If you use the `to` *image* form, the visual effect occurs as a transition from the current card to a completely white, gray, or black screen image, to the inverted image of the current card, or to the image of the next card; `to card` is the default.

Script   The following example handler stacks two visual effects, which occur in succession, so that the transition appears as a fade to black, then to the next card:

```
on fadeOut
  visual effect dissolve to black
  visual effect dissolve to card
  go next card
end fadeOut
```

Notes   Visual effects don't happen when you use the arrow keys or the `show cards` command to change cards; they must be set up in a handler that also contains a `go` command, and they occur when the `go` is executed. If a `go` command is not executed, visual effects set up in the handler are canceled when the handler finishes executing. You can stack up several visual effects that will occur one after the other when you go to the next card.

On a Macintosh II you must use one-bit display mode (choose "2 colors" or "2 grays" on the monitor setup of the Control Panel) to see visual effects.

Wait

```
wait [for] time [seconds]
wait until condition
wait while condition
```

Time is an expression that yields an integer and *condition* is an expression that yields `true` or `false`.

Examples

```
wait 60 seconds
wait until the mouse is down
```

Description

The `wait` command causes HyperCard to pause before executing the rest of the handler, either for a specific length of time, until a specified condition becomes true, or while a specified condition remains true.

Script

The following example handler allows time to view each card:

```
on slideshow
  repeat the number of cards
    visual effect dissolve slowly
    go next card
    wait 2 seconds
  end repeat
end slideshow
```

Note

If `seconds` is not specified for *time,* HyperCard uses `ticks` (¹⁄₆₀ second), which can also be specified explicitly.

Write

Syntax

```
write source to file fileName
```

Source is an expression that yields text, and *fileName* is an expression that yields a file name.

Examples

```
write field "address" to file "myDisk:myFile"
write "first line" & return & "second line" to file "two liner"
```

Description

The `write` command causes HyperCard to copy the specified text into the specified disk file.

Script

The following example handler opens a file specified in a global variable, writes the entire contents of the specified field to the file, then closes the file:

```
on writeFile
  global filename
  open file filename
  write background field 1 to file filename
  close file filename
end writeFile
```

Notes

The file must have been opened previously with the `open file` command and should be closed, when copying is completed, with the `close file` command.

The first `write` command that you execute after opening the file replaces any previous contents. Subsequent `write` commands append to the file's contents.

You must provide the full pathname of the file if it's not at the same directory level as HyperCard. (See "Stack Descriptors" in Chapter 3 for an explanation of pathnames.)

If the file is locked or its disk is full, HyperCard displays an error dialog box and closes the file. HyperCard automatically closes all open files when an `exit to HyperCard` statement is executed, when you press Command-period, or when you quit HyperCard.

See also the `open file`, `close file`, and `read` commands, in this chapter.

Chapter 8

Functions

This chapter describes HyperTalk's built-in functions.

A **function** is a named value that is calculated by HyperCard when a statement in which it's used executes. The value of a function changes according to conditions of the system or according to values of parameters that you pass to the function when you use it. When HyperCard reads a function name in a line of HyperTalk, it places the function's current value—its result—in that location before completing other actions.

Function calls

To make a function call, that is, to use it in a HyperTalk statement, you must either use the word `the` before the function name or append parentheses after it. If a single parameter is passed to a function, the parameter can be enclosed in the parentheses or can follow the word `of`. (When `of` is used in this way to indicate the function call, the word `the` preceding the function name is optional.) If more than one parameter is passed to a function, all parameters must be enclosed in the parentheses and separated from each other by commas. Some examples of function calls are

```
put the time into msg
put time() into background field "Time"
put the length of myVariable into card field "howLong"
put average(total_1,total_2,total_3) into Projection
```

You can define your own functions in HyperTalk using the function handler structure described in Chapter 5.

❖ *Defined functions override built-in ones with same name:* If you define your own function having the same name as a built-in one, yours will override the built-in one if the function call is made with the parentheses syntax (unless the function call is made farther along the hierarchy than the handler's script). Users can call HyperCard's built-in functions directly by using the words `the` or `of`, rather than using the parentheses syntax; however, functions having more than one parameter always require parentheses.

Syntax description notation

The syntax descriptions use the following typographic conventions. Words or phrases in `typewriter type` are Hypertalk language elements or are those that you type to the computer literally, exactly as shown. Words in *italic* type describe general elements, not specific names—you must substitute the actual instances. Square brackets ([ ]) enclose optional elements which may be included if you need them. (Don't type the square brackets.)

It doesn't matter whether you use uppercase or lowercase letters; names that are formed from two words are shown in small letters with a capital in the middle (`likeThis`) merely to make them more readable. The HyperTalk prepositions `of` and `in` are interchangeable—the syntax descriptions use the one that sounds more natural.

The terms *factor* and *expression* are defined in Chapter 4. Briefly, a factor can be a constant, literal, function, property, number, or container, and an expression can be a factor or a complex expression built with factors and operators. Also, a factor can be an expression within parentheses. The term *yields* indicates a specific kind of value, such as a number or a text string, that must result from evaluation of a factor or expression when a restriction applies (for example, the factor or expression used with the `abs` function must yield a number). However, any HyperTalk value can be treated as a text string.

Abs

Syntax
```
the abs of factor
abs (expression)
```
Factor and *expression* yield numbers.

Example
```
put abs(a-b) into field "theOffset"
```

Description
The `abs` function returns the absolute value (makes the sign positive) of the number passed to it.

Annuity

Syntax
```
annuity (rate, periods)
```
Rate and *periods* are expressions that yield numbers

Examples
```
put myPayment*annuity(.015,12) into presentValue
put myPayment*annuity(.015,12)*compound(.015,12) into futureValue
```

Description
The `annuity` function is used to compute the present or future value of an ordinary annuity. *Rate* is the interest rate per period, and *periods* is the number of periods over which the value is calculated. The formula for `annuity` is

$$\text{annuity}\,(\textit{rate, periods}) = (1-(1+\textit{rate})^{-\textit{periods}})\,/\,\textit{rate}$$

The `annuity` function is more accurate than computing the expression above using basic arithmetic operations and exponentiation, especially when *rate* is small.

Notes
See also the `compound` function, later in this chapter.

Atan

the atan of *factor*
atan (*expression*)

Factor and *expression* yield numbers.

Example

```
put atan(1.0) into field "arcTan"   -- yields 0.785398
```

Description

The atan function returns the trigonometric arc tangent (inverse tangent) of the number passed to it; that is, the angle whose tangent is equal to the given value. The result is expressed in radians.

Radians can be converted to degrees by multiplying by 180 and dividing the result by the value of the constant pi.

Script

The following example handler converts a value in radians to degrees and puts the result into the Message box:

```
on radiansToDegrees var
  put round((atan(var)*180)/pi) into msg
end radiansToDegrees
```

Average

Syntax

```
average (list)
```

List is a sequence of comma-separated expressions that yield numbers, or it is a single container that contains such a sequence.

Example

```
put average(1,2,3) into field "avg"
```

Description

The `average` function returns the average of the numbers passed to it.

Script

The following example handler displays the average of a list of numbers contained in one line of a field:

```
on avgSupplyPrice
  put "12.95,10.50,14.75,15.00,9.95" into line 3 of field "suppliers"
  answer "Average widget cost:" && average (line 3 of field "suppliers")
end avgSupplyPrice
```

CharToNum

Syntax

```
the charToNum of factor
charToNum (expression)
```

Factor and *expression* yield a character.

Example

```
put the charToNum of "a" into It -- yields 97
```

Description

The `charToNum` function returns an unsigned integer representing the ASCII equivalent value of the character passed to it.

Notes

If more than one character is passed, `charToNum` returns the ASCII value of the first character. If *source* is a literal, it must appear within quotation marks.

ClickLoc

Syntax
```
the clickLoc
clickLoc()
```

Example
```
put the clickLoc into card field "firstClick"
```

Description
The `clickLoc` function returns the point on the screen where the user most recently clicked before the handler started executing. The location is determined at the time the message is first sent—the mouse could be elsewhere by the time the message is received. The location point is returned as two integers separated by a comma, representing horizontal and vertical pixel offsets measuring from the top-left corner of the card window.

Script
The following example handler, when it is in the script of a locked field, selects a word in the field when the user clicks the word:

```
on mouseUp
  set locktext of me to false -- field must be locked
  click at the clickLoc
  click at the clickLoc
  put "You clicked on the word:" && the selection
  set lockText of me to true -- must lock it again when we leave
end mouseUp
```

CommandKey

Syntax
```
the commandKey
commandKey()
```

Example
```
if the commandKey is up then put "Wow" into the Message box
```

Description
The `commandKey` function returns the constant `up` if the Command key is not pressed or `down` if it is pressed.

Note
The `commandKey` function name can be abbreviated `cmdKey`.

Compound

Syntax

compound(*rate, periods*)

Rate and *periods* are expressions that yield numbers.

Examples

```
put futureValue/compound(.10,12) into presentValue
put presentValue*compound(.10,12) into futureValue
```

Description

The compound function is used to compute the present or future value of a compound interest–bearing account. *Rate* represents the interest rate per period, and *periods* is the number of periods over which the value is calculated. The formula for compound is

compound(*rate, periods*) = $(1 + rate)^{periods}$

The compound function is more accurate than computing the expression above using standard arithmetic operations and exponentiation, especially when *rate* is small.

Script

The following example handler calculates the value in one year of an account earning 7½ percent interest compounded monthly:

```
on calcInterest
  ask "Enter the beginning balance:" with empty
  set numberFormat to ".00" -- dollars and cents format
  put "Value in 1 year $" & it * compound(.075/12,12)
end calcInterest
```

Note

See also the annuity function, earlier in this chapter.

Cos

Syntax

```
the cos of factor
cos (expression)
```

Factor and *expression* yield numbers.

Example

```
put the cos of 2 -- puts -.416147 into the Message box
```

Description

The `cos` function returns the cosine of the angle which is passed to it. The angle must be expressed in radians.

Note

Radians can be converted to degrees by multiplying by 180 and dividing the result by the value of the constant `pi`.

Date

Syntax

```
the [modifier] date
```

Modifier is `long`, `short`, or `abbreviated` (or `abbrev` or `abbr`).

Example

```
put last word of the long date into background field "Year"
```

Description

The `date` function returns a string representing the current date set in your Macintosh. The various forms return strings exemplified by

```
the short date    7/5/87
the long date     Sunday, July 5, 1987
the abbrev date   Sun, Jul 5, 1987
```

Without a modifier the `date` function returns the short date.

Script

The following example handler puts the current date into a field when another field (whose script contains the handler) is changed:

```
on closeField
  put the long date into field "lastUpdate"
end closeField
```

DiskSpace

Syntax

```
the diskSpace
diskSpace()
```

Example

```
if the diskSpace < 100000 then answer "Your disk is getting full."
```

Description

The `diskSpace` function returns an integer representing the number of bytes of free space on the disk that contains the current stack.

Script

The following function handler is used by the second handler (for the `writeFile` message) to ensure that there is enough space on a disk to write to a file on that disk:

```
function checkSpace var
  if the diskSpace > var then return "OK" else return "FULL"
end checkSpace

on writeFile
  global var
  put "MyFilename" into filename
  if checkSpace(card field 1) is "OK" then
    open file filename
    write var to file filename
    close file filename
  else answer "Can't write that file; the disk is full."
end writeFile
```

Exp

Syntax
```
the exp of factor
exp (expression)
```
Factor and *expression* yield numbers.

Example
```
put the exp of 2 -- puts 7.389056 into the Message box
```

Description
The exp function returns the mathematical exponential of its argument (the constant *e*, which equals 2.7182818, raised to the power specified by the argument).

Exp1

Syntax
```
the exp1 of factor
exp1 (expression)
```
Factor and *expression* yield numbers.

Example
```
put the exp1 of 2 -- puts 6.389056 into the Message box
```

Description
The exp1 function returns 1 less than the mathematical exponential of its argument (1 less than the result of the constant *e* raised to the power specified by the argument). That is, it computes:

```
exp (number) - 1
```

Exp2

Syntax

```
the exp2 of factor
exp2 (expression)
```

Factor and *expression* yield numbers.

Example

```
put the exp2 of 16 -- puts 65536 into the Message box
```

Description

The `exp2` function returns the value of 2 raised to the power specified by the argument.

Length

Syntax

```
the length of factor
length (expression)
```

Factor and *expression* yield text strings.

Examples

```
put length("tail") into It -- yields 4
if the length of word n of field 5 > 25 then add 1 to fogIndex
```

Description

The `length` function returns the number of characters (including spaces, tabs, and return characters) in the text string passed to it.

Notes

If *expression* is a literal, it must appear within quotation marks. The `length` function is identical in effect to the following form of the `number` function:

```
the number of characters in factor
```

Ln

Syntax

```
the ln of factor
ln (expression)
```

Factor and *expression* yield numbers.

Example

```
put the ln of 10 -- puts 2.302585 into the Message box
```

Description

The `ln` function returns the base-*e* (natural) logarithm of the number passed to it.

Ln1

Syntax

```
the ln1 of factor
ln1 (expression)
```

Factor and *expression* yield numbers.

Example

```
put the ln1 of 10 -- puts 2.397895 into the Message box
```

Description

The `ln1` function returns the base-*e* (natural) logarithm of the sum of 1 plus the number passed to it. That is, it computes

$$ln (1+number)$$

If *number* is small, the result is more accurate than using standard arithmetic operations.

Log2

Syntax

```
the log2 of factor
log2 (expression)
```

Factor and *expression* yield numbers.

Example

```
put the log2 of 10 -- puts 3.321928 into the Message box
```

Description

The `log2` function returns the base-2 logarithm of the number passed to it.

Max

Syntax

```
max (list)
```

List is a sequence of comma-separated expressions that yield numbers, or it is a single container that contains such a sequence.

Example

```
put max(5,10,7.3) -- puts 10 into the Message box
```

Description

The `max` function returns the highest-value number from a list of numbers passed to it. If the source of the list is a container with more than one line in it, only the first line is used.

Script

The following example handler displays the highest number in a list contained in a variable:

```
on highStock
  put "12.50,10,7.95,14.76,13.70" into stockPrices
  answer "The highest price for the month is:" && max(stockPrices)
end highStock
```

Min

min (*list*)

List is a sequence of comma-separated expressions that yield numbers, or it is a single container that contains such a sequence.

Example

put min(5,10,7.3) -- puts 5 into the Message box

Description

The min function returns the lowest-value number from a list of numbers passed to it. If the source of the list is a container with more than one line in it, only the first line is used.

Script

The following example handler displays the lowest number in a list contained in a variable:

```
on lowStock
  put "12.50,10,7.95,14.76,13.70" into stockPrices
  put "The lowest price for the month is:" && min(stockPrices)
end lowStock
```

Mouse

Syntax

the mouse
mouse()

Example

if the mouse is up put "Press the mouse button" into msg

Description

The mouse function returns the constant up if the mouse button is not pressed, down if it is pressed.

Script   The following example handler determines whether the user has single-clicked or double-clicked the button whose script contains the handler:

```
on mouseUp
  put the ticks into start
  repeat until the ticks-start > 4 -- adjust for comfortable click
    if the mouse is "down" then
      go last card -- put your double-click action here
      exit mouseUp
    end if
  end repeat
  go next card -- put your single-click action here
end mouseUp
```

MouseClick

Syntax
```
the mouseClick
mouseClick()
```

Example
```
if the mouseClick then put the mouseLoc
```

Description   The mouseClick function determines if the mouse button is down. If it is not down, the mouseClick immediately returns the constant false. If the mouse button is down, the mouseClick waits until the mouse button is up, then returns the constant true.

Script   The following example handler demonstrates operation of the mouseClick function by informing the user whether or not it sensed a click during its execution:

```
on mouseUp
  put "Click or don't click..."
  wait 5 seconds
  if the mouseClick then
    put "You clicked."
  else
    put "You didn't click."
  end if
end mouseUp
```

MouseH

Syntax

```
the mouseH
mouseH()
```

Example

```
if mouseH > 512 put "Stop" into msg
```

Description

The mouseH function returns an integer representing the number of horizontal pixels from the left side of the card window to the current location of the mouse pointer. When this number is negative, the mouse has been clicked to the left of the left edge of the card window (possible when you're using a display larger than the original Macintosh display, or if you set the location of the card window different from 0,0).

MouseLoc

Syntax

```
the mouseLoc
mouseLoc()
```

Examples

```
show button "everReady" at the mouseLoc
```

Description

The mouseLoc function returns the point on the screen where the pointer is currently located. This point is returned as two integers separated by a comma, representing horizontal and vertical pixel offsets from the top-left corner of the card window.

Script

The following example handler, in a button script, allows the user to drag the button around the screen:

```
on mouseDown
  repeat until the mouse is up
    show the name of me at the mouseloc
  end repeat
end mouseDown
```

MouseV

Syntax

```
the mouseV
mouseV()
```

Example

```
if mouseV > 342 put "Stop" into msg
```

Description

The `mouseV` function returns an integer representing the number of vertical pixels from the top of the card window, disregarding the title bar, to the current location of the pointer.

Number

Syntax

```
[the] number of objects
[the] number of chunks in factor
```

Objects is `[background] buttons`, `[card] fields`, `backgrounds`, or `cards`. *Chunks* is `characters` (or `chars`), `words`, `items`, or `lines`, and *factor* yields a text string.

Examples

```
put the number of buttons into It
put number of items of line 1 of field 2 into listSize
put the number of chars in msg into line 3 of field 2
if the number of chars in myVar > 10 then put "Big" into msg
```

Description

The `number` function returns the number of buttons or fields on the current card or on its background, the number of backgrounds or cards in the current stack, or the number of chunks of a specified kind in a designated text string.

Script

The following example handler uses the `number` function to delete all the card fields on a card, regardless of how many there are:

```
on deleteFields
  put the tool into oldTool
  choose field tool
  repeat with whichField = the number of card fields down to 1
    -- you must count down like this, not up
    click at the loc of card field whichField
    doMenu clear field
  end repeat
  choose oldTool
end deleteFields
```

Notes

If `backgrounds` is not specified with `buttons`, the number of card buttons is returned; if `card` is not specified with `fields`, the number of background fields is returned. If the `number` function is used with a chunk name, it returns the number of chunks of that kind within the designated container or other factor yielding a text string.

The factor can be a chunk expression, so you can get the number of chunks of one kind within another chunk:

```
the number of chars in first word of field 1
```

You can also use the format that uses parentheses with the `number` function:

```
number(cards)
```

Backgrounds can be specified with the abbreviation `bkgnds`.

See also the `number` property for backrounds, cards, fields, and buttons, in Chapter 9.

NumToChar

Syntax

```
the numToChar of factor
numToChar (expression)
```

Factor and *expression* yield positive integers.

Example

```
put numToChar(67) into word 4 of line 9 of field "ASCII Chart" -- yields C
```

Description

The numToChar function returns the character whose ASCII equivalent value is that of the integer passed to it.

Script

The following example handler turns all of the lowercase letters in a field into uppercase letters:

```
on upperCase
  put card field 4 into temp  -- variables are faster than fields
  repeat with count = 1 to the length of temp
    get character count of temp
    if charToNum of It > 96 and charToNum of It < 123 then
      put numToChar(charToNum(It)-32) into character count of temp
    end if
  end repeat
  put temp into card field 4
end upperCase
```

Notes

See also the charToNum function, earlier in this chapter.

Offset

Syntax

`offset (`*string1*`,` *string2*`)`

String1 and *string2* are both expressions yielding text strings.

Examples

```
put offset("hay",field 1) into the Message box
offset("a","abc") -- typed in msg, returns 1
```

Description

The `offset` function returns the number of characters from the beginning of the *string2* string at which *string1* begins. If *string1* doesn't appear within *string2,* 0 is returned.

Script

The following function handler finds every occurrence of a string within a container, and it replaces every occurrence with a second string:

```
function searchAndReplace container,original,replacement
  repeat until original is not in container
  -- loop until all are replaced
    put offset(original,container) into start
    -- set start to location of original
    put replacement into char start to start + ¬
    (the length of original - 1) of container
  end repeat
  return container
end searchAndReplace
```

Note

The parameters passed to the `offset` function can both be arithmetical or logical (as well as text) expressions; after evaluation, the results are treated as strings.

OptionKey

Syntax

```
the optionKey
optionKey()
```

Example

```
if the optionKey is down then choose button tool
```

Description

The `optionKey` function returns the constant `up` if the Option key is not pressed, `down` if it is pressed.

Param

Syntax

```
the param of factor
param(expression)
```

Factor and *expression* yield integers.

Example

```
if param(1) is empty then answer "Message has no parameters."
```

Description

The `param` function returns a parameter value from the parameter list passed to the currently executing handler. The parameter returned is the *n*th parameter where *n* is the integer derived from *factor* or *expression*. The value of `param(0)` is the message name.

Script

The following example handler sums the numeric arguments passed to it, regardless of how many there are:

```
on addUp -- adds a variable number of arguments
  put 0 into total
  repeat with i = 1 to the paramCount
    add param(i) to total
  end repeat
  put total
end addUp
```

Notes

See also the `paramCount` and `params` functions, in this chapter, and the discussion of parameter passing in Chapter 2, "Handling Messages."

ParamCount

Syntax

```
the paramCount
paramCount()
```

Example

```
if the paramCount < 3 then put "I need at least three arguments."
```

Description

The `paramCount` function returns the number of parameters passed to the currently executing handler.

Script

The following example handler draws an oval differently depending on the number of parameters passed to it:

```
on drawOval
  if the paramCount is 1 then
  -- if 1 param use it as oval size and use default line size
    choose oval tool
    drag from 30,30 to 30 + param(1),30 + param(1)
  else if the paramCount is 2 then
  -- if 2 params use the second as line size
    choose oval tool
    set lineSize to param(2)
    drag from 30,30 to 30 + param(1),30 + param(1)
  end if
  choose browse tool
  reset paint
end drawOval
```

Notes

See also the `param` and `params` functions, in this chapter, and the discussion of parameter passing in Chapter 2, "Handling Messages."

Params

Syntax

```
the params
params()
```

Example

```
put the params into field "messageReceived"
```

Description

The `params` function returns the entire parameter list, including the message name, passed to the currently executing handler.

Script

The following example handler is useful primarily for debugging, to see if the parameters passed to a handler are correct:

```
on myMessage
  put the params
  -- rest of myMessage handler goes here
end myMessage
```

Notes

See also the `param` and `paramCount` functions, in this chapter, and the discussion of parameter passing in Chapter 2, "Handling Messages."

Random

Syntax

```
the random of factor
random(expression)
```

Factor and *expression* yield positive integers.

Example

```
set the loc of button "jumpy" to random(512),random(342)
```

Description

The `random` function returns a random integer between 1 and the integer derived from the *factor* or *expression,* inclusive.

The following example handler draws 10 unique random numbers between 1 and 100:

```
on mouseUp
  global randomList
  put empty into randomList
  repeat until the number of items in randomList is 10
    get random(100)
    if it is not in randomList then put it & "," after randomList
  end repeat
  delete last character of randomList -- get rid of the last comma
  put randomList into msg
end mouseUp
```

Result

Syntax

```
the result
result()
```

Example

```
if the result is not empty then answer "Try again."
```

Description

The result function returns an explanatory text string if an immediately preceding find or go command was unsuccessful. The result is empty if the command executed successfully. The result can also be set by a return statement in a message handler or by an external command. The result is reset by execution of another command and at the end of the handler.

Script   The following example handler searches for a string and displays either the string or the error message if it doesn't find the string:

```
on doMenu var
  if var is "Find..." then
    global findMe
    repeat
      ask "Find what string:" with findMe
      if It is not empty then find It
      else exit doMenu -- cancel clicked
        if the result is not empty then -- there's an error message
          put the result into findMe -- display the error
        next repeat
      else
        put It into findMe -- otherwise display the string
        exit repeat
      end if
    end repeat
  else pass doMenu
end doMenu
```

Notes   It is safer to depend on the empty result of a successful execution, rather than the particular value of some error message, because those values could be different in future versions of HyperCard.

Chapter 5 discusses the `return` statement. Appendix A contains general information about external commands.

Round

Syntax

```
the round of factor
round (expression)
```

Factor and *expression* yield numbers.

Example

```
put round(resultVariable) into field 1
```

Description

The `round` function returns the source number rounded off to the nearest integer.

Any odd integer plus exactly 0.5 rounds up; any even integer (or 0) plus exactly 0.5 rounds down. If the source number is negative, HyperCard internally removes the negative sign, rounds its absolute value, then puts the negative sign back on.

Script

The following function handler rounds off an amount to the nearest dollar:

```
function roundToDollar amount
  set numberFormat to ".00" -- sets dollar format
  return round(amount)
end roundToDollar
```

Seconds

Syntax

```
the seconds
seconds ()
```

Example

```
put (the seconds-startTime) into runTime
```

Description

The `seconds` function returns an integer showing the number of seconds between midnight, January 1, 1904, and the current time set in your Macintosh. The `seconds` function can be abbreviated `secs`.

The following example handler counts the number of seconds the user holds down the mouse button:

```
on stopWatch
  put the long time into now -- what time is it now?
  convert now to seconds
  wait while the mouse is down -- wait until mouse is released
  put the seconds-now into msg -- how many seconds have elapsed?
end stopWatch
```

Notes

See also the `convert` command in Chapter 7, "Commands."

ShiftKey

Syntax

```
the shiftKey
shiftKey()
```

Example

```
if the shiftKey is down then put numToChar(charToNum(msg)-32) into msg
```

Description

The `shiftKey` function returns the constant `up` if the Shift key is not pressed, `down` if it is pressed.

Sin

Syntax

```
the sin of factor
sin(expression)
```

Factor and *expression* yield numbers.

Example

```
put the sin of 2 -- puts 0.909297 into the Message box
```

Description

The `sin` function returns the sine of the angle which is passed to it. The angle must be expressed in radians.

Note

Radians can be converted to degrees by multiplying by 180 and dividing the result by the value of the constant `pi`.

Sound

Syntax
```
the sound
sound()
```

Example
```
wait until the sound is "done"
```

Description

The sound function returns the name of the sound resource currently playing (such as "boing") or the string "done" if no sound is currently playing. The sound function enables you to synchronize sounds with other actions, because scripts continue to run while sounds play.

Script

The following example handler repeats a series of visual effects until a tune specified by the play command finishes:

```
on boogie
  play "harpsichord" tempo 200 ¬
    "ce gq fe ee de ce gq fe ee ce gq fe ee ce"
  repeat until the sound is "done"
    visual effect dissolve to black
    visual effect zoom open to white
    visual effect barn door close to card
    go this card
  end repeat
end boogie
```

Notes

The "done" string is returned as a literal; it's not a HyperTalk constant like up or true. See also the play command, in Chapter 7, "Commands."

Sqrt

Syntax   the sqrt of *factor*
sqrt (*expression*)

Factor and *expression* yield numbers.

Example   put the sqrt of msg -- converts the number in msg to its square root

Description   The sqrt function returns the square root of the positive number passed to it. If you pass a negative number, you get the result NAN(001), which means "not a number."

Tan

Syntax   the tan of *factor*
tan (*expression*)

Factor and *expression* yield numbers.

Example   put the tan of 2 -- puts -2.18504 into the Message box

Description   The tan function returns the tangent of the angle which is passed to it. The angle must be expressed in radians.

Note   Radians can be converted to degrees by multiplying by 180 and dividing the result by the value of the constant pi.

Target

Syntax

```
the target
target()
```

Example

```
if the target is "card id 2875" then pass mouseUp
```

Description

The `target` function returns a string indicating the original recipient of the message. The string returned is one of the following:

```
stack "stackName"
bkgnd of card id number
card id number
bkgnd field id number
card field id number
bkgnd button id number
card button id number
```

For example, the `target` function enables you to tell, in a `mouseUp` handler in a background, whether

☐ the mouse was clicked over a field or button (which either would have had no `mouseUp` handler or would have passed the message on explicitly): `the target` would return the button or field ID

☐ the mouse was clicked outside the area of all buttons and fields: `the target` would return the card ID

☐ the message was sent directly to the background with the `send` command: `the target` would return the background ID

You can use `the target` in place of an object descriptor to determine any of the target's properties:

```
get the short name of the target
```

Script

The following example handler can be placed lower in the hierarchy than any field to display the number of the line clicked (regardless of which field was clicked):

```
on openField
  if style of the target is "scrolling"
  then put scroll of the target into scrollAmount
  else put 0 into scrollAmount
  put (trunc(((item 2 of the clickloc) - (item 2 of the rect of ¬
  the target) + scrollAmount))/(textheight of the target)) + 1) into msg
end openField
```

Note

See also Chapter 9, "Properties."

Ticks

Syntax

```
the ticks
ticks()
```

Example

```
put the ticks into dog
```

Description

The `ticks` function returns an integer representing the number of ticks (⅟₆₀ second) since the Macintosh was turned on or restarted.

Script

The following example handler measures how long it takes to go to the Help stack and find the word ticks:

```
on mouseUp
  put the ticks into startTicks
  go help
  find "ticks"
  put (the ticks - startTicks) into howLong
  answer "It took" && howLong div 60 && "second(s) to find Help."
end mouseUp
```

Time

Syntax

```
the [adjective] time
time()
```

Adjective can be `long`, `short`, or `abbreviated`, (or `abbrev`, or `abbr`).

Example

```
put the time into the Message box
```

Description

The `time` function returns the time as a text string. All forms are the same, returning the hour and minutes, such as `8:55 AM`, except the `long time` form which returns seconds as well, such as `8:55:23 AM`.

Script

The following example records the time at which a field is updated:

```
on closeField
  put return & the time after card field "updateList"
end closeField
```

Note

An adjective can't be used to modify the form of the `time` function that uses parentheses.

Tool

Syntax

```
the tool
tool()
```

Example

```
if the tool is "field tool" then choose browse tool
```

Description

The `tool` function returns the name of the currently chosen tool. Possible values returned by the `tool` function are

```
browse tool        oval tool
brush tool         pencil tool
bucket tool        polygon tool
button tool        rectangle tool
curve tool         regular polygon tool
eraser tool        round rect tool
field tool         select tool
lasso tool         spray tool
line tool          text tool
```

Script

The following example handler chooses the proper tool to manipulate a button or field when you move the pointer over either object:

```
on mouseWithin -- put this in the card, background, or stack script
  if "button" is in the target and the optionKey is down
  then choose button tool
  else if "field" is in the target and the optionKey is down
  then choose field tool
end mouseWithin
```

Notes

See also the `choose` command, in Chapter 7, "Commands."

Trunc

Syntax

```
the trunc of factor
trunc (expression)
```

Factor and *expression* yield numbers.

Example

```
put the trunc of someNumber into msg
```

Description

The `trunc` function returns the integer part of the number passed to it. Any fractional part is disregarded, regardless of sign.

Script

The following example handler draws rectangles in increasing sizes, using the `trunc` function to ensure that the computed values used with the `drag` command are integers:

```
on mouseUp
  reset paint
  choose rectangle tool
  put 50 into left
  put 150 into right
  put 50 into top
  put 150 into bottom
  repeat 5 -- the drag command only takes integers
    drag from left,top to right,bottom
    put trunc(left/1.2) into left
    put trunc(right/1.2) into right
    put trunc(top/1.2) into top
    put trunc(bottom/1.2) into bottom
  end repeat
  choose browse tool
end mouseUp
```

Value

Syntax
```
the value of factor
value (expression)
```

Factor and *expression* yield any values.

Example
```
put the value of field "formula" into field "result"
```

Description
The `value` function evaluates the string derived from *factor* or *expression* as an expression.

Script
The following example handler demonstrates the `value` function by forcing a second level of evaluation of a variable:

```
on mouseUp -- see also the HyperCalc background script
  put "3 + 4" into expression
  put expression -- yields "3 + 4"
  wait 2 seconds
  put value of expression -- yields 7
end mouseUp
```

Version

Syntax
```
the version
version ()
```

Example
```
if the version>1.0 then set textArrows to true
```

Description
The `version` function returns the version number of the HyperCard application currently running.

Chapter 9

Properties

This chapter describes HyperCard properties. **Properties** are the defining characteristics of objects and the HyperCard environment.

Object properties determine how objects look and act. **Global properties** control aspects of the overall HyperCard environment. **Painting properties** control aspects of the HyperCard painting environment, which is invoked when you choose a Paint tool. **Window properties** determine how the Message box and the Tools and Patterns palettes are displayed.

Retrieving and setting properties

HyperTalk lets you get most properties by using the property name as a function in a script or the Message box. You must precede the property name with the word `the` or follow it with `of` if it's an object or window property. You can't use parentheses after the property name, as you do with built-in functions. The following example retrieves the `location` property of button 1 and puts it into the Message box:

```
put the loc of button 1 into msg
```

You set properties with the `set` command:

```
set loc of button 1 to 100,100
```

Some properties can't be set, although other actions affect them. For example, the size of a stack can be changed by compacting it and by adding objects.

Object properties

You can see the value of many object properties by looking at an object's Info dialog box, an example of which is shown in Figure 9-1. (You bring up an object's Info dialog box by choosing the appropriate item from the Objects menu.)

You can also set many properties for the current object from the Info dialog boxes. To set the properties of any object in the current stack, including the current ones, you use the `set` command, either in a script or in the Message box.

Different HyperCard objects have different properties. For example, fields have a property determining their text style, but cards do not. This chapter has a section describing the properties of each of the five types of HyperCard objects.

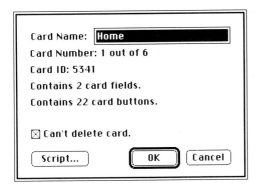

Figure 9-1
An Object Info dialog box

Name property

The name property of an object has three forms—long, abbreviated, and
short. The long name of an object includes the type of object, its name, and the full
pathname of its stack:

```
card button "Rolo" of card "Home" of stack "MyHardDisk:Home"
```

The abbreviated form includes the type of object and its name:

```
card button "Rolo"
```

The short form includes just the name:

```
"Rolo"
```

If you try to retrieve an object's name when it has none, HyperCard returns its ID
number.

ID property

The ID property of an object has three forms which are similar to the three forms of
the name, and which are differentiated by the same adjectives—long,
abbreviated, and short. The long ID of an object includes the type of object, its
ID number, and the full pathname of its stack:

```
card id 2590 of stack "Sila:HyperCard Stacks:Home"
```

The abbreviated form includes the type of object and its ID number:

```
card id 2590
```

The short form includes just the ID number:

```
2590
```

All objects except stacks always have ID numbers; stacks never have ID numbers.

Environmental properties

Some of the global properties, such as the `userLevel` property, can be set on the User Preferences card of the Home stack; others, such as the `lockMessages` property, can be retrieved and set only through HyperTalk. (However, the User Preferences card uses HyperTalk to set properties, and it could be extended to set any others.) The window properties, which pertain to the Message box and the tear-off menus, can be set by clicking and dragging on the windows themselves, as well as through HyperTalk. Painting properties, which pertain to the painting environment, can be controlled with the menus and palettes that appear when a Paint tool is selected, as well as through HyperTalk.

Global properties

You use global properties to choose how particular aspects of the HyperCard environment will perform. You set global properties from any script or from the Message box, and their settings pertain to all objects—if you set `userLevel` to 3, for example, it remains 3 until you reset it (although a protected stack might impose some other user level while you are in that stack).

The global properties, described in this section, are

blindTyping	lockRecent
cursor	lockScreen
dragSpeed	numberFormat
editBkgnd	powerKeys
language	textArrows
lockMessages	userLevel

BlindTyping

```
set blindTyping to true
```

You use the `blindTyping` property to type messages into the Message box and send them (execute them) without having the Message box visible. Blind typing is available only if the user level is set to Scripting, and is usually set with a check box on the User Preferences card (Home stack).

The value of the `blindTyping` property can be `true` or `false`; the default setting is determined at start up and resume time by the setting chosen on the User Preferences card of the Home stack.

If you try to type into the Message box when it's hidden and `blindTyping` is false, HyperCard beeps.

Cursor

```
set cursor to 4
```

The `cursor` property determines the image that appears at the pointer location on the screen. The cursor setting is the ID number or name of a Macintosh 'CURS' resource, which must be available in the HyperCard file itself or in the current stack file. 'CURS' resources can be installed, removed, and created with a Macintosh resource editor.

HyperCard resets the cursor to the one for the current tool at idle, when no other action is happening. The cursors available by default are

1   I-beam
2   crossbar
3   thick crossbar
4   watch indicating "wait"

You can't get the `cursor` property or use it as a function; you can only set it.

DragSpeed

```
set dragSpeed to 144
```

The `dragSpeed` property determines how many pixels per second the pointer will move when manipulated by all subsequent `drag` commands. There are 72 pixels per inch on the Macintosh screen.

At idle time, HyperCard resets the `dragSpeed` property to 0, representing the maximum speed (virtually instantaneous).

EditBkgnd

```
set editBkgnd to true
```

The `editBkgnd` property determines where any painting or creating of buttons or fields happens—on the current card or on its background. It's usually set with the Edit menu and is available only when the user level is Painting (3) or higher.

The value of the `editBkgnd` property can be `true` or `false`; the default setting is `false`.

Language

```
if the language is not "English" then sort international by ¬
field 1
```

You use the `language` property to choose the language in which scripts are written and displayed.

The languages available depend on the translator resources available in your application, Home stack, and stack. The default setting is `English`, and it's always available.

LockMessages

```
set lockMessages to true
```

You use the `lockMessages` property to prevent HyperCard from sending all automatic messages such as `openCard`, `closeCard`, `newCard`, and `deleteCard`.

The value of the `lockMessages` property can be `true` or `false`; the default setting is `false`. HyperCard resets `lockMessages` to `false` at idle time (in effect, at the end of all pending handlers).

Setting the `lockMessages` property to `true` speeds up execution of scripts in which you go to cards, and those in which you create and delete objects. It also prevents execution of handlers invoked by automatic messages, which may be used to set up an environment—hiding the Message box, and so on. It's particularly useful when you want to go to a card momentarily to retrieve or deposit some information, but you don't want to stay there.

LockRecent

```
set lockRecent to true
```

You use the `lockRecent` property to prevent HyperCard from adding miniature representations to the Recent card. (The Recent card is invoked by Command-R or by choosing Recent from the Go menu).

The value of the `lockRecent` property can be `true` or `false`; the default setting is `false`. HyperCard resets `lockRecent` to `false` at idle time (in effect, at the end of all pending handlers).

Setting the `lockRecent` property to `true` speeds up execution of scripts in which you go to cards.

LockScreen

```
set lockScreen to true
```

You use the `lockScreen` property to prevent HyperCard from updating the screen when you go to another card.

The value of the `lockScreen` property can be `true` or `false`; the default setting is `false`. HyperCard resets `lockScreen` to `false` at idle time (in effect, at the end of all pending handlers).

Setting the `lockScreen` property to `true` enables you to open different cards without displaying them on the screen, and it speeds up execution of scripts in which you go to cards. For example, you can lock the screen, then go to another card to read information out of a field, then return to the first card without having the second card appear to the user.

NumberFormat

```
set numberFormat to "00.00" -- displaying 02.20, for example
set numberFormat to "0" -- displaying 2, for same value
set numberFormat to "0.###### " -- displaying 2.2; the default
```

The `numberFormat` property determines the precision with which the results of mathematical operations are displayed in fields and the Message box. Use zeros to show how many digits you want to appear, a period to show where you want the decimal point (if at all), and number signs (#) to the right of the decimal point in places where you want a trailing digit to appear, but only if it has value.

HyperCard resets the `numberFormat` property to its default value, `"0.######"`, at idle time (in effect, at the end of all pending handlers).

When you set the `numberFormat` property, you must enclose the value within double quotation marks if it contains a number sign (#). The `numberFormat` property has no effect on how a number is displayed unless you perform a mathematical operation on it first (for details, see Chapter 4).

PowerKeys

```
set powerKeys to true
```

You use the `powerKeys` property to provide a shortcut for painting. Power keys let you accomplish certain painting actions with single keystrokes. The power key setting is usually done on the User Preferences card of the Home stack. It's available only if the user level is set to Painting (3) or above.

The value of the `powerKeys` property can be `true` or `false`; the default setting is determined at startup and resume time by the setting on the User Preferences card of the Home stack.

TextArrows

```
set textArrows to true
```

The `textArrows` property alters the function of the Right Arrow, Left Arrow, Up Arrow, and Down Arrow keys.

The value of the `textArrows` property can be `true` or `false`; by default it's `false`.

When the `textArrows` property is `false`, the Right Arrow and Left Arrow keys take you to the next and previous cards in the stack, respectively, and the Up Arrow and Down Arrow keys take you forward and backward, respectively, through the cards you've already viewed.

When the `textArrows` property is `true`, the arrow keys move the text insertion point around in a field that you've opened for text editing or in the Message box if you've clicked in it. In the Message box, the Up Arrow and Down Arrow keys move the insertion point to the beginning and end of the line of text, respectively.

When the `textArrows` property is `true`, holding down the Option key while you press the arrow keys produces the same effect as pressing them alone when `textArrows is false`.

❖ *A feature of HyperCard version 1.1:* The `textArrows` property is available only in HyperCard versions 1.1 and later.

UserLevel

```
set userLevel to 5
```

HyperCard's user levels give progressively more power to the user. The levels are Browsing, Typing, Painting, Authoring, and Scripting, as explained in the *HyperCard User's Guide.*

The `userLevel` property can have a value from 1 to 5, with 5 (scripting) providing the most power; the values correlate respectively to the levels listed above. The default setting is determined at start up and resume time by the setting on the User Preferences card of the Home stack.

A script writer can invoke the Protect Stack dialog box from the File menu to impose a limit on the user level available in a stack. In that case, setting the user level higher than the Protect Stack limit has no effect, although it generates no error message. On leaving the protected stack, the user level in effect when the stack was entered is restored.

Window properties

Window properties let you find out about and change the way that the Message box, the card window, the Tools palette, and the Patterns palette are displayed. The names you can use are

```
card window           msg
message [box]         pattern window
message [window]      tool window
```

(`Message`, `message box`, `message window`, and `msg` are synonyms for the Message box.)

The window properties, described in this section, are

```
loc[ation]
rect[angle]
visible
```

Location

```
set loc of tool window to 100,100
```

The `location` property is the location at which the window is displayed. The location is a point, reported as two integers separated by a comma.

The point represents the horizontal and vertical offsets in pixels, respectively, from the top-left corner of the card window to the top-left corner of the specified other window, disregarding the drag bar at the top of the window. The location of the card window is measured from the top-left corner of the screen to the top-left corner of the card window, disregarding the title bar at the top of the card window. On the original Macintosh screen, visible horizontal offsets range from 0 to 511, and visible vertical offsets range from 0 to 341.

The `location` property can be abbreviated `loc`.

Rectangle

```
get the rect of message box -- puts h,v,h,v into It
```

The `rectangle` property is two points, reported as four integers separated by commas.

The points represent the rectangle's top-left (horizontal and vertical) and bottom-right (horizontal and vertical) corner offsets in pixels, respectively, from the top-left corner of the card window. This property can't be set, because the windows are fixed size, but it can be read to determine the exact area of the screen covered by the window.

The `rectangle` property can be abbreviated `rect`.

Visible

```
set the visible of tool window to false
```

The `visible` property determines whether a window is shown or hidden on the screen.

The value of the `visible` property can be `true` or `false`. The Tools and Patterns palettes become visible when you tear them off the menu bar; the Message box can be toggled between being visible and hidden by pressing Command-M.

Setting a window's `visible` property to `false` is the same as clicking its close box or hiding it with the `hide` command.

Painting properties

Painting properties are aspects of the painting environment invoked when you choose a Paint tool from the Tools palette. Most of these properties are usually manipulated from the Options and Patterns menus that appear when a Paint tool is selected. The text attributes pertain to Paint text; they are usually manipulated from the dialog box that appears when you double-click the Paint Text tool in the Tools palette or when you choose Text Style from the Edit menu. Changes to the settings made from HyperTalk are reflected on their respective palettes and menus. The painting properties are described more fully in the *HyperCard User's Guide*.

All of the painting properties can be restored to their default values simultaneously with the `reset paint` command, described in Chapter 7, "Commands."

The painting properties, described in this section, are

```
brush          pattern
centered       polySides
filled         textAlign
grid           textFont
lineSize       textHeight
multiple       textSize
multiSpace     textStyle
```

Brush

```
set brush to 6
```

You use the `brush` property to determine or to change the current brush shape used by the Brush tool. It's normally manipulated from the Brush Shape dialog box invoked by choosing Brush Shape from the Options menu or by double-clicking the Brush.

The value of the `brush` property can be any integer from 1 to 32, each representing a brush shape from the Brush Shape dialog box. The default `brush` setting is 8.

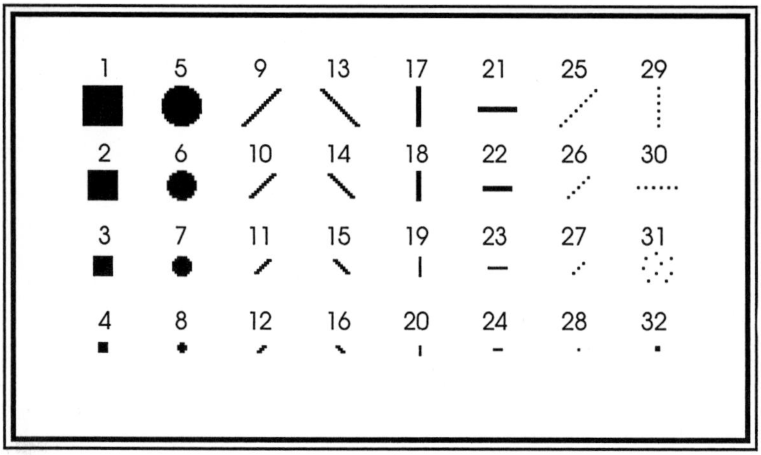

Figure 9-2
Brush Shape dialog box and property values

Centered

```
set centered to true
```

You use the `centered` property to determine or to change the Draw Centered setting. When `centered` is `true`, shapes are drawn from the center, rather than the corner.

The value of the `centered` property can be `true` or `false`; by default it's `false`.

You can also set the `centered` property by choosing Draw Centered on the Options menu.

Filled

```
set filled to true
```

You use the `filled` property to determine or to change the Draw Filled setting. When `filled` is `true`, the current pattern on the Patterns palette is used to fill shapes as they are drawn.

The value of the `filled` property can be `true` or `false`; by default it's `false`.

You can also set the `filled` property by choosing Draw Filled on the Options menu.

Grid

```
set grid to true
```

You use the `grid` property to determine or to change the painting Grid setting. When `grid` is true, movement of many Paint tools is constrained to eight-pixel intervals (just under ⅛ inch).

The value of the `grid` property can be `true` or `false`; by default it's `false`.

You can also set the `grid` property by choosing Grid on the Options menu.

LineSize

```
set lineSize to 8
```

You use the `lineSize` property to determine or to change the thickness of the lines drawn by the line and shape tools.

The value of the `lineSize` property correlates to pixels on the screen and can be 1, 2, 3, 4, 6, or 8; by default it's 1.

You can also set the `lineSize` property by choosing Line Size on the Options menu.

Multiple

```
set multiple to true
```

You use the `multiple` property to determine or to change the Draw Multiple setting. When `multiple` is `true`, multiple images are drawn as you drag a shape tool.

The value of the `multiple` property can be `true` or `false`; by default it's `false`.

You can also set the `multiple` property by choosing Draw Multiple on the Options menu.

MultiSpace

```
set multiSpace to 6
```

You use the `multiSpace` property to determine or to change the amount of space left between edges of the multiple images drawn by the shape tools when the `multiple` property is `true`.

The value of the `multiSpace` property can be an integer ranging from 1 to 9, inclusive; by default it's 1.

Pattern

```
set pattern to 8
```

You use the `pattern` property to determine or to change the current pattern used to fill shapes and to paint with the Brush tool.

The value of the `pattern` property can be any integer from 1 to 40, each representing a pattern on the Patterns palette. The default pattern setting is 12.

The pattern numbers correspond to the 40 positions in the Patterns palette, not to a specific pattern.

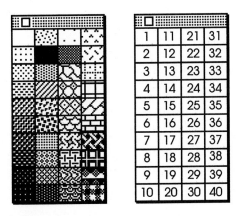

Figure 9-3
Patterns palette and property values

You normally set the `pattern` property from the Patterns palette. You can edit a pattern by double-clicking it on the Patterns palette. Each stack has its own Patterns palette, so when you edit a pattern you change the palette only for the current stack.

PolySides

```
set polySides to 3
```

You use the `polySides` property to determine or to change the number of sides of the polygon created by the Regular Polygon tool.

The value of the `polySides` property can be any integer between 3 and 50. This number correlates to the number of sides in the polygon; its default value is 4. If you set it to a number lower than 3 or higher than 50, it automatically reverts to 3 or 50, respectively. If you choose the circle in the Polygon Sides dialog box, the setting becomes 0 (although you can't set it to 0 using a script).

You normally choose the Polygon Sides setting from a dialog box invoked by choosing Polygon Sides from the Options menu or by double-clicking the Regular Polygon tool.

TextAlign

```
set textAlign to center
```

You use the `textAlign` property to determine or to change the way characters are aligned around the insertion point as you type them with the Paint Text tool.

The value of the `textAlign` property can be `left`, `right`, or `center`; its default value is `left`.

You can also set the `textAlign` property from the Text Style dialog box, which is invoked by choosing Text Style from the Edit menu or by double-clicking the Paint Text tool.

TextFont

```
set textFont to geneva
```

You use the `textFont` property to determine or to change the font in which Paint text appears.

The value which the `textFont` property can have depends on the font resources that you have available in your System file, the HyperCard application, the Home stack, and the current stack. The default value of the `textFont` property is `geneva`.

You can also set the `textFont` property from the Text Style dialog box, which is invoked by choosing Text Style from the Edit menu or by double-clicking the Paint Text tool. If you try to set it to a font that doesn't exist, HyperCard sets it to `chicago`.

TextHeight

```
set textHeight to 20
```

You use the `textHeight` property to determine or to change the space between baselines of Paint text.

The value of the `textHeight` property can be any integer, corresponding to a like number of pixels. By default, the `textHeight` property is set to the value of the `textSize` property plus one-third of that value.

The size of a pixel on the Macintosh screen is about ½ inch, the approximate size of a printer's point.

You can also set the `textHeight` property with the Line Height window of the Text Style dialog box, which is invoked by choosing Text Style from the Edit menu or by double-clicking the Paint Text tool.

TextSize

```
set textSize to 18
```

You use the `textSize` property to determine or to change the font size in which Paint text appears.

The value of the `textSize` property can be any integer, corresponding to a like number of pixels. The default value of the `textSize` property is 12.

The size of a pixel on the Macintosh screen is about ½ inch, the approximate size of a printer's point. Although you can use any integer for `textSize`, exact sizes of fonts available look best. Fonts available can be in your System file, the HyperCard application, the Home stack, or the current stack.

You can also set the `textSize` property from the Text Style dialog box, which is invoked by choosing Text Style from the Edit menu or by double-clicking the Paint Text tool.

TextStyle

```
set textStyle to plain
set textStyle to bold,italic,underline
```

You use the `textStyle` property to determine or to change the style in which Paint text appears.

The `textStyle` property can have a value of `plain` or any combination of the following: `bold`, `italic`, `underline`, `outline`, `shadow`, `condensed`, and `extend` (separated by commas). Its default value is `plain`. If you use `plain` in combination with any of the other values, the others override it.

You can also set the `textStyle` property from the Text Style dialog box, which is invoked by choosing Text Style from the Edit menu or by double-clicking the Paint Text tool.

Stack properties

Stack properties pertain to any stack on any disk or file server currently accessible to your Macintosh. Settable properties of the current stack can be manipulated from a script or through the Stack Info dialog box invoked from the Objects menu.

The stack properties, described in this section, are

```
freeSize        script
name            size
```

FreeSize

```
put the freeSize of stack "addresses" into field "extraSpace"
```

You use the `freeSize` property to determine the amount of free space of the specified stack in bytes. (Free space is created in a stack each time you delete an object.)

The `freeSize` property can be changed only by selecting Compact Stack from the File menu (or executing the HyperTalk command `doMenu compact stack`), which changes its value to 0.

Name

```
set name of this stack to "Robert"
```

You use the `name` property to determine or to change the name of the specified stack, which is its Macintosh file name. The modifiers `long`, `short`, and `abbreviated` can be used with the `name` property as described at the beginning of this chapter.

The value of the `name` property can be any stack name (as described in Chapter 3).

Script

```
put the script of stack "home" into field "Home Script"
```

You use the `script` property to retrieve or to replace the script of the specified stack.

The value of the `script` property is the text string composing the script of the specified stack.

When you set the `script` property using the `set` command, you replace it entirely.

Scripts are normally edited using the HyperCard script editor described in Chapter 1, "HyperCard Basics."

Size

```
get the size of stack "home"
```

You use the `size` property to determine the size of the specified stack in bytes.

The minimum stack size is 4096 bytes; the theoretical maximum is 512 megabytes.

The `size` property can't be changed with the `set` command; it's changed only by adding things to and deleting things from the stack (you must then compact the stack for the deletions to affect its size).

Background properties

Background properties pertain to any background in the current stack. They can be manipulated from a script or from the Message box. Properties of the current background can also be manipulated through the Bkgnd Info dialog box invoked from the Objects menu.

The background properties, described in this section, are

```
ID          number
name        script
```

ID

```
if the ID of background 1 is 2282 then answer "You're Home"
```

You use the `ID` property to determine the permanent ID number of any background in the current stack.

You can't change the ID of any object.

The adjectives `long`, `short`, and `abbreviated` can be used with the `ID` property as described at the beginning of this chapter.

Name

```
if the name of this background is "plain" then go home
```

You use the `name` property to determine or to change the name of any background in the current stack.

The value of the `name` property can be any object name (as described in Chapter 3).

The adjectives `long`, `short`, and `abbreviated` can be used with the `name` property as described at the beginning of this chapter.

Number

```
if the number of this background is 2 then go next card
```

You use the `number` property to determine the number of any background in the current stack.

You can't set the number of the background; it changes when you add or delete backgrounds from the stack.

See also the `number` function in Chapter 8.

Script

```
set the script of second background to empty
put the script of this background into field 1
```

You use the `script` property to retrieve or to replace the script of any background in the current stack.

The value of the `script` property is the text string composing the script of the specified background.

When you set the `script` property using the `set` command, you replace it entirely.

Scripts are normally edited using the HyperCard script editor described in Chapter 1, "HyperCard Basics."

Card properties

Card properties pertain to any card in the current stack. The card is specified as explained in Chapter 3, "Naming Objects." You can manipulate card properties from a script, in the Message box, or through the Card Info dialog invoked from the Objects menu.

Card properties are explained in more detail in the *HyperCard User's Guide* section about the Card Info dialog. The card properties, described in this section, are

```
ID          number
name        script
```

ID

```
get the ID of card 35
```

You use the `ID` property to determine the permanent ID number of any card in the current stack.

You can't change the ID number of any object.

The adjectives `long`, `short`, and `abbreviated` can be used with the `ID` property as described at the beginning of this chapter.

Name

```
set name of this card to "Shark"
if the name of card 1 of next background is "Begin" then go home
```

You use the name property to determine or to change the name of any card in the current stack.

The value of the name property can be any object name (as described in Chapter 3).

The adjectives long, short, and abbreviated can be used with the name property as described at the beginning of this chapter.

Number

```
put the number of last card into msg
get the number of this card
```

You use the number property to determine the number of any card in the current stack.

You can't set the number of a card with the set command; it changes when you add, delete, or sort cards in a stack.

See also the number function in Chapter 8.

Script

```
set the script of this card to field 3
```

You use the script property to retrieve or to replace the script of any card in the current stack.

The value of the script property is the text string composing the script of the specified card.

When you set the script property using the set command, you replace it entirely.

Scripts are normally edited using the HyperCard script editor described in Chapter 1, "HyperCard Basics."

Field properties

Field properties pertain to any card field or background field in the current stack. The field is specified as explained in Chapter 3, "Naming Objects." You can manipulate field properties from a script or from the Message box, or through the Field Info dialog box invoked from the Objects menu. (You must have the Field tool chosen and a specific card or background field selected to activate the Field Info dialog box.)

Field properties are explained in more detail in the *HyperCard User's Guide* section about the Field Info dialog box. The field properties, described in this section, are

```
ID                style
loc[ation]        textAlign
lockText          textFont
name              textHeight
number            textSize
rect[angle]       textStyle
script            visible
scroll            wideMargins
showLines
```

ID

```
put the id of field 1 into msg
```

You use the `ID` property to find out the permanent ID number of any card or background field in the current stack.

You can't change the ID number of any object.

The adjectives `long`, `short`, and `abbreviated` can be used with the `ID` property as described at the beginning of this chapter.

Location

```
set loc of field 1 to 100,100
```

You use the `location` property to determine or to change the location of a card field or background field in the card window.

The location is a point, reported as two integers separated by a comma. The point represents the horizontal and vertical offsets in pixels, respectively, from the top-left corner of the card window to the center of the specified field.

You can also change the field `location` property by dragging the center of the field with the Field tool.

❖ *Offscreen fields:* You can set the location of the field beyond the boundaries of the card window rectangle, putting the field out of reach until you reset its coordinates through HyperTalk.

The `location` property can be abbreviated `loc`.

LockText

```
set lockText of field "safe" to true
```

You use the `lockText` property to prevent or allow editing of text within a field.

When the Browse tool is selected and the pointer is moved over an unlocked field, the pointer changes to an I-beam; clicking then lets you edit the text in the field. If the field is locked, the cursor doesn't change, and the text cannot be edited.

The value of the `lockText` property can be `true` or `false`; by default it's `false`.

You can also change this property by clicking the Lock Text check box in the Field Info dialog box.

Name

```
set name of field 1 to "wheat"
```

You use the `name` property to determine or to change the name of any field in the current stack.

The value of the `name` property can be any object name (as described in Chapter 3).

The modifiers `long`, `short`, and `abbreviated` can be used with the `name` property as described at the beginning of this chapter.

You can also edit the field name by typing in the Field Name box in the Field Info dialog.

Number

```
put the number of field "barley"
```

You use the `number` property to determine the number of a specified field.

You can't change the number with the `set` command; it changes according to the position of the field among the other fields on its card or background. To manipulate the field's position, use the Send Farther and Bring Closer menu commands.

See also the `number` function in Chapter 8.

Rectangle

```
put the rect of field 1 into msg
```

You use the `rectangle` property to determine or to change the location and size of the rectangle occupied by the specified field on its card or background.

The value of the field rectangle is two points, reported as four integers separated by commas. The points represent the rectangle's top-left (horizontal and vertical) and bottom-right (horizontal and vertical) corner offsets in pixels, respectively, from the top-left corner of the card window.

❖ *Offscreen fields:* You can set either of the rectangle points of the field beyond the boundaries of the card window rectangle, putting the field out of reach until you reset its coordinates through HyperTalk.

You can set the bottom-right corner location to a value smaller than the top-left corner location, effectively causing the field to disappear. If you set the field to a size smaller than the minimum (12 by 12 pixels) but large enough to see, HyperCard resets it to the minimum size when you click it.

You can also change the field rectangle by dragging the top-left or bottom-right corner of the field with the Field tool.

The `rectangle` property can be abbreviated `rect`.

Script

```
set script of field "Effect" of first card to empty
```

You use the `script` property to retrieve or to replace the script of any field in the current stack.

The value of the `script` property is the text string composing the script of the specified field.

When you set the `script` property using the `set` command, you replace it entirely.

Scripts are normally edited using the HyperCard script editor described in Chapter 1, "HyperCard Basics."

Scroll

```
put the scroll of field 1 div the textHeight of field 1 into ¬
linesAbove
```

You use the `scroll` property to determine or to change how much material is hidden above the top of a scrolling field's rectangle. Figure 9-4 shows the `scroll` property.

The value of the `scroll` property is an integer representing the number of pixels that have scrolled above the top of the field rectangle; it's 0 if the top of the field is visible. The number of text lines to which the `scroll` property correlates depends on the `textHeight` property of the field.

You normally control how much material is above the top of the rectangle by clicking or dragging in the scroll bar at the right side of the field.

If you try to get or set the `scroll` property of a nonscrolling field, you get an error.

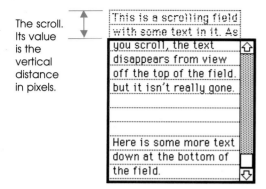

The scroll. Its value is the vertical distance in pixels.

This is a scrolling field with some text in it. As you scroll, the text disappears from view off the top of the field. but it isn't really gone.

Here is some more text down at the bottom of the field.

Figure 9-4
The scroll property

ShowLines

```
set showLines of field three to true
```

You use the `showLines` property to determine or to change whether the text baselines in the field appear or are invisible.

The value of the `showLines` property can be `true` or `false`; by default it's `false`.

You can also change `showLines` by clicking in the Show Lines check box in the Field Info dialog box.

Style

```
set style of field 1 of card 3 to transparent
```

You use the `style` property to determine or to change the style of any field in the current stack.

The value of the field style can be `transparent`, `opaque`, `rectangle`, `shadow`, or `scrolling`.

You can also change the field style by clicking one of the Style radio buttons in the Field Info dialog box.

TextAlign

```
set textAlign of field 1 to left
```

You use the `textAlign` property to determine or to change the way lines of text are aligned in the specified field.

The value of the `textAlign` property can be `left`, `right`, or `center`; by default it's `left`.

You can also set this property by clicking one of the Align radio buttons in the Text Style dialog box. You click the Font button in the Field Info dialog box to invoke the Text Style dialog box, which is described in the *HyperCard User's Guide*.

TextFont

```
set textFont of field 1 to garamond
```

You use the `textFont` property to determine or to change the font in which text in the specified field appears.

The value that the `textFont` property can have is the name of any of the fonts available as font resources in your System file, the HyperCard application, the Home stack, or the current stack. The default value of the `textFont` property is `geneva`.

You can also set this property by selecting one of the font names in the Text Style dialog box. You click the Font button in the Field Info dialog box to invoke the Text Style dialog box, which is described in the *HyperCard User's Guide*. If you try to set the `textFont` property to a font that doesn't exist, HyperCard sets it to `chicago`.

TextHeight

```
set textHeight of field 1 to 20
```

You use the `textHeight` property to determine or to change the space between baselines of text in the specified field.

The value of the `textHeight` property can be any integer, corresponding to a like number of pixels. By default, the `textHeight` property is set to the value of the `textSize` property plus one-third of that value. (The `textSize` property is described later in this section.)

The size of a pixel on the Macintosh screen is about ½ inch, the approximate size of a printer's point.

You can also set this property by typing in the Line Height box in the Text Style dialog box. You click the Font button in the Field Info dialog box to invoke the Text Style dialog box, which is described in the *HyperCard User's Guide.*

TextSize

```
set textSize of field 1 to 18
```

You use the `textSize` property to determine or to change the type size in which text in the specified field appears.

The value of the `textSize` property can be any integer, corresponding to a like number of pixels. The default value of the `textSize` property is 12.

The size of a pixel on the Macintosh screen is about ½ inch, the approximate size of a printer's point. Although you can use any integer for `textSize`, exact sizes of fonts available look best. Fonts available can be in your System file, the HyperCard application, the Home stack, or the current stack.

You can also set this property by selecting one of the font sizes shown or typing directly in the size window in the Text Style dialog box. You click the Font button in the Field Info dialog box to invoke the Text Style dialog box, which is described in the *HyperCard User's Guide.*

TextStyle

```
set textStyle of field 1 to plain
set textStyle of first card field to bold,underline,italic
```

You use the textStyle property to determine or to change the style in which text in the specified field appears.

The textStyle property can have a value of plain or any combination of the following: bold, italic, underline, outline, shadow, condensed, and extend (separated by commas). Its default value is plain. If you use plain in combination with any of the other values, the others override it.

You can also set this property by clicking one of the Style check boxes in the Text Style dialog box. You click the Font button in the Field Info dialog box to invoke the Text Style dialog box, which is described in the *HyperCard User's Guide*.

Visible

```
set visible of field "whereDidItGo" to false
```

You use the visible property to determine or to change whether a field is shown or hidden.

The value of the visible property can be true or false; by default it's true.

You can also set this property with the show and hide commands.

WideMargins

```
set wideMargins of field "nicer" to true
```

You use the wideMargins property to specify whether some extra space is included at the left and right side of each line in the field (to make the text easier to read).

The value of the wideMargins property can be true or false; by default it's false.

You can also change this property by clicking the Wide Margins check box in the Field Info dialog box.

Button properties

Button properties pertain to any card button or background button in the current stack. The button is specified as explained in Chapter 3, "Naming Objects."

You can manipulate the properties of any button in the current stack from a script or from the Message box. Additionally, you can manipulate the properties of a button on the current card or background through the Button Info dialog box invoked from the Objects menu. (You must have the Button tool and a specific card or background button selected to activate the Button Info dialog.)

The button properties, described in this section, are

autoHilite	showName
hilite	style
icon	textAlign
ID	textFont
loc[ation]	textHeight
name	textSize
number	textStyle
rect[angle]	visible
script	

Button properties are explained in more detail in the *HyperCard User's Guide* section about the Button Info dialog.

AutoHilite

```
set autoHilite of the target to true
```

You use the autoHilite property to determine or to change whether the specified button's hilite property is affected by the message mouseDown.

The value of the autoHilite property can be true or false; by default it's false.

When autoHilite is true, mouseDown changes the button's hilite property to true, and mouseUp sets its hilite property to false. The effect is that the button is momentarily highlighted (displayed in inverse video) when the user clicks it, giving visual feedback for the click action.

The autoHilite property can also be changed by clicking the "Auto hilite" check box in the Button Info dialog box.

See also the description of the hilite property, which follows.

Hilite

```
set hilite of button 1 to true
```

You use the `hilite` property to determine or to change whether the specified button is highlighted (displayed in inverse video). To see what highlighting for the various button styles looks like, see the *HyperCard User's Guide.*

The value of the `hilite` property can be `true` or `false`; by default it's `false`.

The `hilite` property can be changed using the `set` command, either from a script or from the Message box, or, if the `autoHilite` property is `true`, by sending the message `mouseDown` to the button. In that case, for all styles of buttons except check boxes and radio buttons, the `hilite` property becomes `true` when the button receives `mouseDown`, and it becomes `false` when the button receives `mouseUp`.

For check boxes and radio buttons with their `autoHilite` property set `true`, the `hilite` property toggles to its opposite state on `mouseDown` and stays that way until it receives another `mouseDown`. That is, when a check box is highlighted, it appears with an "X" check mark in its box; when it's not highlighted, the check mark does not appear. If `autoHilite` is `true`, an unselected check box displays an "X" when you click it; if you click it again, the "X" disappears. The appearance of the check mark correlates to the state of the button's `hilite` property. The situation is similar for radio buttons, except that the `true` highlighted state is indicated by a solid dot inside the button's circle.

See also the description of the `autoHilite` property, immediately preceding.

Icon

```
set icon of button "Bill" to 2002
set icon of button "Bill" to "Bill"
```

You use the `icon` property to determine or to change the icon, if any, that is displayed with the specified button (described in the "Button Info" section of the *HyperCard User's Guide*).

Icons are small images that exist as Macintosh resources and are editable with a Macintosh resource editor. For an icon to be displayed on a button, its resource must be available in the current stack, the Home stack, or the HyperCard application.

The value of the `icon` property is an integer correlating with the ID number of an available icon resource. If a button has no icon, the `icon` property is 0.

The `icon` property can be changed with the `set` command, and it can be set to either the icon's ID number or to its name (if it has one).

The icon can also be changed by clicking the Icon button in the Button Info dialog box, which brings up another dialog box that displays the available icons graphically.

ID

```
put the ID of button 1 into msg
```

The `ID` property lets you determine the permanent ID number of a specified button.

You can't change the ID of any object.

The adjectives `long`, `short`, and `abbreviated` can be used with the `ID` property as described at the beginning of this chapter.

Location

```
set loc of button 1 to 100,100
```

You use the `location` property to determine or to change the location of the specified card button or background button in the card window.

The location is a point, reported as two integers separated by a comma. The point represents the horizontal and vertical offsets in pixels, respectively, from the top-left corner of the card window to the center of the specified button.

You can also change the button `location` property by dragging the center of the button with the Button tool.

❖ *Offscreen buttons:* You can set the location of the button beyond the boundaries of the card window rectangle, putting the button out of reach until you reset its coordinates through HyperTalk.

The `location` property can be abbreviated `loc`.

Name

```
set name of button id 1 of last card to "hole"
```

You use the `name` property to determine or to change the name of the specified button.

The value of the `name` property can be any object name (as described in Chapter 3).

The modifiers `long`, `short`, and `abbreviated` can be used with the `name` property as described at the beginning of this chapter.

The button name can also be edited in the Button Name box in the Button Info dialog box.

Number

```
put the number of button "hole"
```

You use the `number` property to determine the number of the specified button.

The value of the `number` property is an integer.

You can't change the number with the `set` command. The number changes according to the position of the button among the other buttons on its card or background, and that position is manipulated with the Send Farther and Bring Closer menu commands.

See also the `number` function in Chapter 8.

Rectangle

```
put the rect of button 1 into msg
```

You use the `rectangle` property to determine or to change the location and size of the bounding rectangle occupied by the specified button on its card or background.

The value of the button rectangle is two points, reported as four integers separated by commas. The points represent the rectangle's top-left (horizontal and vertical) and bottom-right (horizontal and vertical) corner offsets in pixels, respectively, from the top-left corner of the card window.

❖ *Offscreen buttons:* You can set either of the rectangle points of the button beyond the boundaries of the card window rectangle, putting the button out of reach until you reset its coordinates through HyperTalk.

You can set the bottom-right corner location to a value smaller than the top-left corner location, effectively causing the button to disappear. If you set the button rectangle to a size smaller than the minimum (12 by 12 pixels) but large enough to see, HyperCard resets it to the minimum size when you click it.

You can also change the button rectangle by dragging the top-left or bottom-right corner of the button with the Button tool.

The `rectangle` property can be abbreviated `rect`.

Script

```
set script of button "red" of first card to empty
```

You use the `script` property to retrieve or to replace the script of the specified button.

The value of the `script` property is the text string composing the script of the specified button.

When you set the `script` property using the `set` command, you replace it entirely.

Scripts are normally edited using the HyperCard script editor described in Chapter 1, "HyperCard Basics."

ShowName

```
set showName of button "Hair" to true
```

You use the `showName` property to determine or to change whether the name of the specified button (if it has one) is displayed in its rectangle on the screen.

The value of the ShowName property can be `true` or `false`; by default it's `false`.

You can also change this property by clicking the "Show name" check box in the Button Info dialog box.

Style

```
set style of button 1 to transparent
```

You use the `style` property to determine or to change the style of the specified button.

The value of the `style` property can be `transparent`, `opaque`, `rectangle`, `roundRect`, `checkBox`, or `radioButton`.

Some useful peculiarities of radio buttons and check box buttons are described under the `hilite` property, earlier in this chapter. You can also study the button and card scripts of the User Preferences card in the Home stack.

You can also set this property by clicking one of the Style buttons in the Button Info dialog box.

TextAlign

```
set textAlign of button 1 to left
```

You use the `textAlign` property to determine or to change the alignment of the button name in the button rectangle. To see its effect, the button must have a name and its `showName` property must be `true`.

The value of the `textAlign` property can be `left`, `right`, or `center`; by default it's `left`.

Using the `set` command is the only way to change the alignment of the button name in the button rectangle.

TextFont

```
set textFont of button 1 to Monaco
```

You use the `textFont` property to determine or to change the font in which the name of the specified button appears. To see the effect of `textFont`, the button must have a name and its `showName` property must be `true`.

The value of the `textFont` property can be the name of any of the fonts available as font resources in your System file, the current stack, the Home stack, or the HyperCard application; by default it's `geneva`.

Using the `set` command is the only way to change a button name's typeface. If you set the TextFont property to a font that doesn't exist, HyperCard sets it to `chicago`.

TextHeight

The `textHeight` property determines the amount of space between lines of text. Although you can set this property for a button, it is meaningless because button name text has only one line.

TextSize

```
set textSize of button 1 to 18
```

You use the `textSize` property to determine or to change the type size in which the specified button's name appears. To see the effect of `textSize`, the button must have a name and its `showName` property must be `true`.

The value of the `textSize` property can be any integer, corresponding to a like number of pixels. The default value of the `textSize` property is 12.

The size of a pixel on the Macintosh screen is about ½ inch, the approximate size of a printer's point. Although you can use any integer for `textSize`, exact sizes of fonts available look best. Fonts available can be in your System file, the HyperCard application, the Home stack, or the current stack.

Using the `set` command is the only way to set a button name's type size.

TextStyle

```
set textStyle of button 1 to plain
set the textStyle of button "Fancy" to bold,italic,underline
```

You use the `textStyle` property to determine or to change the style in which the specified button's name appears. To see the effect of `textStyle`, the button must have a name and its `showName` property must be `true`.

The `textStyle` property can have a value of `plain` or any combination of the following: `bold`, `italic`, `underline`, `outline`, `shadow`, `condense`, and `extend` (separated by commas). By default it's `plain`. If you use `plain` in combination with any of the other values, the others override it.

Using the `set` command is the only way to set a button name's style.

Visible

```
set visible of button "it's gone" to false
```

You use the `visible` property to determine or to change whether the specified button is shown or hidden.

The value of the `visible` property can be `true` or `false`; by default it's `true`.

You can also change this property with the `show` and `hide` commands.

Chapter 10

Constants

This chapter describes HyperTalk's built-in constants. A **constant** is a named value that never changes. It's different from a variable because you can't change it, and it's different from a literal because it does not require quotation marks.

The values of some constants are the string of characters making up the name, while others are different. In some cases, it's more convenient to use a constant (such as pi) in place of a long string (such as 3.14159265358979323846). In other cases, it's more convenient to use a constant (such as formFeed) because the only other way to enter that character is with the numToChar function, requiring that you know the ASCII number of the character (as in the numToChar of 12).

You can't name a variable the same as any built-in constant; if you try, HyperCard displays an error dialog box.

Table 10-1 is a list of all the built-in constants in HyperTalk.

Table 10-1
HyperTalk constants

Constant name	Description
down	The value returned by the commandKey, mouse, optionKey, or shiftKey function when the named key (or button, in the case of mouse), is currently pressed. Its value is the same as the literal "down".
empty	The null string, the same as the literal "".
false	The opposite of true; one of the states tested by the if control structure and one of the possible results of evaluation of a logical expression. Its value is the same as the literal "false".
formFeed	The form feed character (ASCII 12), which starts a new page in some file formats.
lineFeed	The line feed character (ASCII 10), which starts a new line in some file formats.
pi	The mathematical value pi to 20 decimal places, denoting the ratio of the circumference of a circle to its diameter, represented by the number 3.14159265358979323846.
quote	The double quotation mark character. It is needed to build a string containing quotation marks because they are stripped out of the string when literals are evaluated:

```
put "george" into It -- quotation marks are not in It
put quote & "george" & quote into It -- quotation marks in
```

Constant name	Description
return	The return character (ASCII 13), which signifies the end of a HyperTalk statement.
space	The space character (ASCII 32), the same as the literal " ".
tab	The horizontal tab character (ASCII 9).
true	The opposite of false; one of the states tested by the if control structure and one of the possible results of evaluation of a logical expression. Its value is the same as the literal "true".
up	The value returned by the commandKey, mouse, optionKey, and shiftKey functions when the named key (or button, in the case of mouse), is not currently pressed. Its value is the same as the literal "up".
zero..ten	The numbers 0 through 10.

Appendixes

Appendix A

External Commands and Functions

This appendix describes HyperCard's external command and function interface. In addition to general information about external commands and functions, this appendix contains specific information that requires a reading knowledge of Pascal or C to be understood. This appendix does not include information about how to write code, nor does it explain how to use a compiler or assembler to create an executable resource.

Definitions, uses, and examples

External commands and functions are extensions to the HyperTalk built-in command and function set. HyperCard includes interface procedures that make extending HyperTalk in this way convenient and practical for expert programmers.

XCMD and XFCN resources

External commands and functions are executable Macintosh code resources, written in a Macintosh programming language (such as Pascal, C, or 68000 assembly language), which are attached to the HyperCard application or a stack with a resource editor such as ResEdit. The resource type of an external command is 'XCMD' and the resource type of an external function is 'XFCN'. They are often named by their resource types: external commands are termed "ex-commands" (written XCMDs), and external functions are "ex-functions" (written XFCNs).

XCMDs and XFCNs are handled in much the same way by HyperCard: they are separately compiled and attached by a resource mover to stacks or the HyperCard application; they use the object hierarchy in the same way; and they communicate with HyperCard through the same parameter block data structure.

A Macintosh code resource is a compiled (or assembled) executable code module. An 'XCMD' or 'XFCN' resource has no header bytes; it is invoked by a jump instruction to its entry point. These resources are simpler than Macintosh drivers: they can't have any global (or static) data, and they can't be larger than 32K bytes in size. (For more details about these restrictions, see "Guidelines for Writing XCMDs and XFCNs," later in this appendix.)

After they have been created and attached to HyperCard or a stack, external commands and functions are called from HyperTalk in much the same way that built-in commands or user-defined message and function handlers are called.

For detailed information on Macintosh resources, see *Inside Macintosh,* published by Addison-Wesley.

Uses for XCMDs and XFCNs

External commands and functions can provide access to the Macintosh Toolbox and to some of HyperCard's own internal routines; they can provide fast processing speed for time-critical operations; and they can override built-in HyperTalk commands to provide custom solutions. XCMDs or XFCNs can be used for serial port input and output routines, custom search-and-replace routines, color graphics display routines, file input and output routines, and so on.

A typical use for an XCMD would be as an interface for a driver, allowing HyperCard to control an external device such as a videodisc player. Such an interface would have three parts: the driver, the XCMD, and a HyperTalk handler. The driver would be completely separate from HyperCard. (See Volume II of *Inside Macintosh* for information about writing drivers.) The XCMD would be small; its purpose would be to convert HyperTalk messages to the appropriate driver calls. The HyperTalk handler would call the XCMD with various parameters directing it to open or close the driver or to perform a specific control call.

Guidelines for writing XCMDs and XFCNs

XCMDs and XFCNs can call most of the Macintosh Toolbox traps and routines, but they have certain limitations and restrictions. They can't do everything that an application can do because they are guests in HyperCard's heap. In that regard they are more like desk accessories than applications. Here are some guidelines for writing XCMDs and XFCNs:

□ Do not initialize the various Macintosh managers by calling their initialization routines. That is, don't call `InitGraf`, `InitFonts`, `InitWindows`, and so on.

□ Do not rely upon having lots of RAM available for your XCMD. There is some extra space in HyperCard's heap, but if HyperCard is running in 750K under MultiFinder™, for example, an XCMD should not be bigger than about 32K.

□ Do not use register A5 of the 68000-family processor. The value in A5 belongs to HyperCard, and it points to HyperCard's global data, jump table, and other things that constitute an "A5 world." XCMDs do not currently have their own A5 world.

□ XCMDs cannot have global data.

□ Because they cannot have global data, XCMDs cannot use string literals with MPW C (MPW C makes string literals into global data). To circumvent this restriction, use 'STR ' resources or put the strings in a short assembly-language glue file.

□ XCMDs cannot have a jump table, so they cannot have code segments. This restriction imposes a 32K limit on the size of XCMDs for 68000-based machines (the 68020 supports longer branches).

□ XCMDs can, however, allocate small chunks of memory by standard `NewHandle` calls. (You can also allocate memory with `NewPtr` calls, but they should be used sparingly to avoid heap fragmentation.)

□ If your XCMD allocates some memory in the heap, it should also deallocate the memory.

□ If an XCMD allocates a handle to save state information between invocations of the XCMD, then you must pass the handle back to HyperCard to be stored somewhere in the current stack, such as in a hidden field. You must to convert the handle from a long integer to a string, because all values are treated as strings by HyperTalk.

□ Since HyperCard jumps blindly to the start of an XCMD's code, it is important that the main routine actually ends up at the start of the XCMD. In other words, the XCMD glue must follow the main routine, so the link order is vitally important.

□ If, as you write, the size of your XCMD begins to approach 32K, consider converting it to a driver.

Flash: an example XCMD

An example external command included with HyperCard is `flash`, which inverts the screen display (changes the black pixels to white and vice versa) a specified number of times. A version of `flash` written and compiled in MPW Pascal has already been attached to the HyperCard application file (that is, to HyperCard itself).

`Flash` is invoked from HyperCard just like a HyperTalk command. That is, you send the message `flash` to HyperCard from the Message box or from an executing script. The flash message takes one parameter: an integer. The `flash` XCMD inverts the screen display twice that many times. For example, the following handler, in response to a `mouseUp` message, sends the `flash` message and its parameter. When the message reaches HyperCard, it invokes the `flash` external command, which inverts the screen display 20 times:

```
on mouseUp
  flash 10
end mouseUp
```

The screen display flashes (is inverted and inverted back again) 10 times.

Flash listing in MPW Pascal

Here's the Pascal listing for `flash`:

```
(*
 * Flash.p - A sample HyperCard XCMD to highlight the screen
 *           - Copyright Apple Computer, Inc.  1987-1988.
 *           - All Rights Reserved.
 *
 * Build instructions:
 *
 * Pascal Flash.p -o Flash.p.o
 * Link Flash.p.o -sg Flash -rt XCMD=0 -m ENTRYPOINT -o StackName
 *
 *)

{$R-}


{$S Flash } { Segment name must be same as command name }
```

```
(*
 * DummyUnit is what HyperTalk jumps to when running the XCMD.
 * Also note that XCMDs do not currently support their own A5 World,
 * thus NO GLOBAL VARIABLES are allowed.  If the link fails then that
 * means the Pascal compiler generated A5-relative code.  (This may
 * happen if you try to use the Pascal libraries, for example.)
 *
 *)


UNIT DummyUnit;

INTERFACE

USES MemTypes, QuickDraw, HyperXCmd;

PROCEDURE EntryPoint(paramPtr: XCmdPtr);

IMPLEMENTATION

TYPE Str31 = String[31];

PROCEDURE Flash(paramPtr: XCmdPtr); FORWARD;

   PROCEDURE EntryPoint(paramPtr: XCmdPtr);
   BEGIN
     Flash(paramPtr);
   END;

   PROCEDURE Flash(paramPtr: XCmdPtr);
   VAR flashCount:  INTEGER;
     again:         INTEGER;
     port:          GrafPtr;
     str:           Str255;
     when:          LongInt;
     ticksPtr:      ^LongInt;

   {$I XCmdGlue.inc }
```

```
  BEGIN
    ZeroToPas(paramPtr^.params[1]^,str); { first param is flash count }
    flashCount := StrToNum(str);
    GetPort(port);
    ticksPtr := Pointer($16A);

    IF (paramPtr^.paramCount <> 1) OR (flashCount < 1)
    THEN flashCount := 3;

    FOR again := 1 TO 2 * flashCount DO
      BEGIN
        when := ticksPtr^ + 4;
        InvertRect(port^.portRect);
        REPEAT UNTIL ticksPtr^ >= when;
      END;
  END;

END.
```

Flash listing in MPW C

Here's a version of `flash` written in MPW C:

```
/*
 *    Flash.c - A sample HyperCard XCMD to highlight the screen
 *              -    Copyright Apple Computer, Inc.  1987-1988.
 *              -    All Rights Reserved.
 *
 *    Build instructions:
 *
 *    C  Flash.c -o Flash.c.o
 *    Link Flash.c.o -sg CFlash -rt XCMD=5 -o StackName
 *
 */

#define __SEG__ CFlash /* Segment name must be the same as command name */

#include <HyperXCmd.h> /* HT interface and #includes Types.h, Memory.h */
#include <QuickDraw.h>

pascal void MacsBug() extern 0xA9FF; /* useful for debugging */
```

```
/*
 *   Your routine MUST be the first code that is generated in the file, as
 *   HyperTalk simply JSRs to the start of the XCMD segment in memory.
 *  Therefore the XCmdGlue.c file must be included after the main routine,
 *   being CFlash in this sample XCMD.  Also note that XCMDs do not currently
 *   support their own A5 World, thus NO GLOBAL VARIABLES are allowed.
 *  If the link fails then that means the C compiler generated A5-relative
 *   code.  (This happens if you try to use the C libraries or use strings
 *   in the code.  Use a STR resource instead.)
 *
 */

pascal void CFlash(paramPtr)
     XCmdBlockPtr paramPtr;
{
     short flashCount,again;
     GrafPtr port;
     Str255 str;

     ZeroToPas(paramPtr,*(paramPtr->params[0]),&str); /* get flash count */
     flashCount = StrToNum(paramPtr,&str);   /* convert to num */
     if (paramPtr->paramCount != 1) flashCount = 3; /* default if no param */
     if (flashCount < 1) flashCount = 3;    /* must be positive */
     GetPort(&port);
     for (again = 1; again <= flashCount; again++) {
          InvertRect(&port->portRect);
          InvertRect(&port->portRect);
     }
}

#include <XCmdGlue.c> /* C routines for HyperCard callbacks */
```

Flash listing in 68000 assembly language

Here's the 68000 assembly language listing for `flash`:

```
*
* Flash.a    - A sample HyperCard XCMD in 68000 Assembly
*            - Copyright Apple Computer, Inc.  1988.
*            - All Rights Reserved.
*
* Build Instructions:
*
*            Asm  Flash.a -o Flash.a.o
*            Link Flash.a.o -sg AFlash -rt XCMD=7 -o StackName
*
*

            INCLUDE 'QuickEqu.a'
            INCLUDE 'Traps.a'

            SEG 'AFlash'                    ; Segname must be same as command name

AFlash      PROC                           ; uses a0,a1,d1
            link    a6,#-4
            move.l  d4,-(sp)               ; save
            move.l  8(a6),a0               ; get paramPtr in a temp reg
            move.l  2(a0),a1               ; get handle to flashCount (as c string)
            move.l  (a1),a1                ; deref
            move.w  #3,d4                  ; StrToNum default result

@1          move.b  (a1)+,d1               ; get a char
            cmp.b   #'0',d1                ; test for a number
            blt.s   @2                     ; less than valid
            cmp.b   #'9',d1
            bgt.s   @2                     ; greater than valid

            and.w   #$000F,d1              ; mask to value of legal char
            move.w  d1,d4                  ; stick value into result

@2          pea     -4(a6)                 ; var result of GetPort
            _GetPort
            bra.s   @4                     ; get into DBRA loop

@3          move.l  -4(a6),a0              ; get port
            pea     portRect(a0)           ; address of portRect
            _InverRect
            move.l  -4(a6),a0              ; get port
            pea     portRect(a0)           ; address of portRect
            _InverRect
```

```
@4          dbra    d4,@3

            move.l  (sp)+,d4                    ; restore
            unlk    a6

            move.l  (sp)+,a0                    ; rts Pascal style
            add.l   #4,a7
            jmp     (a0)

            END
```

Peek: an example XFCN

An example external function is `peek`, which returns the contents of a memory location whose address is passed with the function call. `Peek` is not already attached to the HyperCard application like the `flash` XCMD; you must compile it yourself and attach it to HyperCard or a stack with a resource editor like ResEdit (see "Attaching an XCMD or XFCN" later in this appendix).

Peek listing in MPW Pascal

Here's the Pascal listing for `peek`:

```
(*
 * Peek.p - A sample HyperCard XFCN to return the contents of memory
 *          - Copyright Apple Computer, Inc. 1987,1988.
 *          - All Rights Reserved.
 *
 * Build instructions:
 *
 * Pascal Peek.p -o Peek.p.o
 * Link Peek.p.o -sg Peek -rt XFCN=1 -m ENTRYPOINT -o StackName
 *
 *)

{$R-}

{$S Peek } { Segment name must be same as command name }

(*
 * DummyUnit is what HyperTalk jumps to when running the XCFN.
 * Also note that XCFNs do not currently support their own A5 World,
 * thus NO GLOBAL VARIABLES are allowed.  If the link fails then that
 * means the Pascal compiler generated A5-relative code.  (This may
 * happen if you try to use the Pascal libraries, for example.)
 *
 *)
```

```
UNIT DummyUnit;

INTERFACE

USES MemTypes, HyperXCmd;

PROCEDURE EntryPoint(paramPtr: XCmdPtr);

IMPLEMENTATION

TYPE  Str31 = String[31];
        WordPtr = ^INTEGER;
        LongPtr = ^LongInt;

PROCEDURE Peek(paramPtr: XCmdPtr); FORWARD;

  PROCEDURE EntryPoint(paramPtr: XCmdPtr);
  BEGIN
    Peek(paramPtr);
  END;

  PROCEDURE Peek(paramPtr: XCmdPtr);
  VAR peekAddr,peekSize,peekVal: LongInt;
      str: Str255;

  {$I XCmdGlue.inc }
```

```
BEGIN
  WITH paramPtr^ DO
    BEGIN
      { first param is addr }
      ZeroToPas(params[1]^,str); .
      peekAddr := StrToNum(str);

      { second param, if given, is size }
      peekSize := 1;
      IF paramCount = 2 THEN
        BEGIN
          ZeroToPas(params[2]^,str);
          peekSize := StrToNum(str);
        END;

      CASE peekSize OF
        1: peekVal := BAND($000000FF,Ptr(peekAddr)^);
        2: peekVal := BAND($0000FFFF,WordPtr(BAND($FFFFFFFE,peekAddr))^);
        4: peekVal := LongPtr(BAND($FFFFFFFE,peekAddr))^;
        OTHERWISE peekVal := 0;
      END;

      str := NumToStr(peekVal);
      returnValue := PasToZero(str);
    END;
  END;

END.
```

Peek listing in MPW C

Here's the MPW C code listing for `peek`:

```
/*
 *    Peek.c -  A sample HyperCard XFCN to return the contents of memory
 *              -  Copyright Apple Computer, Inc.  1987,1988.
 *              -  All Rights Reserved.
 *
 *    Build instructions:
 *
 *    C Peek.c -o Peek.c.o
 *    Link Peek.c.o -sg CPeek -rt XFCN=6 -o StackName
 *
 */


#define __SEG__ CPeek /* Segment name must be the same as command name */

#include <HyperXCmd.h> /* HT interface and #includes Types.h, Memory.h */

pascal void MacsBug() extern 0xA9FF; /* useful for debugging */

#define PEEKBYTE(address) *((char *) address)
#define PEEKWORD(address) *((short *) address)
#define PEEKLONG(address) *((long *) address)

/*
 *    Your routine MUST be the first code that is generated in the file, as
 *    HyperTalk simply JSRs to the start of the XFCN segment in memory.
 *  Therefore the XCmdGlue.c file must be included after the main routine,
 *    being CPeek in this sample XFCN.  Also note that XFCNs do not currently
 *    support their own A5 World, thus NO GLOBAL VARIABLES are allowed.
 *  If the link fails then that means the C compiler generated A5-relative
 *    code.  (This happens if you try to use the C libraries or use strings
 *    in the code.  Use a STR resource instead.)
 *
 */
```

```
pascal void CPeek(paramPtr)
    XCmdBlockPtr paramPtr;
{

    char str[256];
    short argc;
    long peekAddr, peekSize, peekVal;
    Handle argv1, argv2;

    argc  = paramPtr->paramCount;
    argv1 = paramPtr->params[0];
    argv2 = paramPtr->params[1];

    ZeroToPas(paramPtr, *argv1, str); /* CtoP string */
    peekAddr = StrToNum(paramPtr, str); /* get address */

    if (argc == 2) {
        ZeroToPas(paramPtr, *argv2, str); /* CtoP string */
        peekSize = StrToNum(paramPtr, str); /* get size */
    }
    else
        peekSize = 1;

    switch(peekSize) {
        case 1:  peekVal = PEEKBYTE(peekAddr); break;
        case 2:  peekVal = PEEKWORD(peekAddr); break;
        case 4:  peekVal = PEEKLONG(peekAddr); break;
        default: peekVal = 0;
    }
    NumToStr(paramPtr, peekVal, str);

    /* XFCN: make sure to return a result, the only change from an XCMD */
    paramPtr->returnValue = PasToZero(paramPtr, str);
}


#include <XCmdGlue.c>
```

Peek is invoked just like a user-defined function handler. That is, you put the function name in a HyperTalk statement followed by one argument within parentheses—an integer representing the memory location whose contents you want HyperCard to return. For example:

```
on mouseUp
  put peek(0) into msg
end mouseUp
```

The current contents of memory address 0 are displayed in the Message box.

Accessing an XCMD or XFCN

You access XCMDs and XFCNs from HyperTalk using the regular message syntax and user-defined function call syntax. The message or function call is passed through the HyperCard object hierarchy.

Invoking XCMDs and XFCNs

You invoke an XCMD as you do a message handler. That is, you type the name of the XCMD followed by its parameters in a HyperTalk script or in the Message box. Separate the parameters (if there are more than one) with commas, and put quotation marks around parameters of more than one word. When the script executes or when you send the Message box contents by pressing Return or Enter, HyperCard sends the message through the normal object hierarchy. For external commands, the Macintosh resource name correlates to the message name—the first word in the message.

Similarly, you call an XFCN in a HyperTalk statement in the same way you would a user-defined function (use parentheses rather than the word `the`), which calls a function handler somewhere farther along the hierarchy. Enclose any parameters within parentheses, separate them (if more than one) with commas, and put quotation marks around parameters of more than one word. If the function takes no parameters, append empty parentheses after it. For external functions, the Macintosh resource name correlates to the function name—the word preceding parentheses in the function call.

You can pass a maximum of 16 parameters to an XCMD or XFCN.

Object hierarchy

External commands and functions use the object hierarchy in the same way as message and function handlers and built-in commands and functions. External commands and functions can be attached to any stack or to the HyperCard application.

If a stack receives a message or function call for which it has no handler, then before passing the message or function call to the next object, it checks to see if it has an external command or function of the same name. When HyperCard receives a message or function call, it checks to see if it has an external command or function *before* it looks for a built-in command or function.

That is, HyperCard searches for message and function handlers, XCMDs and XFCNs, and built-in commands and functions through the hierarchy shown in Figure A-1.

Chapter 2 discusses the message-passing hierarchy, including the dynamic path, in detail.

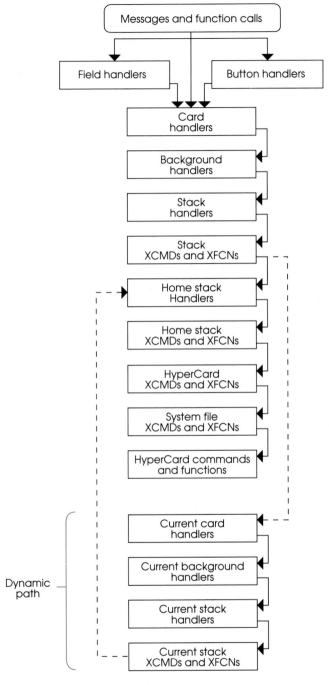

Figure A-1
Message-passing hierarchy, including XCMDs and XFCNs

Parameter block data structure

If HyperCard matches a message or function call with an external command or function, it passes a single argument to the XCMD or XFCN: a pointer to a parameter block called an `XCmdBlock`. All communication between HyperCard and the XCMD or XFCN passes through the parameter block. In Pascal, the parameter block data structure is a `record`; in C it's a `struct`.

HyperCard uses the first two fields of the parameter block to pass information to the XCMD or XFCN before invoking its execution. The XCMD or XFCN uses the other data fields in the `XCmdBlock` to pass back results and to communicate with HyperCard during execution.

The parameter block is listed in both Pascal and C in the respective definition interface files later in this appendix. The Pascal parameter block is also shown here for convenience:

```
TYPE

   XCmdPtr = ^XCmdBlock;
   XCmdBlock =
      RECORD
         paramCount:  INTEGER;
         params:         ARRAY[1..16] OF Handle;
         returnValue: Handle;
         passFlag:    BOOLEAN;

         entryPoint:  ProcPtr;  { to call back to HyperCard }
         request:        INTEGER;
         result:         INTEGER;
         inArgs:         ARRAY[1..8] OF LongInt;
         outArgs:        ARRAY[1..4] OF LongInt;
      END;

END;
```

Passing parameters to XCMDs and XFCNs

Before calling the XCMD or XFCN, HyperCard places the number of parameters and handles to the parameter strings in two fields of the `XCmdBlock`: `paramCount` and `params`.

ParamCount

HyperCard puts an integer representing the parameter count in field `paramCount`. You can pass a maximum of 16 parameter strings.

Params

HyperCard evaluates the parameters and puts their values into memory as zero-terminated ASCII strings. Before it invokes the XCMD or XFCN, HyperCard puts the handles to the parameter strings into the `params` array.

Passing back results to HyperCard

When an XCMD or XFCN finishes executing, HyperCard examines two fields of the `XCmdBlock`: `returnValue` and `passFlag`.

ReturnValue

An XCMD or XFCN can optionally store one zero-terminated string to communicate the result of its execution. HyperCard will look for a handle to the result string in the `returnValue` field of the `XCmdBlock`. Storing a result string is optional for an XCMD; it is expected of an XFCN, but it's not required. If you store a result string handle into `returnValue` in an XCMD, the user can get it by using the HyperTalk function `the result` (useful for explaining why there was an error). For an XFCN, HyperCard uses the `returnValue` string to replace the function call itself in the HyperTalk statement containing the call. If you don't store anything, the result is the empty string.

PassFlag

When an XCMD or XFCN terminates, HyperCard examines the Boolean value of the `passFlag` field. If `passFlag` is false (the normal case), control passes back to the previously executing handler (or to HyperCard's idle state if no handler was executing). If `passFlag` is true, HyperCard passes the message or function call to the next object in the hierarchy. This has the same effect as the `pass` control statement in a script.

Callbacks

The remaining five fields of the `XCmdBlock` record have to do with calling HyperCard back in the middle of execution of an XCMD or XFCN. You use the callback mechanism to obtain data or request HyperCard to perform an action. HyperCard has 29 callback requests (see "Request Codes" later in this appendix). The five `XCmdBlock` fields that compose the callback interface are `entryPoint`, `request`, `result`, `inArgs`, and `outArgs`.

EntryPoint

When HyperCard sets up the `XCmdBlock` data structure before passing control to an XCMD or XFCN, it places an address in `entryPoint`. The XCMD or XFCN uses this address to execute a jump instruction to pass control to HyperCard for the callback.

Request

Before executing the jump instruction, the XCMD or XFCN puts an integer representing the callback request it's making into the `request` field. The request codes are listed in "Callback Procedures and Functions" later in this appendix.

Result

After it completes the callback request, HyperCard places an integer result code in the `result` field. The result code can be 0, 1, or 2. If the callback executed successfully, the result is 0; if it failed, the result is 1; if the callback request is not implemented in HyperCard, the result is 2.

InArgs

The XCMD or XFCN sends up to eight arguments to HyperCard as long integers in the `inArgs` array. Depending on the callback request, HyperCard expects arguments in certain elements of the `inArgs` array. In many callbacks, the arguments are pointers to zero-terminated strings. The callback arguments are shown in Pascal in "Callback Procedures and Functions" later in this appendix.

OutArgs

After it executes the callback request, HyperCard returns up to four long integers (or other types, such as handles) to the XCMD or XFCN as elements of the `outArgs` array. The arguments HyperCard returns from callbacks are shown in Pascal in "Callback Procedures and Functions" later in this appendix.

Callback procedures and functions

If you want to manage a callback to HyperCard yourself, you can define the
`XCmdBlock` data structure in your XCMD or XFCN. Then you can put values you want
to send to HyperCard in `inArgs`, put a request code in `request`, and execute a
jump instruction to the address HyperCard places in `entryPoint`. HyperCard
returns values in `outArgs` and a result code in `result`.

However, if you use MPW Pascal or C, you can take advantage of interface definition
and "glue" files. (The definition and glue files are listed later in this appendix and are
also available on disk from APDA, the Apple Programmer's and Developer's
Association. Information about APDA is listed at the end of this appendix.) The
definition and glue files provide simple procedure and function calls that you can use
inside your XCMD or XFCN to handle callback requests more easily. Include them
when you compile your XCMD or XFCN.

The Pascal code for an XCMD or XFCN should include the definition file
`HyperXCmd.p` at the beginning of the `USES` clause and the glue file
`XCmdGlue.inc` at the end with the `$I` directive. There must be an argument of type
`XCmdPtr` passed by HyperCard to the XCMD or XFCN. In the glue routines, all
strings are Pascal strings unless noted as zero-terminated strings (which have no length
byte; the end of the string is indicated by a null byte). In general, if a handle is
returned, the XCMD or XFCN is responsible for disposing of it.

Definition interface files

The MPW Pascal definition interface file is `HyperXCmd.p`. The MPW C definition
interface file is `HyperXCmd.h`. These files define the `XCmdBlock` parameter block
described earlier in this appendix. They also define the constants representing the
callback result codes and request codes.

Definition file in MPW Pascal

The interface definition file in MPW Pascal is as follows:

```
(*
 * HyperXCmd.p      - Interface to HyperTalk callback routines
 *                  - Copyright Apple Computer, Inc. 1987,1988.
 *                  - All Rights Reserved.
 *
 *)

UNIT HyperXCmd;
```

```
INTERFACE

CONST

    { result codes }
    xresSucc        = 0;
    xresFail        = 1;
    xresNotImp      = 2;

    { request codes }
    xreqSendCardMessage   =  1;
    xreqEvalExpr          =  2;
    xreqStringLength      =  3;
    xreqStringMatch       =  4;
    xreqSendHCMessage     =  5;
    xreqZeroBytes         =  6;
    xreqPasToZero         =  7;
    xreqZeroToPas         =  8;
    xreqStrToLong         =  9;
    xreqStrToNum          = 10;
    xreqStrToBool         = 11;
    xreqStrToExt          = 12;
    xreqLongToStr         = 13;
    xreqNumToStr          = 14;
    xreqNumToHex          = 15;
    xreqBoolToStr         = 16;
    xreqExtToStr          = 17;
    xreqGetGlobal         = 18;
    xreqSetGlobal         = 19;
    xreqGetFieldByName    = 20;
    xreqGetFieldByNum     = 21;
    xreqGetFieldByID      = 22;
    xreqSetFieldByName    = 23;
    xreqSetFieldByNum     = 24;
    xreqSetFieldByID      = 25;
    xreqStringEqual       = 26;
    xreqReturnToPas       = 27;
    xreqScanToReturn      = 28;
    xreqScanToZero        = 39;
```

```
TYPE

  XCmdPtr = ^XCmdBlock;
  XCmdBlock =
    RECORD
       paramCount:      INTEGER;
       params:          ARRAY[1..16] OF Handle;
       returnValue:     Handle;
       passFlag:        BOOLEAN;

       entryPoint:      ProcPtr;  { to call back to HyperCard }
       request:         INTEGER;
       result:          INTEGER;
       inArgs:          ARRAY[1..8] OF LongInt;
       outArgs:         ARRAY[1..4] OF LongInt;
    END;

END;
```

Definition file in MPW C

The interface definition file in MPW C includes the parameter block definition, the result and request code constants, and forward definitions for the glue routines. The definition file is as follows:

```
/*
 *   HyperXCmd.h    - Interfaces for HyperTalk callback routines
 *                  - Copyright Apple Computer, Inc. 1987,1988.
 *                  - All Rights Reserved.
 *
 *   #include this file before your program.
 *   #include "XCmdGlue.c" after your code.
 *
 */

#include <Types.h>
#include <Memory.h>

pascal void Debugger() extern 0xA9FF;
```

```
typedef struct XCmdBlock {
    short      paramCount;
    Handle     params[16];
    Handle     returnValue;
    Boolean    passFlag;

    void       (*entryPoint)();     /* to call back to HyperCard */
    short      request;
    short      result;
    long       inArgs[8];
    long       outArgs[4];
} XCmdBlock, *XCmdBlockPtr;

typedef struct Str31 {
    char       guts[32];
} Str31, *Str31Ptr;


/* result codes */
#define    xresSucc        0
#define    xresFail        1
#define    xresNotImp      2

/* request codes */
#define    xreqSendCardMessage        1
#define    xreqEvalExpr               2
#define    xreqStringLength           3
#define    xreqStringMatch            4
#define    xreqSendHCMessage          5
#define    xreqZeroBytes              6
#define    xreqPasToZero              7
#define    xreqZeroToPas              8
#define    xreqStrToLong              9
#define    xreqStrToNum               10
#define    xreqStrToBool              11
#define    xreqStrToExt               12
#define    xreqLongToStr              13
#define    xreqNumToStr               14
#define    xreqNumToHex               15
#define    xreqBoolToStr              16
#define    xreqExtToStr               17
#define    xreqGetGlobal              18
```

```
#define     xreqSetGlobal              19
#define     xreqGetFieldByName         20
#define     xreqGetFieldByNum          21
#define     xreqGetFieldByID           22
#define     xreqSetFieldByName         23
#define     xreqSetFieldByNum          24
#define     xreqSetFieldByID           25
#define     xreqStringEqual            26
#define     xreqReturnToPas            27
#define     xreqScanToReturn           28
#define     xreqScanToZero             39     /* was supposed to be 29!  Oops! */

/* Forward definitions of glue routines.  Main program
       must include XCmdGlue.c after its routines.   */

pascal void SendCardMessage(paramPtr,msg)
     XCmdBlockPtr        paramPtr;        StringPtr       msg;       extern;
pascal Handle EvalExpr(paramPtr,expr)
     XCmdBlockPtr        paramPtr;        StringPtr       expr;      extern;
pascal long StringLength(paramPtr,strPtr)
     XCmdBlockPtr        paramPtr;        StringPtr       strPtr;    extern;
pascal Ptr StringMatch(paramPtr,pattern,target)
     XCmdBlockPtr        paramPtr;        StringPtr       pattern;
     Ptr  target; extern;
pascal void SendHCMessage(paramPtr,msg)
     XCmdBlockPtr        paramPtr;        StringPtr       msg;       extern;
pascal void ZeroBytes(paramPtr,dstPtr,longCount)
     XCmdBlockPtr        paramPtr;        Ptr dstPtr;
     long      longCount;      extern;
pascal Handle PasToZero(paramPtr,pasStr)
     XCmdBlockPtr        paramPtr;        StringPtr       pasStr;    extern;
pascal void ZeroToPas(paramPtr,zeroStr,pasStr)
     XCmdBlockPtr        paramPtr;        char            *zeroStr;
     StringPtr pasStr;          extern;
pascal long StrToLong(paramPtr,strPtr)
     XCmdBlockPtr        paramPtr;        Str31 *         strPtr;    extern;
pascal long StrToNum(paramPtr,str)
     XCmdBlockPtr        paramPtr;        Str31 *         str;       extern;
pascal Boolean StrToBool(paramPtr,str)
     XCmdBlockPtr        paramPtr;        Str31 *         str;       extern;
pascal void StrToExt(paramPtr,str,myext)
     XCmdBlockPtr        paramPtr;        Str31 *         str;
     extended *    myext;    extern;
```

```
pascal void LongToStr(paramPtr,posNum,mystr)
    XCmdBlockPtr        paramPtr;       long        posNum;
    Str31 *  mystr;     extern;
pascal void NumToStr(paramPtr,num,mystr)
    XCmdBlockPtr        paramPtr;       long        num;
    Str31 *  mystr;     extern;
pascal void NumToHex(paramPtr,num,nDigits,mystr)
    XCmdBlockPtr        paramPtr;       long        num;
    short       nDigits;                Str31 * mystr;      extern;
pascal void BoolToStr(paramPtr,bool,mystr)
    XCmdBlockPtr        paramPtr;       Boolean    bool;
    Str31 *  mystr;     extern;
pascal void ExtToStr(paramPtr,myext,mystr)
    XCmdBlockPtr        paramPtr;       extended * myext;
    Str31 *  mystr;     extern;
pascal Handle GetGlobal(paramPtr,globName)
    XCmdBlockPtr        paramPtr;       StringPtr       globName; extern;
pascal void SetGlobal(paramPtr,globName,globValue)
    XCmdBlockPtr        paramPtr;       StringPtr       globName;
    Handle    globValue;        extern;
pascal Handle GetFieldByName(paramPtr,cardFieldFlag,fieldName)
    XCmdBlockPtr        paramPtr;       Boolean    cardFieldFlag;
    StringPtr       fieldName;      extern;
pascal Handle GetFieldByNum(paramPtr,cardFieldFlag,fieldNum)
    XCmdBlockPtr        paramPtr;       Boolean    cardFieldFlag;
    short       fieldNum;       extern;
pascal Handle GetFieldByID(paramPtr,cardFieldFlag,fieldID)
    XCmdBlockPtr        paramPtr;       Boolean    cardFieldFlag;
    short       fieldID;        extern;
pascal void SetFieldByName(paramPtr,cardFieldFlag,fieldName,fieldVal)
    XCmdBlockPtr        paramPtr;       Boolean    cardFieldFlag;
    StringPtr       fieldName;  Handle    fieldVal;       extern;
pascal void SetFieldByNum(paramPtr,cardFieldFlag,fieldNum,fieldVal)
    XCmdBlockPtr        paramPtr;       Boolean    cardFieldFlag;
    short       fieldNum;               Handle    fieldVal;       extern;
pascal void SetFieldByID(paramPtr,cardFieldFlag,fieldID,fieldVal)
    XCmdBlockPtr        paramPtr;       Boolean    cardFieldFlag;
    short       fieldID;                Handle    fieldVal;       extern;
```

```
pascal Boolean StringEqual (paramPtr,str1,str2)
    XCmdBlockPtr          paramPtr;       Str31 *        str1;
    Str31 *       str2;       extern;
pascal void ReturnToPas (paramPtr,zeroStr,passStr)
    XCmdBlockPtr          paramPtr;       Ptr          zeroStr;
    StringPtr       passStr;       extern;
pascal void ScanToReturn (paramPtr,scanHndl)
    XCmdBlockPtr          paramPtr;       Ptr *      scanHndl;       extern;
pascal void ScanToZero (paramPtr,scanHndl)
    XCmdBlockPtr          paramPtr;       Ptr *      scanHndl;       extern;
```

Glue routines

The MPW Pascal callback glue routines file is `XCmdGlue.inc`. The MPW C definition
file is `XCmdGlue.c`. These files define the interface procedures and functions that
handle callback requests for XCMDs and XFCNs written in the same language. The first
line of each procedure or function definition shows the name and parameters that you
use to call it.

Glue routines in MPW Pascal

The first procedure defines the jump instruction with which the XCMD or XFCN passes
control to HyperCard to carry out its callback request. The MPW Pascal glue routines
are as follows:

```
(*
 * XCMDGlue.inc - Implementation of HyperTalk callback routines
 *                  - Copyright Apple Computer, Inc. 1987,1988.
 *                  - All Rights Reserved.
 *
 *)

{ Assumes the XCMD has included this file and
  has named its argument "paramPtr" }
```

```
PROCEDURE DoJsr(addr: ProcPtr); INLINE $205F,$4E90;


FUNCTION StringMatch(pattern: Str255; target: Ptr): Ptr;
BEGIN
   WITH paramPtr^ DO
      BEGIN
         inArgs[1] := ORD(@pattern);
         inArgs[2] := ORD(target);
         request := xreqStringMatch;
         DoJsr(entryPoint);
         StringMatch := Ptr(outArgs[1]);
      END;
END;


FUNCTION PasToZero(str: Str255): Handle;
BEGIN
   WITH paramPtr^ DO
      BEGIN
         inArgs[1] := ORD(@str);
         request := xreqPasToZero;
         DoJsr(entryPoint);
         PasToZero := Handle(outArgs[1]);
      END;
END;


PROCEDURE ZeroToPas(zeroStr: Ptr; VAR pasStr: Str255);
BEGIN
   WITH paramPtr^ DO
      BEGIN
         inArgs[1] := ORD(zeroStr);
         inArgs[2] := ORD(@pasStr);
         request := xreqZeroToPas;
         DoJsr(entryPoint);
      END;
END;
```

```
FUNCTION StrToLong(str: Str31): LongInt;
BEGIN
   WITH paramPtr^ DO
     BEGIN
        inArgs[1] := ORD(@str);
        request := xreqStrToLong;
        DoJsr(entryPoint);
        StrToLong := outArgs[1];
     END;
END;


FUNCTION StrToNum(str: Str31): LongInt;
BEGIN
   WITH paramPtr^ DO
     BEGIN
        inArgs[1] := ORD(@str);
        request := xreqStrToNum;
        DoJsr(entryPoint);
        StrToNum := outArgs[1];
     END;
END;


FUNCTION StrToBool(str: Str31): BOOLEAN;
BEGIN
   WITH paramPtr^ DO
     BEGIN
        inArgs[1] := ORD(@str);
        request := xreqStrToBool;
        DoJsr(entryPoint);
        StrToBool := BOOLEAN(outArgs[1]);
     END;
END;


FUNCTION StrToExt(str: Str31): Extended;
VAR x: Extended;
BEGIN
   WITH paramPtr^ DO
     BEGIN
        inArgs[1] := ORD(@str);
        inArgs[2] := ORD(@x);
        request := xreqStrToExt;
        DoJsr(entryPoint);
        StrToExt := x;
     END;
END;
```

```
FUNCTION LongToStr(posNum: LongInt): Str31;
VAR str: Str31;
BEGIN
   WITH paramPtr^ DO
      BEGIN
         inArgs[1] := posNum;
         inArgs[2] := ORD(@str);
         request := xreqLongToStr;
         DoJsr(entryPoint);
         LongToStr := str;
      END;
END;



FUNCTION NumToStr(num: LongInt): Str31;
VAR str: Str31;
BEGIN
   WITH paramPtr^ DO
      BEGIN
         inArgs[1] := num;
         inArgs[2] := ORD(@str);
         request := xreqNumToStr;
         DoJsr(entryPoint);
         NumToStr := str;
      END;
END;



FUNCTION NumToHex(num: LongInt; nDigits: INTEGER): Str31;
VAR str: Str31;
BEGIN
   WITH paramPtr^ DO
      BEGIN
         inArgs[1] := num;
         inArgs[2] := nDigits;
         inArgs[3] := ORD(@str);
         request := xreqNumToHex;
         DoJsr(entryPoint);
         NumToHex := str;
      END;
END;
```

```
FUNCTION ExtToStr(num: Extended): Str31;
VAR str: Str31;
BEGIN
   WITH paramPtr^ DO
     BEGIN
        inArgs[1] := ORD(@num);
        inArgs[2] := ORD(@str);
        request := xreqExtToStr;
        DoJsr(entryPoint);
        ExtToStr := str;
     END;
END;


FUNCTION BoolToStr(bool: BOOLEAN): Str31;
VAR str: Str31;
BEGIN
   WITH paramPtr^ DO
     BEGIN
        inArgs[1] := LongInt(bool);
        inArgs[2] := ORD(@str);
        request := xreqBoolToStr;
        DoJsr(entryPoint);
        BoolToStr := str;
     END;
END;


PROCEDURE SendCardMessage(msg: Str255);
BEGIN
   WITH paramPtr^ DO
     BEGIN
        inArgs[1] := ORD(@msg);
        request := xreqSendCardMessage;
        DoJsr(entryPoint);
     END;
END;


PROCEDURE SendHCMessage(msg: Str255);
BEGIN
   WITH paramPtr^ DO
     BEGIN
        inArgs[1] := ORD(@msg);
        request := xreqSendHCMessage;
        DoJsr(entryPoint);
     END;
END;
```

```
FUNCTION EvalExpr(expr: Str255): Handle;
BEGIN
   WITH paramPtr^ DO
      BEGIN
         inArgs[1] := ORD(@expr);
         request := xreqEvalExpr;
         DoJsr(entryPoint);
         EvalExpr := Handle(outArgs[1]);
      END;
END;


FUNCTION StringLength(strPtr: Ptr): LongInt;
BEGIN
   WITH paramPtr^ DO
      BEGIN
         inArgs[1] := ORD(strPtr);
         request := xreqStringLength;
         DoJsr(entryPoint);
         StringLength := outArgs[1];
      END;
END;


FUNCTION GetGlobal(globName: Str255): Handle;
BEGIN
   WITH paramPtr^ DO
      BEGIN
         inArgs[1] := ORD(@globName);
         request := xreqGetGlobal;
         DoJsr(entryPoint);
         GetGlobal := Handle(outArgs[1]);
      END;
END;


PROCEDURE SetGlobal(globName: Str255; globValue: Handle);
BEGIN
   WITH paramPtr^ DO
      BEGIN
         inArgs[1] := ORD(@globName);
         inArgs[2] := ORD(globValue);
         request := xreqSetGlobal;
         DoJsr(entryPoint);
      END;
END;
```

```
FUNCTION GetFieldByName(cardFieldFlag: BOOLEAN; fieldName: Str255): Handle;
BEGIN
   WITH paramPtr^ DO
     BEGIN
        inArgs[1] := ORD(cardFieldFlag);
        inArgs[2] := ORD(@fieldName);
        request := xreqGetFieldByName;
        DoJsr(entryPoint);
        GetFieldByName := Handle(outArgs[1]);
     END;
END;


FUNCTION GetFieldByNum(cardFieldFlag: BOOLEAN; fieldNum: INTEGER): Handle;
BEGIN
   WITH paramPtr^ DO
     BEGIN
        inArgs[1] := ORD(cardFieldFlag);
        inArgs[2] := fieldNum;
        request := xreqGetFieldByNum;
        DoJsr(entryPoint);
        GetFieldByNum := Handle(outArgs[1]);
     END;
END;


FUNCTION GetFieldByID(cardFieldFlag: BOOLEAN; fieldID: INTEGER): Handle;
BEGIN
   WITH paramPtr^ DO
     BEGIN
        inArgs[1] := ORD(cardFieldFlag);
        inArgs[2] := fieldID;
        request := xreqGetFieldByID;
        DoJsr(entryPoint);
        GetFieldByID := Handle(outArgs[1]);
     END;
END;
```

```
PROCEDURE SetFieldByName(cardFieldFlag: BOOLEAN; fieldName: Str255; fieldVal: Handle);
BEGIN
    WITH paramPtr^ DO
      BEGIN
        inArgs[1] := ORD(cardFieldFlag);
        inArgs[2] := ORD(@fieldName);
        inArgs[3] := ORD(fieldVal);
        request := xreqSetFieldByName;
        DoJsr(entryPoint);
      END;
END;


PROCEDURE SetFieldByNum(cardFieldFlag: BOOLEAN; fieldNum: INTEGER; fieldVal: Handle);
BEGIN
    WITH paramPtr^ DO
      BEGIN
        inArgs[1] := ORD(cardFieldFlag);
        inArgs[2] := fieldNum;
        inArgs[3] := ORD(fieldVal);
        request := xreqSetFieldByNum;
        DoJsr(entryPoint);
      END;
END;


PROCEDURE SetFieldByID(cardFieldFlag: BOOLEAN; fieldID: INTEGER; fieldVal: Handle);
BEGIN
    WITH paramPtr^ DO
      BEGIN
        inArgs[1] := ORD(cardFieldFlag);
        inArgs[2] := fieldID;
        inArgs[3] := ORD(fieldVal);
        request := xreqSetFieldByID;
        DoJsr(entryPoint);
      END;
END;


FUNCTION StringEqual(str1,str2: Str255): BOOLEAN;
BEGIN
    WITH paramPtr^ DO
      BEGIN
        inArgs[1] := ORD(@str1);
        inArgs[2] := ORD(@str2);
        request := xreqStringEqual;
        DoJsr(entryPoint);
        StringEqual := BOOLEAN(outArgs[1]);
      END;
END;
```

```
PROCEDURE ReturnToPas(zeroStr: Ptr; VAR pasStr: Str255);
BEGIN
   WITH paramPtr^ DO
     BEGIN
        inArgs[1] := ORD(zeroStr);
        inArgs[2] := ORD(@pasStr);
        request := xreqReturnToPas;
        DoJsr(entryPoint);
     END;
END;


PROCEDURE ScanToReturn(VAR scanPtr: Ptr);
BEGIN
   WITH paramPtr^ DO
     BEGIN
        inArgs[1] := ORD(@scanPtr);
        request := xreqScanToReturn;
        DoJsr(entryPoint);
     END;
END;


PROCEDURE ScanToZero(VAR scanPtr: Ptr);
BEGIN
   WITH paramPtr^ DO
     BEGIN
        inArgs[1] := ORD(@scanPtr);
        request := xreqScanToZero;
        DoJsr(entryPoint);
     END;
END;


PROCEDURE ZeroBytes(dstPtr: Ptr; longCount: LongInt);
BEGIN
   WITH paramPtr^ DO
     BEGIN
        inArgs[1] := ORD(dstPtr);
        inArgs[2] := longCount;
        request := xreqZeroBytes;
        DoJsr(entryPoint);
     END;
END;
```

Glue routines in MPW C

The glue routines in MPW C follow:

```
/*
 *    XCmdGlue.c     - Implementation of HyperTalk callback routines
 *                   - Copyright Apple Computer, Inc. 1987,1988.
 *                   - All Rights Reserved.
 *
 *    #include "HyperXCmd.h" before your program.
 *    #include this file after your code.
 *
 */


pascal void SendCardMessage(paramPtr,msg)
     XCmdBlockPtr   paramPtr;       StringPtr      msg;
     /* Send a HyperCard message (a command with arguments) to the current card.
        msg is a pointer to a Pascal format string.  */
{
     paramPtr->inArgs[0] = (long)msg;
     paramPtr->request = xreqSendCardMessage;
     paramPtr->entryPoint();
}



pascal Handle EvalExpr(paramPtr,expr)
     XCmdBlockPtr paramPtr;         StringPtr      expr;
     /* Evaluate a HyperCard expression and return the answer.  The answer is
        a handle to a zero-terminated string. */
{
     paramPtr->inArgs[0] = (long)expr;
     paramPtr->request = xreqEvalExpr;
    paramPtr->entryPoint();
     return (Handle)paramPtr->outArgs[0];
}
```

```
pascal long StringLength(paramPtr,strPtr)
     XCmdBlockPtr paramPtr;          StringPtr        strPtr;
/* Count the characters from where strPtr points until the next zero byte.
   Does not count the zero itself.  strPtr must be a zero-terminated string. */
{
     paramPtr->inArgs[0] = (long)strPtr;
     paramPtr->request = xreqStringLength;
    paramPtr->entryPoint();
     return (long)paramPtr->outArgs[0];
}


pascal Ptr StringMatch(paramPtr,pattern,target)
     XCmdBlockPtr paramPtr;          StringPtr       pattern;     Ptr target;
/* Perform case-insensitive match looking for pattern anywhere in
   target, returning a pointer to first character of the first match,
   in target or NIL if no match found.  pattern is a Pascal string,
   and target is a zero-terminated string. */
{
     paramPtr->inArgs[0] = (long)pattern;
     paramPtr->inArgs[1] = (long)target;
     paramPtr->request = xreqStringMatch;
    paramPtr->entryPoint();
     return (Ptr)paramPtr->outArgs[0];
}


pascal void SendHCMessage(paramPtr,msg)
     XCmdBlockPtr paramPtr;          StringPtr        msg;
     /* Send a HyperCard message (a command with arguments) to HyperCard.
        msg is a pointer to a Pascal format string.  */
{
     paramPtr->inArgs[0] = (long)msg;
     paramPtr->request = xreqSendHCMessage;
    paramPtr->entryPoint();
}
```

```
pascal void ZeroBytes(paramPtr,dstPtr,longCount)
     XCmdBlockPtr paramPtr;       Ptr dstPtr;   long      longCount;
/* Write zeros into memory starting at destPtr and going for longCount
   number of bytes. */
{
     paramPtr->inArgs[0] = (long)dstPtr;
     paramPtr->inArgs[1] = longCount;
     paramPtr->request = xreqZeroBytes;
    paramPtr->entryPoint();
}



pascal Handle PasToZero(paramPtr,pasStr)
     XCmdBlockPtr  paramPtr;      StringPtr      pasStr;
/* Convert a Pascal string to a zero-terminated string.  Returns a handle
   to a new zero-terminated string.  The caller must dispose the handle.
   You'll need to do this for any result or argument you send from
   your XCMD to HyperTalk. */
{
     paramPtr->inArgs[0] = (long)pasStr;
     paramPtr->request = xreqPasToZero;
    paramPtr->entryPoint();
     return (Handle)paramPtr->outArgs[0];
}



pascal void ZeroToPas(paramPtr,zeroStr,pasStr)
     XCmdBlockPtr paramPtr;       char     *zeroStr;      StringPtr      pasStr;
/* Fill the Pascal string with the contents of the zero-terminated
   string.  You create the Pascal string and pass it in as a VAR
   parameter.  Useful for converting the arguments of any XCMD to
   Pascal strings. */
{
     paramPtr->inArgs[0] = (long)zeroStr;
     paramPtr->inArgs[1] = (long)pasStr;
     paramPtr->request = xreqZeroToPas;
    paramPtr->entryPoint();
}
```

```
pascal long StrToLong(paramPtr,strPtr)
    XCmdBlockPtr    paramPtr;        Str31 *         strPtr;
/* Convert a string of ASCII decimal digits to an unsigned long integer. */
{
    paramPtr->inArgs[0] = (long)strPtr;
    paramPtr->request = xreqStrToLong;
   paramPtr->entryPoint();
    return (long)paramPtr->outArgs[0];
}


pascal long StrToNum(paramPtr,str)
    XCmdBlockPtr    paramPtr;        Str31 *         str;
/* Convert a string of ASCII decimal digits to a signed long integer.
   Negative sign is allowed. */
{
    paramPtr->inArgs[0] = (long)str;
    paramPtr->request = xreqStrToNum;
   paramPtr->entryPoint();
    return paramPtr->outArgs[0];
}


pascal Boolean StrToBool(paramPtr,str)
    XCmdBlockPtr    paramPtr;        Str31 *         str;
/* Convert the Pascal strings 'true' and 'false' to booleans. */
{
    paramPtr->inArgs[0] = (long)str;
    paramPtr->request = xreqStrToBool;
   paramPtr->entryPoint();
    return (Boolean)paramPtr->outArgs[0];
}


pascal void StrToExt(paramPtr,str,myext)
    XCmdBlockPtr    paramPtr;        Str31 *         str;        extended *      myext;
 /* Convert a string of ASCII decimal digits to an extended long integer.
    Instead of returning a new extended, as Pascal does, it expects you
    to create myext and pass it in to be filled. */
{
    paramPtr->inArgs[0] = (long)str;
    paramPtr->inArgs[1] = (long)myext;
    paramPtr->request = xreqStrToExt;
   paramPtr->entryPoint();
}
```

```
pascal void LongToStr(paramPtr,posNum,mystr)
     XCmdBlockPtr  paramPtr;       long       posNum;  Str31 *  mystr;
 /* Convert an unsigned long integer to a Pascal string.  Instead of
    returning a new string, as Pascal does, it expects you to
    create mystr and pass it in to be filled. */
{
     paramPtr->inArgs[0] = (long)posNum;
     paramPtr->inArgs[1] = (long)mystr;
     paramPtr->request = xreqLongToStr;
    paramPtr->entryPoint();
}


pascal void NumToStr(paramPtr,num,mystr)
     XCmdBlockPtr  paramPtr;       long       num;     Str31 *  mystr;
 /* Convert a signed long integer to a Pascal string.  Instead of
    returning a new string, as Pascal does, it expects you to
    create mystr and pass it in to be filled. */
{
     paramPtr->inArgs[0] = num;
     paramPtr->inArgs[1] = (long)mystr;
     paramPtr->request = xreqNumToStr;
    paramPtr->entryPoint();
}


pascal void NumToHex(paramPtr,num,nDigits,mystr)
     XCmdBlockPtr  paramPtr;       long       num;
     short nDigits;       Str31 * mystr;
/* Convert an unsigned long integer to a hexadecimal number and put it
   into a Pascal string.  Instead of returning a new string, as
   Pascal does, it expects you to create mystr and pass it in to be filled. */
{
     paramPtr->inArgs[0] = num;
     paramPtr->inArgs[1] = nDigits;
     paramPtr->inArgs[2] = (long)mystr;
     paramPtr->request = xreqNumToHex;
    paramPtr->entryPoint();
}
```

```
pascal void BoolToStr(paramPtr,bool,mystr)
    XCmdBlockPtr  paramPtr;     Boolean  bool;    Str31 *  mystr;
 /* Convert a boolean to 'true' or 'false'.  Instead of returning
    a new string, as Pascal does, it expects you to create mystr
    and pass it in to be filled. */
{
    paramPtr->inArgs[0] = (long)bool;
    paramPtr->inArgs[1] = (long)mystr;
    paramPtr->request = xreqBoolToStr;
  paramPtr->entryPoint();
}



pascal void ExtToStr(paramPtr,myext,mystr)
    XCmdBlockPtr  paramPtr;      extended *   myext;   Str31 *  mystr;
 /* Convert an extended long integer to decimal digits in a string.
    Instead of returning a new string, as Pascal does, it expects
    you to create mystr and pass it in to be filled. */
{
    paramPtr->inArgs[0] = (long)myext;
    paramPtr->inArgs[1] = (long)mystr;
    paramPtr->request = xreqExtToStr;
  paramPtr->entryPoint();
}



pascal Handle GetGlobal(paramPtr,globName)
    XCmdBlockPtr  paramPtr;      StringPtr     globName;
/* Return a handle to a zero-terminated string containing the value of
   the specified HyperTalk global variable. */
{
    paramPtr->inArgs[0] = (long)globName;
    paramPtr->request = xreqGetGlobal;
  paramPtr->entryPoint();
    return (Handle)paramPtr->outArgs[0];
}
```

```
pascal void SetGlobal(paramPtr,globName,globValue)
    XCmdBlockPtr    paramPtr;        StringPtr        globName;        Handle        globValue;
/* Set the value of the specified HyperTalk global variable to be
   the zero-terminated string in globValue.  The contents of the
   Handle are copied, so you must still dispose it afterwards.  */
{
    paramPtr->inArgs[0] = (long)globName;
    paramPtr->inArgs[1] = (long)globValue;
    paramPtr->request = xreqSetGlobal;
   paramPtr->entryPoint();
}


pascal Handle GetFieldByName(paramPtr,cardFieldFlag,fieldName)
    XCmdBlockPtr    paramPtr;        Boolean    cardFieldFlag;
    StringPtr fieldName;
/* Return a handle to a zero-terminated string containing the value of
   field fieldName on the current card.  You must dispose the handle. */
{
    paramPtr->inArgs[0] = (long)cardFieldFlag;
    paramPtr->inArgs[1] = (long)fieldName;
    paramPtr->request = xreqGetFieldByName;
   paramPtr->entryPoint();
    return (Handle)paramPtr->outArgs[0];
}


pascal Handle GetFieldByNum(paramPtr,cardFieldFlag,fieldNum)
    XCmdBlockPtr    paramPtr;        Boolean    cardFieldFlag;
    short      fieldNum;
/* Return a handle to a zero-terminated string containing the value of
   field fieldNum on the current card.  You must dispose the handle. */
{
    paramPtr->inArgs[0] = (long)cardFieldFlag;
    paramPtr->inArgs[1] = fieldNum;
    paramPtr->request = xreqGetFieldByNum;
   paramPtr->entryPoint();
    return (Handle)paramPtr->outArgs[0];
}
```

```
pascal Handle GetFieldByID(paramPtr,cardFieldFlag,fieldID)
    XCmdBlockPtr  paramPtr;    Boolean  cardFieldFlag;
    short     fieldID;
/* Return a handle to a zero-terminated string containing the value of
   the field whise ID is fieldID.  You must dispose the handle. */
{
    paramPtr->inArgs[0] = (long)cardFieldFlag;
    paramPtr->inArgs[1] = fieldID;
    paramPtr->request = xreqGetFieldByID;
   paramPtr->entryPoint();
    return (Handle)paramPtr->outArgs[0];
}


pascal void SetFieldByName(paramPtr,cardFieldFlag,fieldName,fieldVal)
    XCmdBlockPtr  paramPtr;    Boolean  cardFieldFlag;
    StringPtr fieldName;   Handle    fieldVal;
/* Set the value of field fieldName to be the zero-terminated string
   in fieldVal.  The contents of the Handle are copied, so you must
   still dispose it afterwards. */
{
    paramPtr->inArgs[0] = (long)cardFieldFlag;
    paramPtr->inArgs[1] = (long)fieldName;
    paramPtr->inArgs[2] = (long)fieldVal;
    paramPtr->request = xreqSetFieldByName;
   paramPtr->entryPoint();
}


pascal void SetFieldByNum(paramPtr,cardFieldFlag,fieldNum,fieldVal)
    XCmdBlockPtr  paramPtr;    Boolean  cardFieldFlag;
    short     fieldNum;        Handle    fieldVal;
/* Set the value of field fieldNum to be the zero-terminated string
   in fieldVal.  The contents of the Handle are copied, so you must
   still dispose it afterwards. */
{
    paramPtr->inArgs[0] = (long)cardFieldFlag;
    paramPtr->inArgs[1] = fieldNum;
    paramPtr->inArgs[2] = (long)fieldVal;
    paramPtr->request = xreqSetFieldByNum;
   paramPtr->entryPoint();
}
```

```
pascal void SetFieldByID(paramPtr,cardFieldFlag,fieldID,fieldVal)
    XCmdBlockPtr   paramPtr;      Boolean   cardFieldFlag;
    short     fieldID;           Handle    fieldVal;
/* Set the value of the field whose ID is fieldID to be the zero-
   terminated string in fieldVal.  The contents of the Handle are
   copied, so you must still dispose it afterwards. */
{
    paramPtr->inArgs[0] = (long)cardFieldFlag;
    paramPtr->inArgs[1] = fieldID;
    paramPtr->inArgs[2] = (long)fieldVal;
    paramPtr->request = xreqSetFieldByID;
   paramPtr->entryPoint();
}



pascal Boolean StringEqual(paramPtr,str1,str2)
    XCmdBlockPtr   paramPtr;      Str31 *      str1;    Str31 *      str2;
/* Return true if the two strings have the same characters.
   Case insensitive compare of the strings. */
{
    paramPtr->inArgs[0] = (long)str1;
    paramPtr->inArgs[1] = (long)str2;
    paramPtr->request = xreqStringEqual;
   paramPtr->entryPoint();
    return (Boolean)paramPtr->outArgs[0];
}
```

```
pascal void ReturnToPas(paramPtr,zeroStr,passStr)
    XCmdBlockPtr    paramPtr;        Ptr zeroStr;        StringPtr        passStr;
/* zeroStr points into a zero-terminated string.  Collect the
   characters from there to the next carriage Return and return
   them in the Pascal string passStr.  If a Return is not found,
   collect chars until the end of the string. */
{
    paramPtr->inArgs[0] = (long)zeroStr;
    paramPtr->inArgs[1] = (long)passStr;
    paramPtr->request = xreqReturnToPas;
   paramPtr->entryPoint();
}



pascal void ScanToReturn(paramPtr,scanHndl)
    XCmdBlockPtr    paramPtr;        Ptr *      scanHndl;
/* Move the pointer scanPtr along a zero-terminated
   string until it points at a Return character
   or a zero byte.   */
{
    paramPtr->inArgs[0] = (long)scanHndl;
    paramPtr->request = xreqScanToReturn;
   paramPtr->entryPoint();
}



pascal void ScanToZero(paramPtr,scanHndl)
    XCmdBlockPtr    paramPtr;        Ptr *      scanHndl;
/* Move the pointer scanPtr along a zero-terminated
   string until it points at a zero byte.   */
{
    paramPtr->inArgs[0] = (long)scanHndl;
    paramPtr->request = xreqScanToZero;
   paramPtr->entryPoint();
}
```

Attaching an XCMD or XFCN

To attach an existing XCMD or XFCN (one that has already been compiled or assembled into a resource) to one of your stacks, use a resource editor such as ResEdit. The following steps describe the procedure using ResEdit:

1. Launch ResEdit.

2. Select and open the stack containing the 'XCMD' or 'XFCN' resource you want.

3. Select and open the resource type of 'XCMD' or 'XFCN'.

4. Select and open the particular resource you want by name.

5. Press Command-C to copy the resource.

6. Select and open the stack you want to paste the resource into.

7. If your stack has no resource fork, ResEdit will display a dialog box asking if you want to open one. Click OK. ResEdit will open a window.

8. Press Command-V to paste the resource into your stack.

9. Click the close box on the window. When ResEdit asks if you want to save the file, click Yes.

10. Quit ResEdit.

HyperCard Developer's Toolkit

A disk containing the MPW Pascal and C definition and glue files described in this appendix is available from APDA, the Apple Programmer's and Developer's Association, exclusively to APDA members. You can order the disk and preliminary documentation in a package called the HyperCard Developer's Toolkit.

For membership and ordering information contact:

Apple Programmer's and Developer's Association
290 SW 43rd Street
Renton, WA 98055
Telephone: (206) 251-6548

Appendix B

ControlKey Parameters

This appendix lists the parameter variable values generated by HyperCard in response to different keys pressed in combination with the Control key.

When you press the Control key in combination with another key, HyperCard sends the system message `controlKey` to the current card with one integer parameter value:

`controlKey` *var*

The message can be intercepted by a handler placed anywhere in the object hierarchy between the current card and HyperCard. For example, the following handler causes the Control-P key combination to print the current card:

```
on controlKey whichKey
  if whichKey = 16 then
    doMenu "Print Card"
    exit controlKey
  end if
  pass controlKey
end controlKey
```

The `controlKey` system message is listed in Chapter 6.

Table B-1 lists the parameter values generated by various keys of the Apple Extended Keyboard pressed in combination with the Control key. Parameter values 1 through 31 represent American Standard Code for Information Interchange (ASCII) character code values for combinations of the Control key and letter keys. Some of the parameter values can be generated by more than one key. The parameter value is not affected by pressing the Shift key along with the Control key and the other key.

Table B-1
ControlKey message parameter values

Parameter value	Key(s)	Parameter value	Key(s)
1	a, Home	27	Esc, Clear, Left-bracket ([ )
2	b	28	Backslash (\), Left Arrow
3	c, Enter	29	Right bracket ( ]), Right Arrow
4	d, End	30	Up Arrow
5	e, Help	31	Hyphen (-), Down Arrow
6	f	39	Single Quotation Mark (')
7	g	42	Asterisk (*)
8	h, Delete	43	Plus (+)
9	i, Tab	44	Comma (,)
10	j	45	Minus (−)
11	k, Page Up	46	Period (.)
12	l, Page Down	47	Slash (/)
13	m, Return	48	0
14	n	49	1
15	o	50	2
16	p, all function keys	51	3
17	q	52	4
18	r	53	5
19	s	54	6
20	t	55	7
21	u	56	8
22	v	57	9
23	w	59	Semicolon (;)
24	x	61	Equal (=)
25	y	96	Tilde (~)
26	z	127	Forward Delete

Appendix C

Extended ASCII Table

This appendix lists the character assignments for the 256 single-byte character values used by Macintosh.

There are 256 possible 8-bit binary values, from 00000000 to 11111111. Of these, the first 128 (from 00000000 to 01111111) have been assigned to a standard set of characters and commands used in data processing and communication. These assignments form the ASCII character set. (*ASCII* stands for *American Standard Code for Information Interchange.*)

The remaining 128 binary values, those for which the most significant bit (first digit) is 1 instead of 0, are not assigned in the ASCII standard. Because they have higher numerical values that the first 128 characters, they are often referred to as high-ASCII characters.

This appendix lists all character values by their decimal equivalent.

Table C-1 lists the first 32 characters, the Control characters, which have no printable-character representation, with the standard abbreviation for each and its meaning.

Table C-1
Control character assignments

Value	Name	Meaning	Value	Name	Meaning
0	NUL	Null	16	DLE	Data link escape
1	SOH	Start of heading	17	DC1	Device control 1
2	STX	Start of text	18	DC2	Device control 2
3	ETX	End of text	19	DC3	Device control 3
4	EOT	End of transmission	20	DC4	Device control 4
5	ENQ	Enquiry	21	NAK	Negative acknowledge
6	ACK	Acknowledge	22	SYN	Synchronous idle
7	BEL	Bell	23	ETB	End of transmission block
8	BS	Backspace	24	CAN	Cancel
9	HT	Horizontal tab	25	EM	End of medium
10	LF	Line feed	26	SUB	Substitute
11	VT	Vertical tab	27	ESC	Escape
12	FF	Form feed	28	FS	File separator
13	CR	Carriage return	29	GS	Group separator
14	SO	Shift out	30	RS	Record separator
15	SI	Shift in	31	US	Unit separator

Table C-2 lists the remaining 224 character values with the characters to which they are assigned in the Macintosh Courier font.

Table C-2
Character assignments in Macintosh Courier font

Value	Character	Value	Character	Value	Character	Value	Character	Value	Character
32	SPACE	77	M	122	z	167	ß	212	`
33	!	78	N	123	{	168	®	213	´
34	"	79	O	124	|	169	©	214	÷
35	#	80	P	125	}	170	™	215	◊
36	$	81	Q	126	~	171	´	216	ÿ
37	%	82	R	127	DEL	172	¨	217	Ÿ
38	&	83	S	128	Ä	173	≠	218	⁄
39	'	84	T	129	Å	174	Æ	219	¤
40	(	85	U	130	Ç	175	Ø	220	‹
41	)	86	V	131	É	176	∞	221	›
42	*	87	W	132	Ñ	177	±	222	fi
43	+	88	X	133	Ö	178	≤	223	fl
44	,	89	Y	134	Ü	179	≥	224	‡
45	-	90	Z	135	á	180	¥	225	·
46	.	91	[	136	à	181	µ	226	‚
47	/	92	\	137	â	182	∂	227	„
48	0	93	]	138	ä	183	Σ	228	‰
49	1	94	^	139	ã	184	∏	229	Â
50	2	95	_	140	å	185	π	230	Ê
51	3	96	`	141	ç	186	∫	231	Á
52	4	97	a	142	é	187	ª	232	Ë
53	5	98	b	143	è	188	º	233	È
54	6	99	c	144	ê	189	Ω	234	Í
55	7	100	d	145	ë	190	æ	235	Î
56	8	101	e	146	í	191	ø	236	Ï
57	9	102	f	147	ì	192	¿	237	Ì
58	:	103	g	148	î	193	¡	238	Ó
59	;	104	h	149	ï	194	¬	239	Ô
60	<	105	i	150	ñ	195	√	240	(apple)
61	=	106	j	151	ó	196	ƒ	241	Ò
62	>	107	k	152	ò	197	≈	242	Ú
63	?	108	l	153	ô	198	∆	243	Û
64	@	109	m	154	ö	199	«	244	Ù
65	A	110	n	155	õ	200	»	245	ı
66	B	111	o	156	ú	201	…	246	^
67	C	112	p	157	ù	202	␣	247	~
68	D	113	q	158	û	203	À	248	-
69	E	114	r	159	ü	204	Ã	249	˘
70	F	115	s	160	†	205	Õ	250	
71	G	116	t	161	°	206	Œ	251	·
72	H	117	u	162	¢	207	œ	252	
73	I	118	v	163	£	208	–	253	˝
74	J	119	w	164	§	209	—	254	
75	K	120	x	165	•	210	"	255	ˇ
76	L	121	y	166	¶	211	"		

␣ Stands for a nonbreaking space

Appendix D

Operator Precedence Table

This appendix shows the order of precedence of HyperTalk's operators. In a complex expression containing more than one operator, HyperCard performs the operation indicated by operators with lower-numbered precedence before those with higher-numbered precedence. Operators of equal precedence are evaluated left-to-right, except for exponentiation, which goes right-to-left. If you use parentheses, HyperCard evaluates the innermost parenthetical expression first.

Chapter 4 discusses expression evaluation.

Table D-1
Operator precedence

Order	Operators	Type of operator
1	( )	Grouping
2	−	Minus sign for numbers
	not	Logical negation for Boolean values
3	^	Exponentiation for numbers
4	* / div mod	Multiplication and division for numbers
5	+ −	Addition and subtraction for numbers
6	& &&	Concatenation of text
7	> < <= >= ≤ ≥	Comparison for numbers or text
	is in contains	Comparison for text
	is not in	Comparison for text
8	= is is not <> ≠	Comparison for numbers or text
9	and	Logical for Boolean values
10	or	Logical for Boolean values

Appendix E

HyperCard Limits

This appendix lists various minimum and maximum sizes and numbers of elements defined in HyperCard.

The maximum limits shown in this appendix are theoretical. Some of them are lower in practice. For example, HyperCard currently brings an entire card into memory at once, so the maximum size of a card is limited by available memory. It's possible that a card with a lot of text and long scripts, created while running HyperCard on a Macintosh with 2 megabytes of RAM, would not be able to be opened on a Macintosh with 1 megabyte. The current useful size of a card (or background) is therefore between 50 and 100 kilobytes.

The term *part*, in this appendix and internally in HyperCard, refers to buttons or fields. The value represented by `LongInt` is 2,147,483,647; the value represented by `Integer` is 32,767.

The figures listed in this appendix pertain to version 1.2 of HyperCard; some of them may change in future versions.

Table E-1
HyperCard limits

Item	Limit
Stack limits	
Stack size	512 megabytes
Minimum stack size	4896 bytes
Maximum total number of bitmaps, cards and backgrounds per stack	16,777,216
Maximum stack name size	31 characters
Maximum stack script size	30,000 characters

Background limits

Background size (bytes)	LongInt*
Minimum background size	64 bytes
Maximum parts per background	Integer
Maximum total part size per background (bytes)	LongInt
Maximum background name size	31 characters
Maximum background script size	30,000 characters

Card limits

Card size (bytes)	LongInt*
Minimum card size	64 bytes
Maximum parts per card	Integer
Maximum total part size per card (bytes)	LongInt
Maximum total text size per card (bytes)	LongInt
Maximum card name size	31 characters
Maximum card script size	30,000 characters

Bitmap limit

Largest possible bitmap size	44 kilobytes

Part (button or field) limits

Part size (bytes)	Integer**
Minimum overhead per part	30 bytes
Maximum part name size	31 characters
Maximum part text size	30,000 characters
Maximum part script size	30,000 characters

HyperTalk limits

Maximum nested `repeat` structures	32
Maximum active variables (all pending handlers)	512
Maximum size card name with `go` command	31 characters
Maximum variable name size	31 characters
Maximum number format size	31 characters
Maximum size of command with arguments	254 characters
Maximum handler name size	254 characters
Maximum file I/O buffer size	16,384 bytes
Maximum script size	30,000 characters
Maximum variable value size	Limited by available memory

* Limited by HyperCard stack size; less than 100 kilobytes for practical use.

** The sum of the other elements in the button or field must be less than the part size.

Appendix F

HyperTalk Changes in HyperCard Version 1.2

This appendix explains the differences in HyperTalk introduced with HyperCard version 1.2.

All versions of HyperCard are backward compatible; that is, scripts written for any version of HyperCard will continue to work with later versions. You can ensure that your scripts are using the version of HyperCard they require by including a check of the value returned by the `version` function, described in Chapter 8 (see also enhancements to the `version` function, described in this appendix).

New system messages

HyperCard version 1.2 includes two new HyperTalk system messages, both of which are sent initially to a field. The messages are shown in Table F-1.

Table F-1
New system messages

Message	Meaning
enterInField	Sent to a field when the Enter key is pressed while there is an insertion point or selection in the field. If `enterInField` is not intercepted by a handler and the contents of the field have been changed, HyperCard sends the `closeField` message, as described in Chapter 6.
returnInField	Sent to a field when the Return key is pressed while there is an insertion point or selection in the field. In response to a

returnInField message, HyperCard sends a tabKey message to the field if the following conditions are true:

□ returnInField is not intercepted by a handler

□ the field is not a scrolling field

□ the insertion point or selection is on the last line

□ the field's autoTab property (described in this appendix) is true

Otherwise, HyperCard inserts a return character into the field. The tabKey message, if it's not intercepted, causes HyperCard to place the insertion point in the next field.

New and enhanced commands

HyperCard version 1.2 includes three new HyperTalk commands: lock screen, unlock screen, and select. In addition, three HyperTalk commands have been enhanced: the find command has two new options, and the hide and show commands can operate on the card or background picture.

Lock screen and unlock screen

The lock screen and unlock screen commands have the following syntax:

```
lock screen
unlock screen [with visualEffect]
```

VisualEffect is any of the forms of the visual command described in Chapter 7.

The lock screen command sets the lockScreen global property to true, preventing HyperCard from updating the screen. If you go to another card or do other actions that change the appearance of the screen, those changes are not displayed until the lockScreen property becomes false.

The unlock screen command sets the lockScreen property to false, allowing HyperCard to update the screen. In addition, the with *visualEffect* option specifies a single visual transition that occurs as the screen is updated.

Visual effects can't be compounded using unlock screen, as they can be using the visual command. Visual effects compounded by the visual command are not executed until a go command is encountered. HyperCard flushes unexecuted visual effects and sets lockScreen to false at idle time (in effect, at the end of all pending handlers).

Select

```
select  objectDescriptor
select  [preposition]  chunkExpression of  fieldDescriptor
select  [preposition]  text of  fieldDescriptor
select empty
```

ObjectDescriptor is the descriptor of a button or field, or `me` or `target`; *preposition* is `before` or `after`; and *fieldDescriptor* is the descriptor of a field. (Button and field descriptors and the special descriptor `me` are explained in Chapter 3. The special descriptor `target` is explained in Chapter 2.)

The `select` *objectDescriptor* form chooses the appropriate tool and selects the object specified, as though you had chosen the tool and clicked the object manually with the mouse. The other forms select text in the specified field. `Before` and `after` can be used to place the insertion point relative to the specified text or chunk of text. Using a chunk expression without a preposition selects the entire chunk, highlighting the characters in the chunk. The `select empty` form deselects highlighted text or removes the insertion point. The following lines are examples of the `select` command:

```
select button 1 -- chooses button tool and selects card button 1
select before char 1 of field 2 -- places insertion point at start of field
select after text of field 2 -- places insertion point at end of field
select char 1 to 5 of card field 2 -- selects first five characters of field
```

Find

The new options for the `find` command are invoked by the following forms of syntax in addition to those shown in Chapter 7:

```
find whole expression [in field fieldDesignator]
find string expression [in field fieldDesignator]
```

Expression yields any string of characters, and *fieldDesignator* is a background field name, number, or ID number.

The `find whole` form (also invoked by pressing Shift-Command-F) lets you search for a specific word or phrase, including spaces. For HyperCard to find a match, all the characters must be in the same field, and they must be in the same consecutive order as they appear in the string derived from *expression*.

In the following example, *expression* is a literal, yielding the string of characters between the double quotation marks:

```
find whole "Apple Computer"
```

The example finds a card with a field that has the phrase *Apple Computer* in it; it won't find *Apple Computers* or *This apple is a computer.* (The `find` command without `whole` would find a match in all three cases.) Find `whole` won't find partial-word matches, and it pays no attention to case or diacritical marks: *apple Cømpüter* and *aPPle cOmputer* are seen as the same.

When you use `find` without `whole`, HyperCard finds a card that contains every word in the string derived from *expression,* but the words can appear in different order or in different fields. That is, with `find whole`, interword spaces are part of the search string; without `whole` the spaces delimit separate search strings. With every form of `find`, you can limit the search to a specific background field.

The `find string` form lets you search for a contiguous string of characters, including spaces, regardless of word boundaries. (Find `whole` searches for characters at the beginnings of words.) For HyperCard to find a match, all the characters must be in the same field, and they must be in the same order as in the string derived from *expression.* For strings without spaces, `find string` works the same as `find chars`.

In this example:

```
find string "ple Computer"
```

HyperCard finds the string in *Apple computers* but not in *computers, not apples.* (The `find` command without `string` would not find a match in either case.)

Hide and show

The `hide` and `show` commands in version 1.2 operate on the bitmap pictures on cards and backgrounds, as well as the menu bar, card window, Message box, Tools and Patterns palettes, and buttons and fields, as described in Chapter 7. The syntax for the new forms is:

```
hide card picture
hide picture of cardDescriptor

hide background picture
hide picture of backgroundDescriptor

show card picture
show picture of cardDescriptor

show background picture
show picture of backgroundDescriptor
```

CardDescriptor yields the descriptor of a card in the current stack, and *backgroundDescriptor* yields the descriptor of a background in the current stack, as described in Chapter 3, "Naming Objects."

The `picture` form of the `hide` command removes from view the graphic bitmap on the card or background, and the `picture` form of the `show` command displays it.

Hidden card and background pictures are not displayed when the Browse, Button, or Field tools are chosen, but if you attempt to use a Paint tool manually, a dialog box appears asking if you want to make the picture visible; clicking OK displays the picture. (You can draw on hidden pictures from a script.) Whether or not you are in Edit background mode determines whether your actions pertain to the card or background picture.

The following example,

```
show picture of card 3
```

makes the graphic bitmap of the third card in the current stack visible, setting the card's `showPict` property to `true`. If the picture were visible before you issued the `show picture` command, of course, there would be no effect.

New and enhanced functions

HyperCard version 1.2 has two enhancements to existing functions and nine new functions.

Enhancement to number function

The `number` function has been enhanced by the following form:

```
the number of cards of backgroundDescriptor
```

BackgroundDescriptor yields the descriptor of a background in the current stack, as described in Chapter 3, "Naming Objects."

This form of the `number` function returns the number of cards that are associated with the specified background. For example,

```
get the number of cards of background 3
```

Enhancement to version function

The `version` function has been enhanced by the two following forms:

```
the [long] version [of HyperCard]
the version of stackDescriptor
```

StackDescriptor yields the descriptor of any stack currently available to your Macintosh, as described in Chapter 3, "Naming Objects."

The `long` modifier, when used with the `version [of HyperCard]` form, returns the standard Macintosh version resource format (see *Inside Macintosh* for details). For example,

```
put the long version -- returns 01208000 for HyperCard version 1.2
```

The `version of` *stackDescriptor* form returns a five-item string including the following items:

☐ the version of HyperCard that created the stack

☐ the version of HyperCard last used to compact the stack

☐ the oldest version of HyperCard that changed the stack since it was last compacted

☐ the version of HyperCard that last changed the stack

☐ the date when the stack was most recently modified and closed (in seconds since midnight, January 1, 1904)

All versions are returned in the `long` form, and the version numbers are separated by commas. Items 1 through 4 are set to 00000000 if the version of HyperCard is less than 1.2. For example, if `old stack` were created with HyperCard version 1.1, then edited and compacted with version 1.2,

```
put the version of stack "old stack"
```

would put the following value in the Message box:

```
00000000,01208000,01208000,01208000,2660687462
```

You can use the `convert` command, described in Chapter 7, to change item 5 into a more readable format.

Functions for found text

```
the foundText
the foundChunk
the foundLine
the foundField
```

These functions return information about text found by the `find` command. The `foundText` function returns the characters that are enclosed in the box after the `find` command has executed successfully; for example, the commands

```
find "Hyper"
put the foundText
```

would put `HyperCard` in the Message box if it were the word containing the matching string. The `foundChunk` function returns a chunk expression describing the location of the text in the box; for example, if field 1 contained *Now is the time,* the commands

```
find "Now"
put the foundChunk
```

would put `char 1 to 3 of bkgnd field 1` into the Message box. The `foundLine` function returns a chunk expression describing the line in which the beginning of the text was found, in a form such as `line 1 of card field 2`. The `foundField` function returns the descriptor of the field in which the text was found, in a form such as `card field 2`.

Functions for selected text

```
the selectedText
the selectedChunk
the selectedLine
the selectedField
```

These functions return information about text that is currently selected. The `selectedText` function returns the selected text itself. The `selectedChunk` function returns a chunk expression describing the location of the selected text, the `selectedLine` returns a chunk expression describing the line containing the selected text, and the `selectedField` returns the descriptor of the field containing the selected text. The forms of the expressions returned by these functions are like those returned by the functions for found text, described in the previous section.

ScreenRect function

```
the screenRect
screenRect()
```

The `screenRect` function returns the rectangle of the screen in which HyperCard's menu bar is displayed; the value returned is four integers, separated by commas, representing the pixel offsets of the left, top, right, and bottom edges, respectively, from the top-left corner of the screen.

See also "Properties of screen rectangles," in the next section.

New and enhanced properties

HyperCard version 1.2 has five new HyperTalk properties: `autoTab`, `cantDelete`, `cantModify`, `showPict`, and `userModify`. All five properties can have values of `true` or `false`. In addition, version 1.2 has an enhanced `cursor` global property and eight new ways to specify aspects of the screen rectangles of buttons, fields, and windows.

AutoTab

```
set autoTab of field 3 to true
```

The `autoTab` property pertains to any nonscrolling field in the current stack. When `autoTab` is `true`, pressing Return with the insertion point in the last line of that field moves the insertion point to the next field on that card by sending the `tabKey` message to the current card.

(Normal tabbing order is followed: if the field you're leaving is a card field, the insertion point moves to the next higher-numbered card field or to the lowest-numbered background field if no higher-numbered card field exists; if the field you're leaving is a background field, the insertion point moves to the next higher-numbered background field or to the lowest-numbered card field if no higher-numbered background field exists.)

The `autoTab` property can also be set by clicking the Auto Tab check box in the Field Info dialog box of the nonscrolling field.

CantDelete

```
set cantDelete of this card to true
```

The `cantDelete` property pertains to any card or background in the current stack, or to any stack accessible to your Macintosh. It controls whether or not the user can delete the specified card, background, or stack. This property checks or unchecks the "Can't delete" option in the object Info dialog box of the specified object.

The `cantDelete` property is also automatically set when the user sets `cantModify`, as described in the following section.

CantModify

```
set cantModify of this stack to true
```

The `cantModify` property pertains to any stack accessible to your Macintosh. It controls whether or not the stack can be changed in any way. This property checks or unchecks both the "Can't modify" stack option and the "Can't delete stack" option in the Protect Stack dialog box. (If the user has checked "Can't delete stack," however, and a script sets `cantModify` to `true` and then `false`, "Can't delete stack" is left checked.)

When you set `cantModify` from a script, you override whatever the user has set by hand in the Protect Stack dialog box. Setting `cantModify` to `false` does not, however, override protection provided by media that are write-protected in other ways.

See also the `userModify` property, later in this appendix.

ShowPict

```
set showPict of this card to false
```

The `showPict` property pertains to a card or a background in the current stack. It controls whether or not the specified card or background picture is displayed. Setting the `showPict` property of a card or background to `false` is the same as hiding it with the `picture` form of the `hide` command, described in this appendix; setting it to `true` is the same as showing it with the `picture` form of the `show` command.

When the `showPict` property of the current card or background is `false` and you attempt to use a Paint tool on it manually, a dialog box appears asking if you want to make the picture visible; clicking OK sets the `showPict` property to `true` and the picture appears. (You can draw on hidden pictures from a script.)

UserModify

```
set userModify to true
```

The `userModify` property is a global property pertaining to HyperCard itself. It controls whether or not a user can type into fields or use Paint tools on a card that has been write-protected. A card is write-protected under the following circumstances:

☐ The stack is on a CD-ROM.

☐ The stack is on a file server in a folder whose access privileges are set to Read Only.

☐ The "Locked" box is checked in the stack's Get Info dialog box in the Finder's File menu.

☐ The stack is on a locked 3.5-inch disk.

☐ "Can't modify stack" is checked in the stack's Protect Stack dialog box.

Cursor

```
set cursor to busy
```

The `cursor` property has been enhanced to accept eight cursor names by default: `arrow`, `busy`, `cross`, `hand`, `iBeam`, `none`, `plus`, and `watch`. You can also set the cursor to the ID number or name of any available 'CURS' resource, as explained in Chapter 9. The `busy` cursor is HyperCard's beach ball—each time it's set, it turns 45° clockwise, so you can make it appear to spin by setting it inside a `repeat` loop:

```
on mouseUp
  repeat until the mouseClick
    set cursor to busy
    wait 2 ticks
  end repeat
end mouseUp
```

Properties of screen rectangles

The properties described in this section pertain to the screen rectangles of buttons and fields, the Tools and Patterns palettes, the Message box, and the card window.

`the left of` *partOrWindow*

ParOrWindow yields the descriptor of a button or field in the current stack, as described in Chapter 3, "Naming Objects," or the name of one of the windows listed above, as described in Chapter 9, "Properties."

You use the `left` property to determine or change item 1 of the value of the `rectangle` property (left, top, right, bottom) when applied to the specified object or window.

the top of *partOrWindow*

You use the `top` property to determine or change item 2 of the value of the `rectangle` property (left, top, right, bottom) when applied to the specified object or window.

the right of *partOrWindow*

You use the `right` property to determine or change item 3 of the value of the `rectangle` property (left, top, right, bottom) when applied to the specified object or window.

the bottom of *partOrWindow*

You use the `bottom` property to determine or change item 4 of the value of the `rectangle` property (left, top, right, bottom) when applied to the specified object or window.

the topLeft of *partOrWindow*

You use the `topLeft` property to determine or change items 1 and 2 of the value of the `rectangle` property (left, top, right, bottom) when applied to the specified object or window.

the bottomRight of *partOrWindow*

You use the `bottomRight` property to determine or change items 3 and 4 of the value of the `rectangle` property (left, top, right, bottom) when applied to the specified object or window. The `bottomRight` property can be abbreviated `botRight`.

the width of *partOrWindow*

You use the `width` property to determine the horizontal distance in pixels occupied by the rectangle of the specified object or window. You can change the width of a button or field rectangle with the `set` command, but you can't set that property of a window.

the height of *partOrWindow*

You use the `height` property to determine or change the vertical distance in pixels occupied by the rectangle of the specified object or window. You can change the height of a button or field rectangle with the `set` command, but you can't set that property of a window.

When you set the width or height of a button or field, its `location` property (center coordinate) remains the same.

New operator

HyperCard version 1.2 has one new operator: `within`. It pertains to the screen rectangles of buttons and fields, the Tools and Patterns palettes, the Message box, and the screen on which HyperCard's menu bar is displayed. The syntax of an expression in which `within` is valid is the following:

point is [not] `within` *rectangle*

Point is an expression that yields a list of two integers separated by a comma and *rectangle* is an expression that yields a list of four integers separated by commas.

The `within` operator tests whether or not a point lies inside a rectangle; it results in a Boolean value: `true` or `false`. The following example handler, placed in a button script, is invoked when you click the button. It waits until you move the pointer outside the button rectangle, then beeps when you move the pointer back inside the button rectangle:

```
on mouseUp
  wait until the mouseLoc is not within rect of me
  repeat until the mouseLoc is within rect of me
    set cursor to busy -- spin beach ball while we wait
  end repeat
  beep
end mouseUp
```

New synonyms

HyperCard version 1.2 has twelve new synonyms (or abbreviations) for HyperTalk terms, which are shown in Table F-2. (The new abbreviations are additions, not replacements for the older terms.)

Table F-2
New HyperTalk synonyms

New synonym	Term
bg	background
bgs	backgrounds
btns	buttons
cd	card
cds	cards
fld	field
flds	fields
grey	gray
pict	picture
sec	secs or seconds
second	secs or seconds
tick	ticks

New shortcuts

HyperCard version 1.2 has several new keyboard shortcuts that allow you to edit scripts of objects more easily.

Command-Tab

In all versions of HyperCard, pressing Command-Tab chooses the Browse tool. In version 1.2, two additional shortcuts are available: holding down the Command key and pressing Tab twice in rapid succession chooses the Button tool; holding down the Command key and pressing Tab three times in rapid succession chooses the Field tool. The period of time defining *rapid succession* is 30 ticks (one-half second).

Command-Option

While using the Browse tool, you can press the Command and Option keys simultaneously to display the outline of all visible buttons (those whose visible property is `true`). While the buttons are displayed this way, you can click one to edit its script.

While using the Button tool, you can use the Command-Option combination to display all buttons (visible and hidden). However, the click-to-edit shortcut works for the visible buttons only. The user level must be set to Scripting to edit scripts.

Shift-Command-Option

While using the Browse tool, you can press the Shift, Command, and Option keys simultaneously to display the outline of all visible fields (those whose visible property is `true`). While the fields are displayed this way, you can click one to edit its script.

While using the Field tool, you can use the Shift-Command-Option combination to display all fields (visible and hidden). However, the click-to-edit shortcut works for the visible fields only. The user level must be set to Scripting to edit scripts.

Other Command-Option key combinations

When you're using any tool, Command-Option-C edits (invokes the script editor for) the script of the current card, Command-Option-B edits the script of current background, and Command-Option-S edits the script of the current stack.

The shortcuts introduced with HyperCard version 1.2 are summarized in Table F-3.

Table F-3
New shortcuts

Key press	Effect
Command-Tab	Choose Browse tool
Command-Tab(2x)	Choose Button tool
Command-Tab(3x)	Choose Field tool
Command-Option	Display buttons; click to edit script
Shift-Command-Option	Display fields; click to edit script
Command-Option-C	Edit script of current card
Command-Option-B	Edit script of current background
Command-Option-S	Edit script of current stack

Appendix G

HyperTalk Syntax Summary

This appendix lists HyperTalk's built-in commands and functions, showing the syntax of their parameters.

HyperTalk's built-in commands and functions are described in more detail in Chapters 7 and 8, respectively. A brief description and page reference for each is included in Appendix G.

Syntax description notation

The syntax descriptions use the following typographic conventions. Words or phrases in `typewriter type` are Hypertalk language elements or are those that you type to the computer literally, exactly as shown. Words in *italic* type describe general elements, not specific names—you must substitute the actual instances. Square brackets ([]) enclose optional elements which may be included if you need them. (Don't type the square brackets.) In some cases, optional elements change what the message does; in other cases they are helper words that have no effect except to make the message more readable.

It doesn't matter whether you use uppercase or lowercase letters; names that are formed from two words are shown in small letters with a capital in the middle (`likeThis`) merely to make them more readable. The HyperTalk prepositions `of` and `in` are interchangeable—the syntax descriptions use the one that sounds more natural.

The terms *factor* and *expression* are defined in Chapter 4. Briefly, a factor can be a constant, literal, function, property, number, or container, and an expression can be a factor or a complex expression built with factors and operators. Also, a factor can be an expression within parentheses.

Table G-1
HyperTalk command syntax

---

add *expression* to *destination*

answer *question* [with *reply* [or *reply2* [or *reply3*]]]

arrowKey *keyName*

ask [password] *question* [with *defaultAnswer*]

beep *count*

choose *toolName* tool

click at *location* [with *key*[, *key2*[, *key3*]]]

close file *fileName*

close printing

convert *container* to *format* [and *format*]

delete *chunk* [of *container*]

dial *expression* [with modem [*modemCommands*]]

divide *destination* by *expression*

doMenu *menuItem*

drag from *start* to *finish* [with *key*[, *key2*[, *key3*]]]

edit script of *object*

enterKey

find [chars] *expression* [in field *fieldDesignator*]

find [word] *expression* [in field *fieldDesignator*]

functionKey *keyNumber*

get *expression*

go [to] [stack] *stackName*

go [to] *bkgndDescriptor* [of [stack] *stackName*]

go [to] *cardDescriptor* [of *bkgndDescriptor*] [of [stack] *stackName*]

help

hide menuBar

hide *window*

hide *part*

multiply *destination* by *expression*

open [*document* with] *application*

open file *fileName*

open printing [with dialog]

play "*voice*" [tempo] ["*notes*"]

play stop

pop card [*preposition destination*]

print card

print *expression* cards

print *cardDescriptor*

print *document* with *application*

push *cardDescriptor*

put *expression* [*preposition destination*]

read from file *fileName* until *character*

read from file *fileName* for *numberOfCharacters*

```
reset paint
returnKey
set [the] property [of object] to value
show number cards
show menuBar
show window [at h, v]
show part [at h, v]
sort [direction] [style] by expression
subtract expression from destination
tabKey
type expression [with key[, key2[, key3]]]
visual [effect] effectName [speed] [to image]
wait [for] time [seconds]
wait until condition
wait while condition
write source to file fileName
```

Table G-2
HyperTalk function syntax

───

```
the abs of factor
abs (expression)
annuity (rate, periods)
the atan of factor
atan (expression)
average (list)
the charToNum of factor
charToNum (expression)
the clickLoc
clickLoc ()
the commandKey
commandKey ()
compound (rate, periods)
the cos of factor
cos (expression)
the [modifier] date
the diskSpace
diskSpace ()
the exp of factor
exp (expression)
the exp1 of factor
exp1 (expression)
the exp2 of factor
exp2 (expression)
the length of factor
```

```
length (expression)
the ln of factor
ln (expression)
the ln1 of factor
ln1 (expression)
the log2 of factor
log2 (expression)
max (list)
min (list)
the mouse
mouse ()
the mouseClick
mouseClick ()
the mouseH
mouseH ()
the mouseLoc
mouseLoc ()
the mouseV
mouseV ()
[the] number of objects
[the] number of chunks in factor
the numToChar of factor
numToChar (expression)
offset (string1, string2)
the optionKey
optionKey ()
the param of factor
param (expression)
the paramCount
paramCount ()
the params
params ()
the random of factor
random (expression)
the result
result ()
the round of factor
round (expression)
the seconds
seconds ()
the shiftKey
shiftKey ()
the sin of factor
sin (expression)
the sound
```

```
sound()
the sqrt of factor
sqrt(expression)
the tan of factor
tan(expression)
the target
target()
the ticks
ticks()
the [adjective] time
time()
the tool
tool()
the trunc of factor
trunc(expression)
the value of factor
value(expression)
the version
version()
```

Appendix H

HyperTalk Vocabulary

This appendix lists, in alphabetical order, HyperTalk's native vocabulary—the names of its built-in commands and functions, its system messages, keywords, the names of objects and their properties, and various adjectives, constants, ordinals, and other terms.

This list is not exhaustive—there are other terms with specific meanings recognized by HyperCard in particular contexts, and they are described with the primary term to which they relate. For example, the names of the various visual effects are listed with the `visual` command in Chapter 7.

The parameter syntax of HyperTalk's built-in commands and functions is shown in Appendix G.

Table H-1
HyperTalk vocabulary

Term	Category	Page	Meaning
abbr[ev[iated]]	Adjective	145, 175	Modifies the value returned by the `date` function or the `name` or `ID` properties.
abs	Function	140	Returns absolute value of a number.
add	Command	88	Adds the value of an expression to a value in a container.
after	Preposition	122	Used with `put` command, directing HyperCard to append a new value following any preexisting value in a container.
all	Adjective	127	Specifies total number of cards in stack to `show cards` command.
annuity	Function	140	Computes present or future value of an ordinary annuity.

Table H-1 *(continued)*
HyperTalk vocabulary

Term	Category	Page	Meaning
answer	Command	89	Displays a dialog with question and reply buttons.
any	Ordinal	37	Special ordinal used with object or chunk to specify a random element within its enclosing set.
arrowKey	Command	90	Takes you to another card.
arrowKey	System message	82	Sent to current card when an arrow key is pressed.
ask	Command	92	Displays a dialog box with a question and default answer.
atan	Function	141	Returns trigonometric arc tangent of a number.
autoHilite	Property	203	Determines whether or not the specified button's `hilite` property is affected by the message `mouseDown`.
average	Function	142	Returns the average value of numbers in a list.
background	Object	3, 34	Generic name of background object; used with specific designation (`go to next background`). Also used to specify containing object for buttons and, optionally, fields (`background button 2`).
backgrounds	Object type	154	Specifies backgrounds as type of object to the `number` function.
beep	Command	93	Causes Macintosh to make a beep sound.
before	Preposition	122	Used with `put` command, directing HyperCard to place a new value at the beginning of any preexisting value in a container.
bkgnd	Object	34	Abbreviation for `background`.
bkgnds	Object type	155	Specifies backgrounds as type of object to the `number` function.
blindTyping	Property	176	Allows typing into Message box when hidden.
browse	Tool	94, 170	Name of tool from Tools palette; used with `choose` command or returned by the `tool` function.
brush	Property	184	Determines the current brush shape.
brush	Tool	94, 170	Name of tool from Tools palette; used with `choose` command or returned by the `tool` function.
btn	Object	34	Abbreviation for `button`.

Term	Category	Page	Meaning
bucket	Tool	94, 170	Name of tool from Tools palette; used with `choose` command or returned by the `tool` function.
button	Object	34	Generic name of button object; used with a specific designation (`hide button one`).
button	Tool	94, 170	Name of tool from Tools palette; used with `choose` command or returned by the `tool` function.
buttons	Object type	154	Specifies buttons as type of object to the `number` function.
card	Object	34	Generic name of a card object; used with a specific designation (`go to card "fred"`). Also used to specify containing object for fields and, optionally, buttons (`card field "date"`).
cards	Object type	154	Specifies cards as type of object to the `number` function.
centered	Property	184	Determines the Draw Centered setting.
char[acter]	Chunk	54	A character of text in any container or expression.
char[acter]s	Chunk type	154	Specifies characters as type of chunk to the `number` function.
charToNum	Function	142	Returns ASCII value of a character.
choose	Command	94	Changes the current tool.
click	Command	95	Causes same actions as clicking at a specified location.
clickLoc	Function	143	Returns location of most recent click.
closeBackground	System message	183	Sent to current card just before you leave the current background.
closeCard	System message	80	Sent to current card just before you leave it.
closeField	System message	79	Sent to unlocked field when it closes.
closeStack	System message	83	Sent to current card just before you leave the current stack.
close file	Command	97	Closes a previously opened disk file.
close printing	Command	98	Ends a print job.
commandKey	Function	143	Returns state of the Command key: `up` or `down`.
compound	Function	144	Computes present or future value of a compound interest–bearing account.
controlKey	System message	82	Sent to current card when a combination of the Control key and another key is pressed.
convert	Command	98	Converts a date or time to specified format.

Term	Category	Page	Meaning
cos	Function	145	Returns the cosine of the angle that is passed to it.
cursor	Property	177	Sets image appearing at pointer location on screen. You can only set cursor; you can't get it.
curve	Tool	94, 170	Name of tool from Tools palette; used with `choose` command or returned by the `tool` function.
date	Function	145	Returns a string representing the current date.
delete	Command	100	Removes a chunk of text from a container.
deleteBackground	System message	83	Sent to current card just before the background is deleted.
deleteButton	System message	77	Sent to a button just before it is deleted.
deleteCard	System message	80	Sent to current card just before it is deleted.
deleteField	System message	79	Sent to a field just before it is deleted.
deleteStack	System message	83	Sent to the current card just before a stack is deleted.
dial	Command	101	Generates touch-tone sounds through audio output or modem attached to serial port.
diskSpace	Function	146	Displays the amount of free space available on the disk containing the current stack.
divide	Command	102	Divides the value in a container by the value of an expression.
do	Keyword	72	Sends the value of an expression as a message to the current card.
doMenu	Command	103	Performs a specified menu command.
doMenu	System message	83	Sent to current card when any menu item is chosen.
down	Constant	213	Value returned by various functions to describe the state of a key or the mouse button.
drag	Command	104	Performs same action as a manual drag.
dragSpeed	Property	177	Sets pixels-per-second speed at which pointer moves with `drag` command.
editBkgnd	Property	177	Determines whether manipulation of buttons, fields or paintings occurs on current card or background.
edit script	Command	105	Opens the script of a specified object.
eight	Constant	213	String representation of the numerical value 8.
eighth	Ordinal	36	Designates object or chunk number eight within its enclosing set.

Term	Category	Page	Meaning
else	Keyword	70	Optionally follows `then` clause in an `if` structure to introduce an alternative action clause.
empty	Constant	213	The null string; same as the literal `""`.
end	Keyword	61, 64, 70, 71	Marks the end of a message handler, function handler, `repeat` loop, or multiple-statement `then` or `else` clause of an `if` structure.
enterKey	Command	105	Sends contents of Message box to the current card.
eraser	Tool	94, 170	Name of tool from Tools palette; used with `choose` command or returned by the `tool` function.
exit	Keyword	61, 64, 69	Immediately ends execution of a message handler, function handler, or `repeat` loop.
exp	Function	147	Returns the mathematical exponential of its argument.
exp1	Function	147	Returns one less than the mathematical exponential of its argument.
exp2	Function	148	Returns the value of 2 raised to the power specified by the argument.
false	Constant	213	Boolean value resulting from evaluation of a comparative expression and returned from some functions.
field	Container	45	Generic name of field container; used with specific designation (`put the time into card field "time"`).
field	Object	2, 34	Generic name of field object; used with specific designation (`get name of first field`).
field	Tool	94, 170	Name of tool from Tools palette; used with `choose` command or returned by the `tool` function.
fields	Object type	154	Specifies fields as type of object to the `number` function.
fifth	Ordinal	36	Designates object or chunk number five within its enclosing set.
filled	Property	185	Determines the Draw Filled setting.
find	Command	106	Searches card and background fields for text strings derived from an expression.

Table H-1 *(continued)*
HyperTalk vocabulary

Term	Category	Page	Meaning
first	Ordinal	36	Designates object or chunk number one within its enclosing set.
five	Constant	213	String representation of the numerical value 5.
formFeed	Constant	213	The form feed character (ASCII 12), which starts a new page in some file formats.
four	Constant	213	String representation of the numerical value 4.
fourth	Ordinal	36	Designates object or chunk number four within its enclosing set.
freeSize	Property	190	Determines the amount of free space available in a specified stack.
functionKey	Command	108	Performs Undo, Cut, Copy, or Paste operations with parameter values of 1, 2, 3, or 4, respectively.
functionKey	System message	82	Sent to current card when any function key on the Apple Extended Keyboard is pressed.
get	Command	109	Puts the value of an expression into the local variable It.
global	Keyword	73	Declares specified variables to be valid beyond current execution of current handler.
go	Command	110	Takes you to a specified card or stack.
grid	Property	185	Determines the Grid setting.
help	Command	111	Takes you to the first card in the stack named Help.
hide	Command	111	Hides the specified window from view.
hilite	Property	204	Determines whether a specified button is highlighted.
icon	Property	204	Determines the icon that is displayed with a specified button.
ID	Property	35, 192	Determines the permanent ID number of a specified background, card, field, or button. (See also pages 193, 195, and 205.)
idle	System message	81	Sent to the current card repeatedly whenever nothing else is happening.
if	Keyword	70	Introduces a conditional structure containing statements to be executed only if a specified condition is true.
into	Preposition	122	Used with put command, directing HyperCard to replace any preexisting value in a container with a new value.

Table H-1 *(continued)*
HyperTalk vocabulary

Term	Category	Page	Meaning
It	Container	47	Local variable that is the default destination for `get`, `ask`, `answer`, `read`, and `convert` commands.
item	Chunk	55	A piece of text delimited by commas in any container or expression.
items	Chunk type	154	Specifies items as type of chunk to the `number` function.
language	Property	178	Used to choose language in which scripts are displayed.
lasso	Tool	94, 170	Name of tool from Tools palette; used with `choose` command or returned by the `tool` function.
last	Ordinal	37	Special ordinal used with object or chunk to specify the element whose number is equal to the total number of elements in its enclosing set.
length	Function	148	Returns the number of characters in the text string derived from an expression.
line	Chunk	55	A piece of text delimited by return characters in any container.
line	Tool	94, 170	Name of tool from Tools palette; used with `choose` command or returned by the `tool` function.
lineFeed	Constant	213	The line feed character (ASCII 10), which starts a new line in some file formats.
lines	Chunk type	154	Specifies lines as type of chunk to the `number` function.
lineSize	Property	185	Determines the thickness of lines drawn with line and shape tools.
ln	Function	149	Returns the base-*e* (natural logarithm) of the number passed to it.
ln1	Function	149	Returns the base-*e* (natural logarithm) of the sum of the number passed to it plus 1.
loc[ation]	Property	182	Determines the location at which a window, field, or button is displayed. (See also pages 196 and 205.)
lockMessages	Property	178	Prevents HyperCard from sending all automatic messages such as `openCard`.
lockRecent	Property	178	Prevents HyperCard from adding miniature representations to the Recent card.
lockScreen	Property	179	Prevents updating of the screen from card to card.

Table H-1 *(continued)*
HyperTalk vocabulary

Term	Category	Page	Meaning
lockText	Property	196	Allows or prevents text editing in a specified field.
log2	Function	150	Returns the base-2 logarithm of the number passed to it.
long	Adjective	145, 175	Modifies value returned by date function and by name and ID properties.
max	Function	150	Returns the highest-value number from a list of numbers.
me	Object	37	Specifies object containing the executing handler.
message [box]	Container	48	The Message box.
mid[dle]	Ordinal	37	Special ordinal used with object or chunk to specify the element whose number is equal to one more than half the total number of elements in its enclosing set.
min	Function	151	Returns the lowest-value number from a list of numbers.
mouse	Function	151	Returns state of the mouse button: up or down.
mouseClick	Function	152	Determines whether the mouse button has been clicked.
mouseDown	System message	77, 79, 80	Sent to a button, unlocked field, or the current card when the mouse button is pressed down.
mouseEnter	System message	78, 79	Sent to a button or field when the pointer is first moved inside its rectangle.
mouseH	Function	153	Returns the horizontal offset in pixels of the pointer from the left edge of the card window.
mouseLeave	System message	78, 79	Sent to a button or field when the pointer is first removed from its rectangle.
mouseLoc	Function	153	Returns the point on the screen where the pointer is currently located.
mouseStillDown	System message	77, 79, 80	Sent to a button, unlocked field, or the current card repeatedly when the mouse button is held down.
mouseUp	System message	77, 79, 80	Sent to a button, unlocked field, or the current card when the mouse button is released after having been previously pressed down within the same object's rectangle.
mouseV	Function	154	Returns the vertical offset in pixels of the pointer from the top of the screen.

Table H-1 *(continued)*
HyperTalk vocabulary

Term	Category	Page	Meaning
mouseWithin	System message	78, 79	Sent to a button or field repeatedly while the pointer remains inside its rectangle.
msg [box]	Container	48	The Message box.
multiple	Property	186	Determines the Draw Multiple setting for drawing multiple shapes.
multiply	Command	113	Multiplies the value in a container by the value derived from an expression.
multiSpace	Property	186	Determines the space between objects drawn with the Draw Multiple setting activated.
name	Property	35, 190	Determines the name of a stack, background, card, field, or button. (See also pages 192, 194, 197, and 205.)
next	Keyword	69	Ends execution of current iteration of a repeat loop, beginning next iteration.
next	Object modifier	37	Used with card or background to refer to the one following the current one.
newBackground	System message	82	Sent to the current card as soon as a background has been created.
newButton	System message	77	Sent to a button as soon as it has been created.
newCard	System message	80	Sent to a card as soon as it has been created.
newField	System message	79	Sent to a field as soon as it has been created.
newStack	System message	83	Sent to the current card as soon as a stack has been created.
nine	Constant	213	String representation of the numerical value 9.
ninth	Ordinal	36	Designates object or chunk number nine within its enclosing set.
number	Function	154	Returns the number of buttons or fields on the current card or background, or the number of a specified type of chunk within a value.
number	Property	36, 192	Determines the number of a background, card, field, or button. (See also pages 194, 197, and 206.)
numberFormat	Property	44, 179	Determines the precision with which results of mathematical operations are displayed.
numToChar	Function	156	Returns the character whose ASCII equivalent value is that of the integer passed to it.
offset	Function	157	Returns the number of characters from the beginning of the source string.
one	Constant	213	String representation of the numerical value 1.

Table H-1 *(continued)*
HyperTalk vocabulary

Term	Category	Page	Meaning
open	Command	114	Launches the specified application.
openBackground	System message	83	Sent to a card when you go to it and its background is different from the one you were formerly on.
openCard	System message	80	Sent to a card when you go to it.
openField	System message	79	Sent to a field when you place the insertion point in it for text editing.
open file	Command	115	Opens the data fork of the specified file.
open printing	Command	116	Begins a print job.
openStack	System message	83	Sent to a card when you go to it and it's in a stack different from the one containing the card you were formerly on.
optionKey	Function	158	Returns the state of the Option key: up or down.
oval	Tool	94, 170	Name of tool from Tools palette; used with choose command or returned by the tool function.
param	Function	158	Returns a parameter value from the parameter list passed to the currently executing handler.
paramCount	Function	159	Returns the number of parameters passed to the currently executing handler.
params	Function	160	Returns the entire parameter list passed to the currently executing handler.
pass	Keyword	62, 65	Ends execution of a message handler or function handler and sends the invoking message or function call to the next object in the hierarchy.
pattern	Property	186	Determines the Paint pattern.
pencil	Tool	94, 170	Name of tool from Tools palette; used with choose command or returned by the tool function.
pi	Constant	213	The mathematical value pi to 20 decimal places, equal to the number 3.14159265358979323846.
play	Command	117	Starts HyperCard's sound-playing feature.
browse	Tool	94, 190	Name of tool from Tools palette; used with choose command or returned by the tool function.
poly[gon]	Tool	94, 170	Name of tool from Tools palette; used with choose command or returned by the tool function.

Table H-1 *(continued)*
HyperTalk vocabulary

Term	Category	Page	Meaning
`polySides`	Property	187	Determines the number of sides created by the Regular Polygon tool.
`pop card`	Command	118	Returns you to last card saved with the push card Command.
`powerKeys`	Property	180	Keyboard equivalents of commonly used painting actions.
`prev[ious]`	Object modifier	37	Used with `card` or `background` to refer to the one preceding the current one.
`print card`	Command	119	Prints the the current card or a specified number of cards beginning with the current card.
`print`	Command	120	Prints the specified document.
`push`	Command	121	Saves the identification of a specified card in a LIFO memory stack for later retrieval.
`put`	Command	122	Copies the value of an expression into a container.
`quit`	System message	84	Sent to the current card when you choose Quit HyperCard from the File menu (or press Command-Q), just before HyperCard goes away.
`quote`	Constant	213	The straight double quotation mark character.
`random`	Function	160	Returns a random integer between 1 and the integer derived from a specified expression.
`read`	Command	123	Reads a file previously opened with the `open file` command into the local variable `It`.
`rect[angle]`	Property	182	Determines the rectangle occupied by a specified window, field, or button. (See also pages 197 and 206.)
`rect[angle]`	Tool	94, 170	Name of tool from Tools palette; used with `choose` command or returned by the `tool` function.
`reg[ular] poly[gon]`	Tool	94, 170	Name of tool from Tools palette; used with `choose` command or returned by the `tool` function.
`repeat`	Keyword	66	Introduces a `repeat` loop, an iterative structure containing a block of one or more statements executed multiple times.
`reset paint`	Command	125	Reinstates the default values of all the painting properties.

Table H-1 *(continued)*
HyperTalk vocabulary

Term	Category	Page	Meaning
result	Function	161	Returns the status of find or go command previously executed in current handler.
resume	System message	84	Sent to the current card when HyperCard resumes running after having been suspended.
return	Keyword	62, 65	Returns a value from a function handler or message handler.
returnKey	Command	125	Sends any statement in the Message box to the current card.
returnKey	System message	81	Sent to current card when Return key is pressed.
round	Function	163	Returns the number derived from an expression, rounded off to the nearest integer.
round rect [angle]	Tool	94, 170	Name of tool from Tools palette; used with choose command or returned by the tool function.
script	Property	191	Retrieves or replaces the script of the specified stack, background, card, field, or button. (See also pages 193, 194, 198, and 207.)
scroll	Property	198	Determines the amount of material that is hidden above the top of the specified scrolling field's rectangle.
second	Ordinal	36	Designates object or chunk number two within its enclosing set.
seconds	Function	163	Returns the number of seconds between midnight, January 1, 1904, and the current time.
select	Tool	94, 170	Name of tool from Tools palette; used with choose command or returned by the tool function.
selection	Container	47	Currently selected area of text in a field.
send	Keyword	74	Sends a specified message directly to a specified object.
set	Command	126	Changes the state of a specified global, painting, window, or object property.
seven	Constant	213	String representation of the numerical value 7.

Table H-1 *(continued)*
HyperTalk vocabulary

Term	Category	Page	Meaning
seventh	Ordinal	36	Designates object or chunk number seven within its enclosing set.
shiftKey	Function	164	Returns the state of the Shift key: up or down.
short	Adjective	145, 175	Modifies value returned by date function and by name and ID properties.
show cards	Command	127	Displays a specified number of cards in the current stack.
showLines	Property	199	Determines whether or not the text baselines are visible in a field.
showName	Property	207	Determines whether or not the name of a specified button is displayed in its rectangle on the screen.
show	Command	128	Displays a specified window or object.
sin	Function	164	Returns the sine of the angle that is passed to it.
six	Constant	213	String representation of the numerical value 6.
sixth	Ordinal	36	Designates object or chunk number six within its enclosing set.
size	Property	191	Returns the size of a specified stack.
sort	Command	130	Puts all of the cards in a specified stack in order, according to a specified key expression.
sound	Function	165	Returns the name of the sound that is currently playing.
space	Constant	213	The space character (ASCII 32); same as the literal " ".
spray [can]	Tool	94, 170	Name of tool from Tools palette; used with choose command or returned by the tool function.
sqrt	Function	166	Returns the square root of a number.
stack	Object	38	Generic name of stack object; used with specific name (go to stack "help").
startUp	System message	80	Sent to the current card (first card of the Home stack) when HyperCard first begins running.
style	Property	199	Determines the style of a specified field or button. (See also page 207.)
subtract	Command	131	Subtracts the value of an expression from the value in a container.

Table H-1 *(continued)*
HyperTalk vocabulary

Term	Category	Page	Meaning
suspend	System message	83	Sent to the current card when HyperCard is suspended by launching another application with the `open` command.
tab	Constant	213	The horizontal tab character (ASCII 9).
tabKey	Command	131	Places the insertion point in the next unlocked field on the current background and card.
tabKey	System message	81	Sent to current card when Tab key is pressed.
tan	Function	166	Returns the tangent of an angle.
target	Function	167	Indicates the object that initially received the message that initiated execution of the current handler.
ten	Constant	213	String representation of the numerical value 10.
tenth	Ordinal	36	Designates object or chunk number ten within its enclosing set.
text	Tool	94, 170	Name of tool from Tools palette; used with `choose` command or returned by the `tool` function.
textAlign	Property	188	Determines the alignment of characters created with the Paint Text tool, or those in a field, or those in the name of a button. (See also pages 200 and 208.)
textArrows	Property	180	Determines the functions of the arrow keys.
textFont	Property	188	Determines the font of characters created with the Paint Text tool, or those in a field, or those in the name of a button. (See also pages 200 and 208.)
textHeight	Property	188	Determines the space between the baseline and characters created with the Paint Text tool or those in a field. (See also page 201.)
textSize	Property	189	Determines the size of Paint text or text in a field or in the name of a button. (See also pages 201 and 209.)
textStyle	Property	189	Determines the style of Paint text or the text in a field or in the name of a button. (See also pages 202 and 209.)

Term	Category	Page	Meaning
the	Special	138	Precedes a function name to indicate a function call to one of HyperCard's built-in functions. You can't call a user-defined function with `the`. Also allowed, but not required, preceding special container names (`the Message box`) and properties.
then	Keyword	70	Follows the conditional expression in an `if` structure to introduce the action clause.
third	Ordinal	36	Designates object or chunk number three within its enclosing set.
this	Object modifier	37	Used with `card`, `background`, or `stack` to refer to the current one.
three	Constant	213	String representation of the numerical value 3.
ticks	Function	168	Determines the number of ticks since the Macintosh was turned on or restarted.
time	Function	169	Returns the current time as a text string.
tool	Function	170	Returns the name of the currently chosen tool.
true	Constant	213	Boolean value resulting from evaluation of a comparative expression and returned from some functions.
trunc	Function	171	Determines the integer part of a number.
two	Constant	213	String representation of the numerical value 2.
type	Command	132	Inserts the specified text at the insertion point.
up	Constant	213	Value returned by various functions to describe the state of a key or the mouse button.
userLevel	Property	181	Determines the user level from 1 to 5.
value	Function	172	Evaluates an expression.
version	Function	172	Returns the version number of the currently running HyperCard application.
visible	Property	183	Determines whether or not a window, field, or button appears on the screen. (See also pages 202 and 209.)
visual	Command	133	Sets up a specified visual transition to the next card opened.
wait	Command	135	Causes HyperCard to pause before executing the rest of the current handler.

Table H-1 *(continued)*
HyperTalk vocabulary

Term	Category	Page	Meaning
wideMargins	Property	202	Determines whether or not additional space is displayed in the margins of a specified field.
word	Chunk	54	Piece of text in delimited by spaces in any container or expression.
words	Chunk type	154	Specifies words as type of chunk to the number function.
write	Command	136	Copies specified text into a specified disk file.
zero	Constant	213	String representation of the numerical value 0.

Glossary

actual parameters: See **parameters.**

background: A type of HyperCard object; a basic template which is shared by a number of cards. The background is composed of the **background picture, background field,** and **background button.**

background button: A button that belongs to a background; it appears on, and its actions are the same for, all cards with the same background. Contrast with **card button.**

background field: A field that belongs to a background; its size, position, and text attributes remain constant on all cards associated with that particular background, but its text changes from card to card. Contrast with **card field.**

background picture: A picture that belongs to a background; it applies to a series of cards. You see the Background picture by choosing Background from the Edit menu. Contrast with **card picture.**

browse: To wander through HyperCard's stacks.

Browse tool: The tool you use to click buttons and to set the insertion point in fields.

button: A type of HyperCard object; an action object or "hot spot" on the screen. For example, clicking a button with the Browse tool can take you to the next card. See also **background button, card button.**

Button tool: The tool you use to create, change, and select buttons.

card: A type of HyperCard object; HyperCard's basic unit of information.

card button: A button that belongs to a card; it appears on, and its actions apply to, a single card. Contrast with **background button.**

card field: A field that belongs to a card; its size, position, text attributes, and contents are limited to the card on which the field is created. Contrast with **background field.**

card picture: A picture that belongs to and which applies only to a specific card. Contrast with **background picture.**

chunk: A piece of the character string representing a value. Valid chunks are characters, words, items, and lines.

Command key: The key at the lower-left side of the keyboard that has a propeller-shaped symbol. On some keyboards this key also has an Apple symbol and might be called the *Apple key.*

command: A response to a particular message; a command is a built-in message handler residing in HyperCard. See also **external command.**

constant: A named value that never changes. For example, the constant empty stands for the null string, a value that can also be represented by the literal expression " ".

container: A place where you can store a value. Containers are: **fields,** the **Message box,** the **selection,** and **variables.**

control structure: A block of HyperTalk statements defined with keywords that enables you to control the order or the conditions under which it executes.

current: (adj.) The card, background, or stack you're using now. For example, the current card is the one you can see on your screen.

dynamic path: A series of extra objects inserted into the path through which a message passes when its **static path** does not include the current card. The dynamic path comprises the current card, current background, and current stack.

expression: A description of how to get a value; a **source of value** or complex expression built from sources and operators.

external command: A command written by a programmer to extend HyperCard's built-in command set, attached to a stack or in HyperCard.

factor: A single element of value in an expression. See also **value.**

field: A **container** in which you type regular (as opposed to Paint) text. Also, the tool you use to create a field. HyperCard has two kinds of fields—**card fields** and **background fields.**

Field tool: The tool you use to create, change, and select fields.

formal parameters: See **parameter variables.**

function: A named value that HyperCard calculates each time it is used. The way in which the value is calculated is defined internally for HyperTalk's built-in functions, and you can define your own functions with function handlers.

function call: The use of a function name in a HyperTalk statement or in the Message box, invoking either a function handler or a built-in function.

function handler: A handler that executes in response to a function call matching its name.

General tool: Any HyperCard tool that isn't a Paint tool. The General tools are Browse, Button, and Field.

global properties: The properties that determine aspects of the overall HyperCard environment. For example, `userLevel` is a global property which determines the current **user level** setting.

global variable: A variable that is valid for all handlers in which it is declared with the `global` keyword. Contrast with **local variable.**

handler: A block of HyperTalk statements contained in the script of an object that executes in response to a message or a function call matching the handler's name. HyperTalk has **message handlers** and **function handlers.**

hierarchy: See **object hierarchy.**

Home card: The first card in the Home stack; it is generally used as a pictorial index to stacks. Choose Home from the Go menu to get to Home (or press Command-H). You can also type `go home` in the Message box or include it as a statement in a handler.

HyperTalk: HyperCard's built-in script language for HyperCard users.

identifier: A character string of any length, beginning with an alphabetic character, containing any alphanumeric character and, optionally, the underscore character. Identifiers are used for **variable** and **handler** names.

keyboard equivalent key: A key you press together with the Command key to issue a menu command.

keyword: Any one of the 14 words that have a predefined meaning in HyperTalk. Examples of keywords are `on`, `if`, `do`, and `repeat`.

layer: The order of a button or field relative to other buttons or fields on the same card or background. The object created most recently is ordinarily the topmost object (that is on the front layer).

literal: An expression denoted by double quotation marks at either end of a character string; its value is the string itself.

local variable: A variable that is valid only within the handler in which it is used (local variables need not be declared). Contrast with **global variable.**

message: A character string you send to an object from a **script** or the Message box, or which HyperCard sends in response to an event. Some examples of HyperTalk messages are `mouseUp`, `go`, and `push card`.

Message box: a **container** that you use to send messages to objects or to evaluate expressions.

message handler: A handler that executes in response to a message matching its name.

number: a character string consisting of any combination of the numerals 0 through 9, optionally including one period (.) representing a decimal value. A number can be preceded by a hyphen or a minus sign to represent a negative value.

object: An element of the HyperCard environment that sends and receives messages. There are five kinds of HyperCard objects: **buttons, fields, cards, backgrounds,** and **stacks.**

object descriptor: Designation used to refer to an object. An object descriptor is formed by combining the name of the type of object with a specific name, number, or ID number. For example, `background button 3` is an object descriptor.

object hierarchy: The ordering of HyperCard objects that determines the path through which **messages** pass.

object properties: The properties that determine how HyperCard objects look and act. For example, the `location` property of a button determines where it appears on the screen.

on-line help: assistance you can get from an application program while it's running. In this guide, on-line help refers to HyperCard's disk-based Help system.

operator: a HyperTalk language element that you use in an **expression** to manipulate or calculate **values.**

Paint text: Text you type using the Paint Text tool. Paint text can appear anywhere, while **regular text** must appear in a field created with the Field tool. When you finalize Paint text by clicking, it becomes part of a card or background picture.

Paint tool: Any HyperCard tool you use to make pictures. Tools include Lasso, Brush, Spray, Eraser, and many others.

painting properties: The properties that control aspects of HyperCard's painting environment, which is invoked when you choose a Paint tool. For example, the `brush` property determines the shape of the Brush tool.

palette: The name for a **tear-off menu** when it's been torn off. A palette remains visible on the screen so you can use it without having to pull down the menu. HyperCard has two palettes— Tools and Patterns.

parameters: Values passed to a handler by a message or function call. Any expressions after the first word in a message are evaluated to yield the parameters; the parameters to a function call are enclosed in parentheses or, if there is only one, it can follow `of`.

parameter variables: Local variables in a handler which receive the values of parameters passed with the message or function call initiating the handler's execution.

picture: Any graphic or part of a graphic, created with a Paint tool or imported from an external file, which is part of a card or background.

point: In printing, the unit of measurement of the height of a text character; one point is about ½₂ of an inch. When you select a font, you can also select a point size, such as 10-point, 12-point, and so on. Also, a location on the screen described by two integers, separated by a comma, representing horizontal and vertical offsets, measured in pixels from the top-left corner of the card window or (in the case of the card window itself) of the screen.

power key: One of a number of keys on the Macintosh keyboard you can press to initiate a menu action when a Paint tool is active. Power keys are enabled when you choose Power Keys from the Options menu or you check Power Keys in the User Preferences card in the Home stack.

properties: The defining characteristics of any HyperCard object and of HyperCard's environment. See also **global properties, object properties, painting properties,** and **window properties.**

Recent: A special dialog box that holds pictorial representations of the last 42 unique cards viewed. Choose Recent from the Go menu to get the dialog box. Also, as in `recent card`, an adjective describing the card you were on immediately prior to the current card.

recursion: The continued repeating of an operation or group of operations. Recursion occurs when a handler calls itself.

regular text: Text you type in a field. You use the Browse tool to set an insertion point in a field and then type. Regular text is editable and searchable, while **Paint text** is not.

script: A collection of handlers written in HyperTalk and associated with a particular object.

search path: The route the computer must follow to retrieve a file you ask for.

selection: A container that holds the currently selected area of text. Note that text found by the `find` command is not selected. See also **container.**

source of value: HyperTalk's most basic expressions; the language elements from which values can be derived: **constants, containers, functions, literals,** and **properties.**

stack: A type of HyperCard object which is a collection of cards; a HyperCard document. See also **card.**

static path: The message-passing route defined by an object's own hierarchy. For example, the static path followed by a message sent to (but not handled by) a button would include the card to which the button belongs, the background associated with that card, and the stack containing them. Contrast with **dynamic path.**

System file: Software your computer uses to perform its basic operations.

system message: Message sent to an object by HyperCard in response to an event such as a mouse click or the creation or deletion of an object.

target: The object which first receives a message.

tear-off menu: A menu that you can convert to a **palette** by dragging the pointer beyond the menu's edge. HyperCard has two tear-off menus— Tools and Patterns.

text field: See **field.**

text property: A quality or attribute of a character's appearance. Properties include style, font, and size.

tool: An implement you use to do work. HyperCard has tools for browsing through cards and stacks, creating text fields, editing text, making buttons, and creating and editing pictures.

user level: The property of HyperCard ranging from 1 to 5, usually chosen on the User Preferences card in the Home stack, that lets you use HyperCard's tools and abilities. The five user levels are: Browsing, Typing, Painting, Authoring, and Scripting.

value: The information on which HyperCard operates. All HyperCard values can be treated as strings as characters.

variable: A named container that can hold a value consisting of a character string of any length. HyperCard has **local variables** and **global variables.** See also **container.**

window properties: The properties that determine how the Message box and the Tool and Pattern palettes are displayed. For example, the `visible` property determines whether or not the specified window is displayed on the screen.

Index